After You, Prime Minister

After You, Prime Minister

James Douglas-Hamilton

Foreword by Sir Malcolm Rifkind

STACEY
INTERNATIONAL

After You, Prime Minister

Published by
Stacey International
128 Kensington Church Street
London W8 4BH
Tel: +44 (0)20 7221 7166 Fax: +44 (0)20 7792 9288
E-mail: info@stacey-international.co.uk
www.stacey-international.co.uk

ISBN: 978-1-906768-06-5

Cover illustration © Steve Bright

Picture credits:
The following photographers and institutions are gratefully acknowledged for their
contributions:

© Gilman and Soame (6), © The Herald (3, 19), © Mrs Alexandra Hildebrandt
(12), © Alan McTavish (27), © Lady Moore of Wolvercote (13), © The Oxford
Mail (4, 5, 7), © Scotsman Publications Limited (2, 11, 14, 16, 20, 22, 24), ©
Scottish Parliamentary Corporate Body (25), © Strawberry Productions
Photographic Studios (18), © Susie Selkirk (9, 10, 26), © Universal Pictorial Press
and Agency Limited (23), © Valentine and Sons Limited (1)

British Library Catalogue in Publication Data:
A catalogue record for this book is available from
the British Library.

Printed in the UK by TJ International, Cornwall

Contents

	List of Illustrations	vi
	Acknowledgements	vii
	Foreword by Sir Malcolm Rifkind	ix
1	The Coronation and fighting for fun	1
2	Oxford Union President and demonstrations over South Africa	23
3	Cape to Cairo and a teach-in on Rhodesian UDI	40
4	Rudolf Hess, MI5 and Albrecht's secrets	55
5	An advocate, a councillor, a married man and an MP	79
6	The House of Commons and the fall of a Labour Government	101
7	Dominica, the Falklands and the smallest majority in Scotland	113
8	A Parliamentary Private Secretary and Mrs Margaret Thatcher's Minister	134
9	The Scottish Office and the tragedy of Lockerbie	153
10	The Earldom of Selkirk – Earl for four days	182
11	Out of office and out of power	204
12	On the trail of two heroes – Mussert's flag and Roosevelt's home	216
13	A new MSP and a new Parliament	233
14	Concorde and Parliament at work	251
15	Family connections – the Black Douglas, the Selkirk Settlers and John Buchan's Canda	263
	Postscript – Afghanistan and the future of devolution	275
	Index	283

List of Illustrations

Between pages 84 and 85

1   The Crown of Scotland
2   The Thistle Ceremony
3   Boxing on the sands of North Berwick
4   Boxing against Cambridge
5   Boxing against Loughborough
6   Oxford Union group photograph
7   Oxford Union debate
8   Edinburgh Castle
9   Engagement photograph
10   Family photograph
11   Constructing Edinburgh Castle's tunnel
12   Albrecht Haushofer
13   Geordie and PM Lee Kuan Yew

Between pages 180 and 181

14   Victory in the 1983 General Election
15   The Whips' Office
16   The Scottish Office Ministers
17   With Margaret Thatcher
18   With the PM and Mr and Mrs Mowat
19   The author at Foxbar
20   The firearms amnesty
21   With John Major
22   With Paddy Ashdown
23   Author as a Life Peer
24   The opening of the Scottish Parliament
25   Taking the oath in the Scottish Parliament
26   With family in Iceland
27   Statue of the 5th Earl of Selkirk

Acknowledgements

I can testify that it is not strictly necessary to die in order to see your whole life flash before your eyes. It is possible to write a memoir instead.

This can cover childhood dreams, the hopes of youth, the prospect of achievement and later a willingness to realise that the pursuit of excellence has to come to terms with reality.

So why write a memoir at all? It was the actress Mae West who said "Keep a diary and someday it will keep you!" There is no diary in my case but an attempt to set the record straight, to entertain of course, but also to give a bird's eye view of some of the political highlights of the last 50 years.

A number of people have helped me along the way including my old friends Harold Lind and Charles Edward Lysaght who gave their valuable views on the early drafts of the manuscript.

Frances Horsburgh used her journalistic skills to help with the initial editing of the memoir and advised on what might most engage the reader's interest.

I would also like to thank Dr Maria Castrillo of the National Library of Scotland who allowed me access to some of the necessary papers and photographs. Similarly Patrick Vollmer and his colleagues in the House of Lords Library assisted with checks on Parliamentary facts.

Then there is Tom Stacey, the renowned author and publisher, who made it clear he would read the memoir and agreed to put it into print. As a result Charles Powell of Stacey International took on the task of copy reading and creating the final shape of the book.

Finally I would like to thank my wife Susie who encouraged the project from the start, added her own reflections and cheerfully put up with all the time I spent at a busy computer.

I am very grateful to those who gave permission to use their photographs or qotations. We have endeavoured to make contact with all copyright holders and will seek to make appropriate settlement with all those whom we were unable to contact.

Any incompleteness in what has been recalled is my responsibility.

James Douglas-Hamilton

Foreword

I first met James Douglas-Hamilton at a student debate at Edinburgh University in 1964. We were both undergraduates in the Law Faculty but that was where the similarity ended.

James had arrived at Edinburgh with a somewhat awesome reputation. Already, the year before, he had been President of the Oxford Union. He had a boxing blue from Oxford and, what was more, he was Lord James, younger son of the Duke of Hamilton.

Within a year he had become President of Debates and had organised a Teach-in on Rhodesia, attended by over a thousand people including a galaxy of Ministers and statesmen, which was broadcast live on television for three hours by the BBC.

That was, and has remained, typical of James' strengths throughout a remarkably varied career. He possesses an impressive mixture of courage, tenacity, integrity and oratorical skill. But he combines it with a diffidence, a modesty and a hesitancy on social occasions which is both endearing to his friends and, often, puzzling to those who do not know him well.

But do not be fooled. As this excellent book demonstrates, James has had various targets in his public and political life. To a very considerable extent he has achieved them. He is a Privy Counsellor, an advocate at the Scots Bar, and has been a Minister of State and a Member of Parliament. He was one of the founding members of the Scottish Parliament and now sits in the House of Lords as Lord Selkirk of Douglas.

Unlike many politicians he, also, has a varied and significant hinterland. He has written three books, apart from this one. His first, *Motive for a Mission*, about Rudolf Hess's flight to Britain, won a literary award. He was active in the Territorial Army and is now an Honorary Air Commodore in the Reserves.

James is as nice as he seems but he is no saintly figure. He has been as ambitious as most politicians and has always landed on his feet. Take, for example, the chapter in this book about his renunciation of the Earldom of Selkirk because of his determination to remain an MP and assist John Major's Government with its slender majority.

All this is true but consider the course of events. James renounces the peerage thereby earning the gratitude of his Prime Minister and his Party. A year later, like many of us, he loses his seat in the 1997 General Election. John Major then sends him to the House of Lords in his Resignation Honours. Within a year the hereditary peers are expelled from the House of Lords by Tony Blair. James, however, is unaffected as he is a Life Peer not a hereditary earl! How is that for forward planning!

I have had the privilege of having James not just as a friend for over forty years but also as a colleague, as my Parliamentary Private Secretary in the Foreign Office, and as one of my Ministers when I was Secretary of State for Scotland.

He was a splendid Minister, especially at the Dispatch Box. On one occasion, at the height of the poll tax controversy, he was answering questions in the House on Burns Day. An Opposition MP tried to discomfit him by suggesting that if Robert Burns had been alive he would have described the Government Front Bench as "[sic] a parcel of rogues in the nation". James, completely unfazed, begged to disagree. He politely reminded the House that Scotland's bard had, after all, been a tax collector!

His greatest pride was representing his constituents in West Edinburgh. I recall one remarkable example of his persistence and organisational skills on their behalf. Proposals for a Western Relief Road in his constituency needed to be approved by the House of Commons. Because it was a local matter the division was going to be late at night when the House would, normally, be empty as there were no whipped votes.

James, not only, wrote to every Conservative MP requesting their presence. He also persuaded the Prime Minister, Margaret Thatcher, to leave a dinner she was attending in the House with MPs from the North West of England to vote in the division lobbies. The 30 Tory MPs that she was dining with came too, albeit with varying degrees of enthusiasm. One was heard to mutter that he had no idea why he was there but it was difficult to refuse James.

Parliament has had its ups and downs over the many centuries of its existence. MPs have been subject to particularly strong criticisms in recent months. That is often right and proper. James Douglas-Hamilton has always, quite rightly, been held in the highest respect by his fellow MPs and by the public.

The main loves of his life have been, and continue to be, Susie and his four stalwart sons, Andrew, Charles, Harry and Jamie. These personal satisfactions have been combined with a great love of Scotland and a very deep sense of public duty.

He completes these excellent memoirs by urging young people to get involved in political activity and public service. I hope they do. If they use James Douglas-Hamilton as their role model they won't go far wrong and their country will be the better for it.

Sir Malcolm Rifkind

CHAPTER 1

The Coronation and fighting for fun

One young page at Queen Elizabeth's Coronation was lost. He had been in Westminster Abbey for hours and all the magnificent ceremonial was over. Having done all that was required of him, he could not remember where he was supposed to go next!

I was ten years old and had received the imposing invitation to be present on this great State occasion from the Earl Marshal. It was a call which could not be refused as it came, "By Command of the Queen."

Why was I fortunate enough to receive such a special command? It was all down to my grandmother Helen Dowager Duchess of Northumberland who was Mistress of the Robes to the Queen Mother. The historic title originally conferred responsibility for the Queen's clothes and jewellery but more recently involved arranging rotas for ladies in waiting and performing certain duties at State ceremonies. My grandmother had become Mistress of the Robes to the then Queen Elizabeth in 1937 and remained with her during her years as Queen Mother until 1964. Now I was to act as page carrying my grandmother's coronet into the Abbey and walking behind her in the Queen Mother's procession.

As 2 June 1953 dawned I told my mother it was the most important day of my life – so far! After putting on my rather resplendent page's outfit, my grandmother and I went by taxi to Westminster and we assembled in the Abbey. I remember being allowed to sit on a chair near the peeresses during the ceremony. One of the highlights for me was Prince Philip's words of allegiance to the new Queen in which he promised to "become your liege man of life and limb and of earthly worship". I noticed that the Moderator of the General Assembly of the Church of Scotland had a key role along with the Archbishop of Canterbury in presenting the Bible to the new monarch. The Moderator Dr Pitt Watson with great dignity said "Here is wisdom; this is the royal Law; these are the lively oracles of God." I also remember the exhilarating fanfares of trumpets and the triumphant airs of Handel and Elgar. While I enjoyed the magnificent music, sitting among the huge audience were a certain Lord and Lady Tweedsmuir – none of us knew it then, but 20 years or so later I would marry their daughter Susan Buchan.

With the Coronation proceedings over, I found myself in the Abbey annexe where everyone was purposefully dispersing – everyone except me that is. Then I remembered somebody had given me a small card which enabled me to get access to the Royal Gallery in the House of Lords. An officer of the Parliament showed me the way.

There I was greeted by my father who informed me that the benign, splendidly attired gentleman standing a few feet away was the Prime Minister, Sir Winston Churchill. He was wearing the robes of the Order of the Garter over the very grand uniform of the Lord Warden of the Cinque Ports.

"Would you like to meet him?" my father asked. "I have been talking to him and he has been very moved by the day's events. In fact all he could say was 'Wonderful, wonderful,' as tears ran down his cheeks."

Since so great a man as Sir Winston had been overcome by the splendour of the proceedings, I felt I too was entitled to be overawed and I thought it best not to intrude on his emotions at such a moment. I did, however, become a lifelong fan and his colourful writings and quotes have provided me with a literary quarry to be mined ever since.

When I became an MP I remember a Conservative colleague, the late Julian Critchley, claiming that when Sir Winston used to enter the voting lobby in the House of Commons the ranks of the younger members would divide to make way for him and they would "watch history pass them by."

The Coronation is one of my most vivid boyhood memories and it was soon to be followed by the Procession of Honours in Scotland. My father, as Duke of Hamilton, had the duty of presenting the Crown of Scotland to the Queen in St Giles Cathedral, with myself as his page. This was a tremendous opportunity for the Scots to welcome their new monarch amidst substantial applause and it was a great success on the day.

However there were some disturbances involving the blowing up and defacing of pillar boxes, leading up to this event. Some Scots objected to their Queen being referred to as EIIR, since unlike England, Scotland had never had a Queen Elizabeth before. My father told me that he had written a long letter to the Prime Minister, Sir Winston Churchill, urging him to explain in detail the reasons for the higher numeral. He feared however that his point had not been taken. He said his letter was on more than one page of paper and if in the future I ever wrote a letter to the Prime Minister it must never exceed one page, advice which years later I always took.

Playing even a small role at the Coronation had been an unforgettable experience and for more than half a century since that day I have carried the memories of those carriages and coronets and all the brilliant technicolour pageantry with me.

I was born in 1942 at Dungavel House near Strathaven. After my older brother Angus and myself came three younger brothers Hugh, Patrick and David. Hugh was a romantic and a poet who acquired a wide knowledge of Scottish history and who sadly died in his forties. Patrick and David became talented musicians.

My mother Elizabeth Percy, who died in 2008, at the age of 92, was the daughter of the Duke and Duchess of Northumberland and was brought up in Alnwick Castle. Life at Alnwick in those days was conducted in grand style and my mother was related to a remarkable number of Dukes, including her grandfather the Duke of Gordon and her brother-in-law the Duke of Sutherland. She and her sister Diana were taught by a governess and never went to school. Their father died from appendicitis when my mother was only 13. After her sheltered upbringing, it must have been quite a change when she reached the age of 18 and was taken by my grandmother on a world tour which included China.

In 1937 she married my father Douglas, a man of action who was 14 years older, who had boxed for Scotland as Scotland's Middleweight Boxing Champion, and who already had a reputation as a pioneering aviator. They had a happy marriage for 36 years until he died suddenly at the age of 70. She was a clever, serene and tenacious person who had a love of music and the arts. When my brothers and I were young she enjoyed reading to us and would give wise counsel, advising that in life we should always make the best of the hand which we were given to play.

One of my mother's most interesting artistic projects was to arrange, on the advice of my brother Hugh, for the famous Austrian painter, Oskar Kokoschka, whose work Hitler had denounced as degenerate, to paint my father and her. The artist himself had warned against such a plan claiming his art was "brutal" but my mother was not to be dissuaded. The end result was dramatic and unusual. It captured my mother's calmness and serenity but was somewhat less flattering to my father. Should anyone wish to see it the painting is now in the possession of the Scottish National Portrait Gallery.

After her five sons grew up my mother directed her considerable energies towards founding the charity The Lamp of Lothian and was successful in raising funds to restore St Mary's Church in Haddington as well as other buildings which became a focal centre of the community. She also took pride in supporting her friend the great violinist, Yehudi Menuhin, by chairing the Governors' meetings of the school named after him in Surrey.

After she died, my cousin, Iain, an elephant expert in Kenya, wrote a poem in her honour which contains the line "We loved her for her presence in her day, for welcoming the fatherless to stay." This refers to the fact that Iain's father David, my father's youngest brother, had been killed serving as a photo reconnaissance pilot with the RAF in 1944. Years later I wrote a book entitled *The Air Battle for Malta* based on David's diaries as Squadron Commander of 603 (City of Edinburgh) Squadron, which had earlier achieved distinction for shooting down more enemy aircraft than any other in the Battle of Britain. In Malta in early 1942 the Spitfire pilots of his squadron were outnumbered by more than ten to one. In spite of everything, including starvation rations and being bombed four times a day, they won a decisive victory on 10 May 1942 recovering air supremacy over the strategic island. This was a turning point in the war for control of the Mediterranean, North Africa and the Middle East and the RAF, with the other services, had effectively raised the siege imposed on the island by Germany and Italy.

My mother's kindness and way with words was also evident when she wrote to a student friend of mine whose mother had died tragically long before her time. She wrote "I so much hope that your mother moved and touched and changed your life as my mother did for me." Years later after my mother's death my friend told me that "Reading those immensely consoling words, I remembered again all the good my mother had done and was glad."

Dungavel, a big house on a lonely Lanarkshire moor, became the family home when Hamilton Palace was pulled down in 1922. When I was six years old we moved to Lennoxlove in East Lothian. Dungavel House was subsequently sold to the National Coal Board and later purchased by the Government and turned into an open prison. Now it has become a reception centre for asylum seekers.

Many years later I went back there as the Scottish minister responsible for prisons. It was a strange feeling to see the rooms with which I had been familiar as a child converted into cells and I could still remember the way the pigeons had cooed in the pine trees outside as darkness fell.

One of my clearest memories of living at Dungavel was the presence of the Royal Air Force in the field opposite the house, the place where my father used to land, piloting a light aircraft. The servicemen were training on gliders and one day I had the pleasure of being wheeled in one of them across the field. I asked why we could not actually fly and was told that because of my small size I might fall out!

Looming large in my childhood memories is Nanny Chalmers, who we children regarded with much respect and a good deal of affection. Nanny was a disciplinarian who used to wield a wooden spoon to make sure her orders and wishes were obeyed. She was, unsurprisingly, very efficient and was regarded as something of an institution in the family.

When we were young my father enjoyed reading to us, one of his favourites was the heroic poem "Horatius" about the Roman soldier who prevented the city from being overwhelmed by a large hostile army. Horatius had held the bridge over the Tiber with two volunteers until it could be chopped down to stop the invaders crossing the river. It was the story of one man and his two friends standing up to a mighty multitude and triumphing. Thomas Macaulay who wrote it, was an MP for Edinburgh in 1838 and was obviously a man of strong convictions. The Prime Minister Lord Melbourne was supposed to have said of him "I wish I could be as certain of anything as Tom Macaulay is of everything."

Lennoxlove, which my father bought in 1948 was a house with a fascinating history. The original keep had been built in the twelfth century and had been added to over the years. It had previously been called Lethington and one of its owners Sir Richard Maitland had served as Secretary to Mary, Queen of Scots.

I remember as a boy wandering up and down the avenue of huge lime trees beyond the house and garden known as "the Politicians Walk" and conjuring up in my mind a vision of the troubled Queen treading delicately over the grass, deep in conversation with her minister.

The house also had a romantic connection with another famous woman – la Belle Stewart, who modelled for the figure of Britannia on coins. Her beauty had entranced King Charles II who showered her with gifts including a wonderful tortoiseshell cabinet which was destined to be housed at Lennoxlove and which I grew up admiring, being especially intrigued by its secret drawers. I also admired the full length portraits of Frances Stewart and her husband by the court painter Sir Peter Lely which my father, urged on by my mother, had bought along with the house and where he felt they belonged.

When she died in 1702, Frances Stewart, who had married the Duke of Richmond and Lennox, left a legacy to her nephew Alexander Blantyre with the condition that her trustees were to buy a house for him to be called "Lennox love to Blantyre." Lethington was purchased and in time the new name was shortened memorably to Lennoxlove.

I learnt that Lennoxlove also had a violent past. When preparations for the 21st birthday, of my brother Angus were being made, a trench was dug across the lawn to help create outside toilets and to our astonishment a number of cannonballs were uncovered. They had remained embedded there, probably the result of some English incursion centuries ago. When they had been fired they had apparently failed to penetrate the 15 feet thick walls and simply disappeared into the ground.

After we moved to Lennoxlove I remember going on a one-boy deputation to see my father. He had planned to send all his sons to Summerfield School in Oxford but I wanted to go to a school in Scotland. He agreed and I was enrolled as a boarder at Belhaven Hill School in Dunbar. My French master there was called Colin Mason and we were all impressed that his brother James, to whom he bore a strong resemblance, was a famous film star who had starred as Field Marshal Rommel in *The Desert Fox* and also as the dashing and unscrupulous Rupert of Hentzau in *The Prisoner of Zenda*.

When I was eight years old I remember my father taking my older brother and myself out in a small boat. He proceeded to row it from the harbour in North Berwick to the island of Craigleith. Leaving the boat some way up the bank we made our way to the top of the island. It was then that we discovered how quickly the weather can change in the Firth of Forth. A terrific wind blew up with such strength that you could lie against it without sinking to the ground.

We returned to the boat to head for home but by now the waves were huge. The boat was launched, with myself, sitting in the bow. A wave swept over it drenching me from head to foot. My brother was sitting in the stern of the boat and my father began to row. He took a great stroke with the oars and the boat advanced only to be hurled back by a monstrous wave.

Slowly the strength of my father began to prevail and some sixty minutes later we were a good distance from the island but still a worryingly long way from the harbour. I had only learnt to swim a few weeks earlier and was not a strong performer. As soon as we were 150 yards from the island amidst the mountainous waves I began seriously to doubt whether I would make it all the way back if the boat sank!

It was not long after that when I saw a welcome sight. The pilot boat from North Berwick was churning its way towards us – the result, I later learned, of a worried telephone call to the coastguard from my mother. My father kept rowing. He had got into his rhythm and was slowly defeating the elements. Only when the pilot boat circled around us did he agree to receive assistance.

Our vessel was tied to the pilot boat and the captain turned his craft in the direction of Norway. As he put on full power both boats leapt forward. We did not know what was in his mind but he told us that two students had hired the other rowing boat and had last been seen disappearing into the far distance of an increasingly stormy North Sea.

Eventually, when we could hardly see the Scottish mainland, the captain and his boat came close to the students. They were in deep distress and probably already suffering from hypothermia. The captain on circling their boat roared at them "Keep rowing you wet shower." I felt like saying to him that these were just ordinary students while my father had been middleweight boxing champion of Scotland so it was not surprising he had done better at the oars. One look at the captain however told me that he was not in the mood to receive such information.

Having been safely towed ashore, I walked home along the beach reflecting this had been a great adventure. My father on the other hand did not see it in quite the same light. All he said on the way back to our house was "No need to say anything about this to your mother!"

It was this episode which left me with an acute awareness of my father's great physical strength and which made me think about trying my hand at boxing. He had taught me the basics on the seashore near our home in North Berwick and I was eager to learn more.

The opportunity came when I arrived at Eton College aged 13. It was here that my training began in earnest, under the tutelage of former professional boxer, Reg Hoblin.

Eton in the 1950s was an archetypal English boys-only public school with more than a thousand pupils. It had been founded by

King Henry VI in 1440 for scholars then considered to be well qualified. We were told that the school had gone into mourning in 1820 upon the death of King George III who had been a great benefactor and the boys had taken to wearing dark tailcoats. Apparently the state of sorrow has continued for when I arrived the black coats were worn by all pupils. All, that is, except for those who were less than 5 feet and 4 inches in height who had to wear a shortened jacket, contemptuously referred to as a "bumfreezer", an indignity which did not come my way – thankfully I was of sufficient height.

One advantage of the school was that every boy had his own study/bedroom, and therefore had the opportunity to work hard without interruption before important exams. The teaching was of a very high standard and the "beaks" had a good relationship with the pupils. On one occasion I was astonished by our French teacher, Hubert Hartley, saying that we were the best class he had ever taught and he had arranged a surprise for us. He had indeed. Halfway through the class two ladies entered the classroom with bowls of strawberries and ice-cream. Sadly this was the only time that I was the recipient of such largesse while at school.

Younger boys under 15 had to undertake a certain amount of "fagging", which was the right of the most senior boys to insist on chores being carried out for their benefit. Also the Head of the House had the right to beat other boys for transgressions, if the House Master gave permission. I recall that a willowy garden cane was used, and that the Head of the House would take a run of about eight steps so as to wield the cane with maximum effectiveness. I thought little about such matters then, but later I came to the view that such practices and punishments were out of date and a distraction from work.

Years later when I was Minister for Education I was surprised to be presented by the Scottish Council for the Curriculum with a tawse, the leather strap used by teachers of state schools in Scotland to inflict corporal punishment. This action very much annoyed the civil servants with me, who considered it to be in very bad taste. A day or so later I telephoned the National Museums of Scotland, in case they might like a well worn tawse. After a search the National Museums confirmed they had no such historical item and would like to have it, so I gave it to them as a curiosity for future generations.

Sport was a big part of life at Eton and, for those who preferred rowing to cricket, one excitement was the opportunity to row and compete in races on the river. The 4th of June was always a day of tremendous celebration with a Procession of Boats in the evening, the highlight being when the boys in the boats would raise their oars and stand upright. The families on the bank would watch in fascination and with perhaps a touch of amusement in case the rowers' skills were less than perfect and one of the boats capsized. However if any rower were to deliberately cause a capsize catapulting all eight oarsmen into the river along with the cox he could anticipate an "Eight Tanning". This would be administered by the Captain of the Eight and was one of the most severe forms of corporal punishment at that time. Capsizing was not totally unknown but normally it just did not happen!

At the end of term we would sing the "Eton Boating Song", an extremely confident ditty accompanied by a most rousing tune. I also enjoyed the singing of American Civil War songs which was encouraged by the Head Master Robert Birley.

Another pleasure was playing with the Eton Golfing Team which gave me an insight into the splendour of the Berkshire

Courses, which were very good, although not in quite the same league as St Andrews or Muirfield in Scotland. A friend of mine on the golf team, Ewan Harvie-Watt, was also Scottish and our homeland was envied for more than just its golf courses. We were given what was known as "Scots Leave" at the end of term and allowed to depart from the school a day earlier than everyone else. On one such occasion while travelling to Scotland on the sleeper train, I remember, rather appropriately, reading the well-known thriller *The Thirty Nine Steps* by John Buchan. It was so enthralling I could not put it down but of course I did not have an inkling then that I would marry the author's granddaughter, some twenty years later.

While at Eton I joined the School Cadet Corps under the charismatic leadership of the Commanding Officer, Willie Gladstone, the great grandson of the illustrious Liberal Prime Minister. The year I joined, the Corps Camp was based at Loch Ewe in the North West Highlands of Scotland. For the first exercise I had to go on board a minesweeper and jump off it into water in which I was well out of my depth and make my way to shore. I quickly learnt that when you jump into deep water with a pack, pouches and a rifle you sink like a stone and swimming underwater becomes alarmingly difficult. To make matters worse I let go of the rifle and had to scrabble desperately for it in the murky depths. At last I found the weapon at my feet and struggled to the surface, my lungs bursting for air. Swimming became easier if I turned on my back and held my rifle in front of me and I made it to dry land.

A few hours later I and some other cadets were charged with the job of defending a bridge which was due to be attacked by regular soldiers from no less a unit than Her Majesty's Parachute Regiment! When the assault began the Paras gave us an all too real taste of battle when they fired a heavy smoke bomb from a mortar. This went off with a very loud bang between two cadets and just about fifteen feet from where I had taken up a defensive position. When they attacked fortunately the Paras fired only blank cartridges. I later learnt that if the smoke bomb had hit any of us on the head the chances of survival would have been slim. Being young, we made light of it. After all a miss is as good as a mile!

Before my time at Eton came to an end I had boxed 18 times for the school and won 14 bouts, narrowly losing four. As luck would have it I won my first five fights including the annual tournament of boxing between Eton, Bedford, Haileybury and Dulwich. On this occasion, as was often the case, I was taller than my opponents, who tended to be short with chests like barrels and punches like the kick of a horse. Therefore it was my purpose to use my longer reach to knock them dizzy long before they could get anywhere near me, tactics which worked well for a bit.

Squaring up to someone who is actually allowed to hit you is a unique experience. It is of course the art of self-defence and should involve getting hit as little as possible. Every now and then however a hard punch to the head gets through and you feel dizzy for a moment. Then your training kicks in and you fight back.

I remember four bouts in particular. Playing golf at North Berwick on one occasion, a friend told me that at Charterhouse School they had a brilliant boxer called Dyson, who had become something of a legend. Apparently he had had five fights and in each case had finished off his opponent in the first round. I put this daunting piece of information to the back of my mind until the next term, when I was informed that I had been selected to

14

fight Charterhouse, and that I had nothing to worry about, since my opponent had only had five fights and lacked my experience. I asked what his name was and was told that it was Dyson.

To say that I was alarmed would be an understatement. When I told Reg Hoblin who it was I was up against he advised me to move round to my right, so that if my opponent had a very powerful right hand punch it would have further to travel and would not have the same force if I was moving away from it. For about thirty to forty seconds I did as Reg had said and then he came for me with fists flailing. To my shame I forgot everything I had ever learned and started hurling punches back. I was wondering why my punches were having no effect when all of a sudden I found the referee in front of me shouting at me to go to a corner. Behind him, in the middle of the ring, was Dyson, sitting on his bottom. It was only when I arrived in the corner that I realised that I had hit him with a right just as he was coming forward which had doubled the force of the blow. It occurred to me that this was what he was supposed to be doing to me, but before I could think any further the referee told him he had had enough and it was over. My relief knew no bounds.

However, life in the ring was not always as simple. I was expected to win my weight in the school boxing, but there was a boy called Charles Verey, who was a magnificent defensive fighter. In a large ring he would leap from one side to another dodging punches, rather like a panther, delivering huge punches in exchange. I came up against him in the semi-finals and adopted entirely the wrong procedure. I should have boxed him but I did not. I went straight for him with maximum aggression and in defence he was always at his best. By the middle of the third round I thought I was well ahead, but overconfidence proved to be my undoing. I left my chin unguarded for a brief moment and he hit me with a superb right hand punch over my guard, which in normal circumstances would have been a knockout punch. I must have been very fit, because although I went down I was back on my feet a split second later, my head singing like a tea kettle. I remember thinking, I am so far ahead it is not going to matter, but I was wrong. By a split majority of the three judges Charles Verey got the decision. I knew that one day I would have to fight him again.

That fight came in the semi-finals next year when I was feeling under the weather with an extremely bad cold, but I knew I had to fight Charles just the same. Again instead of boxing him I chose the wrong tactics and attacked him from beginning to end, and in the middle of the third round he hit me with a tremendous punch under the heart. I remember feeling very weak, but this time I was genuinely so far ahead it did not make any difference and I got the decision. Afterwards I had difficulty in breathing and a great pain in my chest. I was taken to the sanatorium with, as it turned out, a punctured lung.

When the next boxing season came around I had recovered and won all my remaining fights for Eton. I used to train with an extremely strong middleweight called Robin Watson, who later captained the Oxford Boxing Team. I boxed at lightweight and recognised that Robin had a mighty punch. Usually I could skip out of the way, but during one afternoon of training I ran out of luck, and he caught me with a punch in the pit of the stomach which knocked all the wind out of me. It was a good number of seconds before I could continue.

During my next fight against Bradfield I had an opportunity to put into practice what I had so painfully learned from Robin Watson. I noticed that my opponent was not guarding his stomach and gave him a straight left to his solar plexus. The effect was electrifying. He let out a loud howl which reverberated around the gym into the street beyond. Anyone passing who was not aware of the finer points of the noble art of self-defence would have thought someone was being bushwhacked! Naturally I knew what to do which was to take up the posture of a victorious fighter who knows his opponent has had enough.

What happened next I still remember as one of the most disagreeable episodes in my life. The referee said "Douglas-Hamilton will you keep your punches up." I knew with absolute certainty that my punch had been a good six inches above the belt but to my dismay he said it again. I had no desire to punch my opponent again and could tell from his body language that he feared me. Just as sharks circle when there is blood on the water, I walked around him knowing that I could not risk a further body punch. Finally I caught him with a left hook and he went down on the canvas and this time it was all over.

Sometime later I passed the referee in the gym and to my astonishment he apologised to me. He told me that I had delivered a perfect punch but because the boy's father had been sitting next to him, he felt he had to say something. Since the referee was likely to be in charge of further matches, in which I might be involved, I decided not to reply but felt that he had done neither of us any favours by giving a misleading impression.

One of my sparring partners at that time was the now famous explorer Sir Ranulph Fiennes. He later told a newspaper that I had a weird way of sidestepping. In fact I was keeping out of the way of his punches. He was very strong, and I reckoned that if I ever had to fight him for real, it would be extremely tough since he could hit harder than anyone of his weight or age group.

My last fight in the school boxing competition was just before the welcome news arrived that I had got a place at Balliol College, Oxford University. A year later I found myself training with the Oxford Boxing team. The first fight I had for Oxford was against the then Loughborough College and I was up against an army sergeant, who was tough but did not have a good guard. When I delivered a right hand punch he went down and the second time he received a right hand punch he went down again. While he was on the canvas I was given a dressing down from the referee for putting my hand on the ropes before going to a neutral corner. Despite these extra seconds my opponent could not beat the count of ten.

Pride comes before a fall, as I was soon to learn. I was sent to box the Sandhurst team where all the cadets, dressed in full military uniform, had come to watch the fun. Regrettably the first two Oxford boxers were knocked down and their fights stopped. When I got in the ring I had not the slightest idea that I would be up against one of the toughest soldiers in the British Army, David le Sueur. Blissfully unaware I sallied forth in the hope that I would knock him out with all possible speed. I caught him with two solid rights and, although his knees seemed to wobble, to my surprise he did not go down. Then it all happened. He closed with me in what can only be described as a fearsome scrimmage in a corner of the ring and I found myself on the floor with a violent pain in my right knee but a clear head. I got up immediately but my knee gave way a second time and again I was on the floor. I was not dizzy and I was unaware of any heavy punches coming my way, but at the beginning of the second round the referee could see I was having trouble with my knee and stopped the match. It was the only time in my life that I did not complete a fight.

Knowing that something was wrong with me, I alerted my father who summoned me to London where he had laid on a meeting with the top surgeon, Dr Reginald Watson-Jones, who informed me that I had ripped my cartilage at both ends, an injury which often came the way of footballers. He wanted to operate immediately but, wishing to spend Christmas at home, I volunteered to go in to an Edinburgh hospital. This caused Dr Reginald Watson-Jones to send a very long telegram to my father informing him that his qualifications were such that there was no need for me to go elsewhere. However, when he was told that the leading Edinburgh surgeon, Mr Lawson-Dick, would be responsible, he withdrew his opposition and the operation went ahead.

A few weeks later back at Oxford I felt I had to make up for lost time. Training recommenced and I was selected to fight the Belsize Boxing Club in Chelsea Town Hall. I remember getting in the ring and hearing somebody in the audience shout "Let's see what the bloody aristocracy can do." I glanced in the direction of the shout and saw a group of men in pinstripe suits with a haze of cigarette smoke above their heads. The coach, Alf Gallie, former boxing champion of Wales, told me to pay no attention and the fight commenced. At the end of the first round I was ahead on points and at the very beginning of the second round my opponent came straight at me throwing numerous punches. I immediately planted a right hand punch on the side of his jaw. When I had done that sort of thing to David le Sueur at Sandhurst he had just shaken his head and carried on as though nothing had happened. But this opponent collapsed across the ring on to the ropes. I went for him with the intention of bringing the fight to an end, but as I did so the referee shouted "Stop" and I realised he was not going to allow me to punch him again.

In training for the Oxford against Cambridge match of 1962, I was still getting trouble from my knee and went to a physiotherapist who happened to be blind. He brought me good luck by helping enormously in the preparations for the fight against Cambridge. Provided my knee did not give way, I would have a chance. Here it has to be admitted that Oxford versus Cambridge bouts are not like other boxing matches, since both sides go flat out to knock out their opponents as quickly as possible.

One of the very strict rules was that each boxer had to weigh in at no more than his correct weight division. I had to take off a few pounds to qualify for the lightweight division, so I stopped drinking any fluids the day of the weigh-in. Having hit the mark, I thankfully consumed a lot of water. I asked about my opponent, Roger Houghton, and was told he was Cambridge's vice captain and that he had knocked out his Oxford opponent the year before. Apparently he boxed rather like an expert chess player, sizing up the other man's weaknesses before going in to finish the fight.

At this point I wondered why on earth I had taken up this sport and then I remembered. My father had been a champion as well as being captain of Oxford's boxing team and his example had fired my enthusiasm. He had been known as "the Boxing Marquis" and maybe I hoped that some of his skill would rub off on me. On this occasion I felt I was under particular pressure as the captain of our team, Malcolm Faber, had also invited my father to give away the prizes.

As the match approached I was having my hands bandaged to avoid breaking any thumbs and was informed that two of my team mates had already been knocked out. This was unsettlingly swift – my boxing gloves still had to be pulled on. I sized up my opponent as I walked down towards the ring and noticed that he had the same height and build as myself.

During the first round the punches came thick and fast and I tried out my best manoeuvre. I feinted with the left and delivered a right hand punch followed by a left hook, but I had not put my full weight behind the punch and he covered up like a hedgehog. In the second round it was his turn and after an exchange of blows, I felt my knee give way and I went back on the ropes. In the last round we both tried furiously to land a knockout punch. Our fists met in midair before the final bell. It had been one of the longest nine minutes of my life and at the end of it I genuinely did not know who had won.

The fight was staged in Oxford Town Hall with more than 1,000 people in the audience. I got the decision – as well as a broken nose. My victory turned the tide and Oxford beat Cambridge by one fight. When my proud father gave away the prizes he said it had been "a jolly good show." My brother Angus, who was in the audience, later said nothing about the boxing only that he thought our father's contribution was a bit over the top. Later Roger Houghton wrote on my programme "Grand fight. Well done. Good luck for next year."

Boxing at Eton was abolished shortly after I left and at many other fee-paying schools as well. The British Medical Association has expressed grave reservations about the sport and I am well aware that some people think it should be banned.

I venture to disagree. No sport or adventurous outdoor activity is without some risk. Of course boxing should have strict medical safeguards which amateur boxing already has. To ban it altogether could drive it underground where the risks involved would be far greater. In my opinion the noble art of self-defence teaches youngsters how to look after themselves in difficult circumstances and can greatly increase self-confidence and physical fitness.

21

I think something of the thrill and excitement of the ring was caught by the poet John Masefield when he wrote "Who never felt a boxer's trim, Of brain divinely knit to limb, Nor felt the whole live body go, One tingling health from tip to toe."

My last fight for Oxford was against the captain of the German Universities whom I beat on points, but when I hung up my boxing gloves that night I had a feeling I would not fight again. I wanted to try my hand at something else and stood for office in the Oxford Union.

CHAPTER 2

Oxford Union President and demonstrations over South Africa

By a stroke of good luck, towards the end of my time at Eton, Willie Gladstone became my moral tutor. He never lectured me about unbecoming conduct but he did tell me exactly what studies I would have to undertake if I were to have any prospect of getting a place at university.

He warned me in June 1960 that any possibility of getting into Balliol College, at Oxford University was a "far higher hurdle" than I could be expected to jump. Even so I reckoned that by the time I had absorbed his teaching I might be able to make it, and on 17 December that year I was informed that I had been admitted to Balliol to read History.

He wrote to me a few months later recommending books to read and the merits of the Territorial Army. Taking his advice, I joined the 6/7th Battalion Cameronians Scottish Rifles immediately.

Willie Gladstone had the gift of imparting his own skill at putting together a persuasive essay and making the best use of limited knowledge. Before tutorials his enthusiastic encouragement was often preceded by the playing of stimulating music by such composers as Corelli and Vivaldi.

My interest in debating was kindled by him, and at Oxford I attended virtually every single Union debate. Speaking there was, to me, a much more frightening experience than boxing, as you have to think on your feet and respond to a vociferous audience.

The Union is probably the most famous debating society in the world and has a well-established reputation for attracting high quality speakers from all walks of life. In the summer of 1962 I took my first step on the road to realising my ambition to be President of this prestigious body by being elected to the Union's Library Committee.

A friend at Balliol introduced me to Harold Lind who had been a Chairman of the Labour Club, and had received a First Class Honours Degree. He was referred to by some as "the Brain of Britain" as he had won a TV quiz. Harold sent me pamphlets on the subject of anarchy on the grounds that if I was to debate successfully in the Union I would have to know what arguments my most extreme opponents wished to support. By the time I was asked to give a main speech I was prepared for those with ultra left wing tendencies, and it went well.

In due course I allowed my name to go forward for the position of Secretary against Jonathan Aitken, a prominent Union member and polished performer, who was expected to win. However after four recounts I was found to be ahead by two votes. I telephoned Harold Lind with the result, and there was a long silence. He had given me tips as an old professional assists a young novice, but he had never expected me actually to win.

In the summer term of 1963 I worked for the new President Jeffrey Jowell, who allowed me to speak in favour of a motion calling for sanctions to be imposed against the Apartheid regime in South Africa. This seemed to capture the mood of the students and I sought to justify the case by ending with these words:

"It is a way of helping the people of South Africa towards the most peaceful solution, and towards the end of the present atmosphere of hate. One day, we hope that South Africa will come back into the Commonwealth – a South Africa where there is a real unity of races. Mr. President, the white man's burden is now his conscience."

This went down well with Union members and at the end of term I was elected to the position of Librarian of the Union, only one step away from the Presidency. It was at this time I was informed that Desmond Donnelly MP, with whom I had spoken in a debate, had recommended me for the Junior Konigswinter Trip. This meant a chance to attend a conference in Germany of British and German students interested in peaceful development in Europe. I accepted the invitation and travelled to West Berlin, where I met Donald Dewar for the first time and future Tory Leader Michael Howard.

Donald was a student at Glasgow University and I soon learnt was one of the very best debaters of his generation having won the Observer Mace competition. In Berlin he was devastating with his scorn and contempt towards all grandees at the top of the Conservative Party from Prime Minister Harold Macmillan downwards. He was very polemical in his language as well as being extremely entertaining.

Overshadowing our visit and the conference was the presence of the Berlin Wall, which had been built two years earlier by Walter Ulbricht's Communist Government to prevent East Germans from making their way to the West. We were taken as a group to see the Wall and the death zone in the no man's land between the east and west parts of the city. In particular we were shown the spot where the first person attempting to get over the Wall was shot by Communist border guards and left to die without medical attention. His name was Peter Fechter. I remember the West Berlin police becoming very agitated and displeased when one of us ventured too close to the Wall.

One particular episode clearly illustrated the grim circumstances of the Cold War. We were asked by the German English Interchange Council to take presents to East Berlin families and to tell the authorities that we were simply visiting friends. The packages we carried included food and clothing. We travelled by underground railway and when armed communist border guards stopped us, our leader, a nervous looking young man, was taken to an adjacent room for interrogation. The rest of us were detained in a large room for several hours while Donald Dewar let us know how annoyed he was at being treated in this way. As for the rest of us we all took a good look at the border guard with the loaded machine gun sitting at the entrance before saying too much.

Eventually all our parcels were confiscated but we were allowed to enter East Berlin. Donald, Harold Lind and I visited the Soviet war memorial which consisted of an enormous statue of a Russian soldier trampling on a swastika and at the other end a mother mourning the human sacrifice of war. As we walked through the streets the difference between the two parts of the divided city was all too obvious, West Berlin being a showpiece of consumer choice in comparison with the impoverished East.

A day or two before our brush with the Communist border guards we had been told that we were all going to be taken to the Central Square of West Berlin, where the US President, John F Kennedy, was to address a vast audience of West Berliners.

I was standing with Donald Dewar and Harold Lind, about

100 feet away from the dais which was erected in front of the city hall, when a young sunburnt man full of charisma and vitality emerged. It was of course President Kennedy and he proceeded to make the most powerful address I had ever heard. His speech implied that an attack by the Soviet Union on the enclave of West Berlin would be interpreted in the same way as an attack on London or Washington.

Each sentence was given in English, and then translated into German. When it became clear what he was saying the crowd of hundreds of thousands of Berliners went wild with enthusiasm. Kennedy told them "And there are some who say in Europe and elsewhere we can work with the Communists. Let them come to Berlin." It was a catchphrase which echoed throughout the speech.

He had begun by recalling "Two thousand years ago the proudest boast was 'Civis Romanus sum' [I am a Roman citizen]. Today in the world of freedom, the proudest boast is 'Ich bin ein Berliner.'" He ended with the rallying cry "All free men wherever they may live are citizens of Berlin, and, therefore, as a free man, I take pride in the words 'Ich bin ein Berliner.'"

Later some of the commentators engaged in a grammatical and semantic argument that the word "Berliner" used in that way actually meant a doughnut. All I can say having been there, is that not a single person at the time doubted he was identifying himself with the unique importance of keeping West Berlin free.

When the speech ended I remember the huge crowd began to shout with intense enthusiasm "Kenn-e-dy, Kenn-e-dy!" What he had said had made a tremendous impact upon them. They believed, as would other Western European nations, that the American President had given an ultimatum to the Russians to back off from contemplating an attack on West Berlin. That night on Air Force

One a weary but happy President Kennedy apparently acknowledged to aide and speech writer Ted Sorensen "We'll never have another day like this one as long as we live." He had the ability to leave his audience full of optimism and hope. To me that day, he represented youth, idealism and courage – none of us then could have guessed that sadly he had only a few months to live.

When I returned home I told my father about being present at this historic occasion. To my astonishment he had just come back from Washington where he had represented British Building Societies as their President and he had been welcomed by none other than John F Kennedy at a chance meeting in the White House.

It seems everyone can recall where they were when the tragic news from Dallas came through on 22 November 1963. I was in the Oxford Union and refused to accept what I had heard. I walked back to Balliol College and as I looked through the window of the Junior Common Room I saw a group of my friends, one of whom was holding up a radio with tears running down his cheeks. He was the American Rhodes scholar Walt Slocombe, who would later become US Under Secretary of Defence. It was then I knew that President Kennedy was dead. I later attended the university tribute to the President when we stood in respectful silence near the Bodleian Library.

Strangely enough, almost a decade earlier I had met Mr Khrushchev, the Russian leader, who was President Kennedy's sparring partner during the tense days of the Cuban Missile Crisis. My father as Duke of Hamilton was Hereditary Keeper of Holyrood Palace and he had also been appointed Lord Steward of the Queen's Household. He had been asked to welcome Mr Bulganin, the Soviet premier and Mr Khrushchev, then first secretary of the Communist Party (known collectively as B and K in the British tabloids) to tea there during their visit to Britain in 1955. I was invited to attend and vividly remember being surprised by the twinkle in Mr Khrushchev's eye. Mr Bulganin was being charming to my mother as she gave him tea at a small table while my father did the same for Mr Khrushchev, who liked china tea. My father told him he had visited Moscow when he was MP for East Renfrew in the 1930s and the Russian leader claimed that everything had changed since then – an apparent reference to the process of DeStalinisation.

Back at the Oxford Union in the winter of 1963 the candidates for the presidency all took part in a debate on the motion that the House of Commons was not an effective democratic assembly. I was asked to defend the Commons and hoped that Christopher Mayhew, the Labour MP, who was a former president of the Union, would be asked to speak with me. However the current President Tony Hart overruled me saying he had invited Lord Lambton whom he claimed was not a reactionary and was a good House of Commons man, while Mayhew was said to be "very dogmatic."

During the debate the Liberal Candidate for the presidency Garth Pratt got the better of Lord Lambton in an exchange. The next day Pratt was elected president of the Union with myself coming in second and Jonathan Aitken third. I was determined to stand again.

My chance came when my Trotskyite opponent Richard Kirkwood agreed to debate the motion "This House would destroy Liberal Democracy." He arranged to propose this motion with the support of Paul Foot, nephew of Michael Foot, the future Leader of the Labour Party.

It seemed likely that Paul Foot would speak in favour of revolutionary action so I laid an ambush for him and on the night in question he did exactly what was expected of him. The Oxford

Union's audience at that time was in the main liberal and left of centre but certainly not totalitarian in outlook. This gave me the opportunity to engage in sustained ridicule of my opponents to the delight of the audience. I began:

"When somebody thinks that he is right and everyone else is wrong in politics it is called prejudice, in religion it is called bigotry, in a lunatic asylum it is called normality and in the Oxford Union it is sometimes called Richard Kirkwood.

"I have listened with great interest to the proposers and now realise where they stand politically. They are looking at society through contact lenses overlaid by pages of Marxism, overlaid by pages of Trotskyism, not to mention revisionism and left-wing deviationism, with a touch of right-wing Kautskyism and modern dogmatism. But the isms which they support most fervently, and vehemently of all are obscurantism and bourgeois intellectualism. The result is their left hand does not always know what their left hand is doing...

"The Proposition said it is no good for the people trying to achieve anything through democratic means, because they will be frustrated by monopolies, free competition and the Press Barons. But who would have thought in 1900 when all these things existed in a more controlled form that the few men gathered round Keir Hardie were going to start a Party which would become the Government within 24 years.

"Yet because there was a need for the Labour Party, and because people wanted it, it came into existence. Of course it was a struggle but monopolies, competition, Press Barons and the lot would not prevent the Labour Party from coming to power.

"That is why we defend Liberal Democracy, because views can be expressed and parties can be formed when the people think that there is a need for them. We can guarantee you safeguards against the eternal control of one group or an all-wise ruler. The Proposition cannot ...

"Now after listening to the frightening militancy of Mr. Paul Foot and the Treasurer it is self-evident that they could not even break up a Vicarage Sunday school tea-party, let alone the whole of Britain...

"The fatalist defeatism expressed in this Motion is saying that rule by coercion or benevolent paternalism is better than government by consent... As Mill said 'if all mankind minus one were of one opinion and only one person were of the contrary opinion, mankind would be no more justified in silencing that one person, than he if he had the power would be justified in silencing mankind.' It is this respect for the dignity of the individual which makes liberal democracy an ideal of government to which men should aspire and not look on with shame... It is clear Mr. President that we would rather have respect for human dignity than accept the politics of superstition."

The next day to my surprise I received a supportive letter from an American student called David Boren, who would later become a US Senator. He wrote:

"I certainly expect you to win this election... I have heard

31

few speeches that matched yours in technical oratorical proficiency, but that was not what impressed me most. I was impressed by your obvious sincerity and integrity coupled with a sizeable proportion of intellectual rigour. I don't think that anyone ever doubted that you had these qualities, but the ability to project the qualities through the mechanism of oratory is a unique one…

"What I hope is that you will recognise that you have these capabilities which I think showed themselves fully for the first time last night and that you will have enough confidence in them to consider a political career your life's work."

Strengthened by such a message of support, I learnt at the end of the count that I won by an overall majority. However, David Boren's enthusiasm for my election was not shared by everyone.

Randolph Churchill, Sir Winston's son, wrote an article in the *Spectator* on 13 March 1964 complaining that while my election as President of the Oxford Union had been reported by the *Daily Sketch*, the *Daily Express* and the *Daily Mail*, they had not reported the election of Charles Edward Lysaght as President of the Cambridge Union. He wrote "The trouble is that while Mr Lysaght is tolerably well connected he does not have any handle to his name to furnish any snob appeal to the readers of the popular press."

I had once heard Randolph speaking to the Union, delivering an attack on "the Gutter Press", and since this was yet another criticism of journalists which had nothing to do with me, I noted Randolph's views without comment. I began to prepare for the debates of the summer term, deliberately including what may have been the

Oxford Union's first inter-university debate. A highlight turned out to be the debate on the motion "That Southern Rhodesia should not be permitted independence until there is majority rule." This would be supported by Iain Macleod and former Prime Minister of Rhodesia, Garfield Todd. It was opposed by the Earl of Sandwich and Stephen Hastings, a Tory MP. Robin Day, another ex-President of the Union, along with Philip Whitehead, helped organise the televising of key elements of this debate. When Iain Macleod and Garfield Todd won, with a majority of more than 15 to 1, Lord Sandwich graciously accepted defeat and claimed that Oxford had always been the home of lost causes.

Towards the end of that term I was out of circulation sitting degree exams, which were not without incident. During my first paper the Chairman of the Examiners stood over me glowering and informed me that I was wearing brown shoes which were not allowed under the examination rules. He said "If you are not wearing black shoes in the next exam, I will send you straight out." This caused me considerable alarm as there were only a few minutes between exams and I would have had no time to buy new shoes. I dashed off to see my great friend, sadly now the late, Neil MacCormick, later Regius Professor of Law at Edinburgh University and more recently a special adviser to SNP First Minister Alex Salmond. He very generously lent me a large pair of somewhat leaky but very definitely black shoes. I always attributed full responsibility for my Oxford MA to him!

The Chairman of the Examiners had another go at me some weeks later. I had to attend an interview on my degree exams and having submitted my thesis on Singapore and its transition from colonialism to self-government, he proceeded to cross-examine me on it. Somewhere I had written down a sentence about the exploitation of raw materials in developing countries, which had seemed like a good idea at the time. But he alleged that this was Marxist-Leninist dialectic and made me a crypto-Marxist. Since I had been a recent President of the Conservative Association I did not consider that I needed to reply to his preposterous suggestion and happily the rest of the interviewing board did not take his remarks seriously.

The Degree exams were finished but they turned out to be just a lull before the real storm – a major row which would receive national news coverage was about to erupt in the Oxford Union. Without my knowledge, the President of the Conservative Association, Stephen Dollond, had invited the South African Ambassador, Mr Carel De Wet, to come to Oxford to address a meeting of the Association. The visit had been arranged in secret while I was occupied with sitting degree exams. Had I known, I would have advised against it because of the strength of hostile feeling towards the Apartheid Regime. In any case I would have argued that arranging such a secret meeting would be asking for trouble, as the news would be sure to leak. That is exactly what happened and busloads of hardened demonstrators appeared from London.

Stephen Dollond had booked a room in the Union to give a glass of sherry to the Ambassador before his speech that evening. I noticed that the Treasurer of the Union, the student radical Tariq Ali, was present and being somewhat excited, he hissed when the South African Ambassador came on to the premises. The former President of the Union, Garth Pratt, also objected to the Ambassador coming on to the Union premises on the grounds that there was currently a boycott of South African goods and said to me "You are the bloody President. Turn them off." Since nobody had broken any Union rules, I took no action and Pratt put a Motion on the board deploring that

I as President had allowed the South African Ambassador to use the Union as a place of refuge, and that I had allowed the police onto the premises without the permission of the Union's Standing Committee, thereby causing inconvenience to members.

The Ambassador was taken to the hall opposite to make his speech and the demonstration began, consisting I thought of about 250 protestors. Some demonstrators attempted to let down the tyres of the Ambassador's car when he tried to leave after the meeting and during the course of the evening four arrests were made. Towards the end Tariq Ali addressed the crowd urging them to come to the Union on the next night and to vote for the Motion which would be presented.

The next day Garth Pratt's Motion, which had more than 100 signatures put down in support, was withdrawn and Tariq Ali put down his Motion deploring those responsible for allowing the police and Ambassador to come on to the Union premises as this produced disturbances. Apparently Eric Abrahams, the next President, urged Tariq Ali to withdraw his Motion which he subsequently did. Then another student called Roderick Floud decided to put down a Motion of Censure on me.

That evening I welcomed the guest speakers and I was told that if I made a full and complete apology to the House, Floud would consider withdrawing his Motion, but I paid no attention. During the debate I called Floud and asked John McDonnell to take the chair. Floud moved his Censure Motion and then I was called. Making a strong plea for freedom of expression I said:

> "There is no rule of the Society to exclude any guest of any member because the majority of the Society disapprove of what he stands for. The boycott rule does not apply to South

Africans... and this is no precedent. Several years ago Sir Oswald Moseley, whose views are equally unpopular actually spoke in a debate. I would not have asked him but that is neither here nor there.

"Indeed last winter I introduced on to Union premises two men whose views I do not agree with from the People's Republic of China, and I might add that it was the first time they had ever spoken to a university in this country... Those who really believe in freedom of expression believe in that for every human being and not just for those whom we like."

In the midst of my speech John McDonnell had an exchange with Tariq Ali, accusing him of ushering the Ambassador around the Union premises. This was not quite correct since he had opened the door but he had hissed as he did so. Tariq Ali replied "That is a lie, a malicious lie and unless you withdraw I shall walk out." John McDonnell refused to withdraw, whereupon Ali walked out, the lights in the Union went off and 150 of the 800 in the audience followed.

In order to get proceedings operational again, I persuaded another former President, Jeffrey Jowell, to take the chair, the lights went on and the 150 returned. I finished saying "Whether you vote for me or against me, you will never convince me that I as one person had a moral right to discriminate against someone because I detested their views. In any case I make no apology whatsoever." Jeffrey Jowell called two more speakers, Michael Beloff spoke against me and Harold Lind spoke for me. The Adjournment Motion was declared overwhelmingly defeated and I returned to the chair.

Meanwhile Tariq Ali and Roderick Floud went out and another exodus occurred, this time about 120 leaving and we proceeded with a debate that the Commonwealth Immigration Act should be rigidly applied to the Celtic Fringe, a bit of humorous light relief after what had gone before.

One of the speakers that night was William Douglas-Home, brother of the Conservative Prime Minister. He made a very entertaining speech about "the Douglas Cause", a subject my father had told me never to mention, and about which William had also written a play.

In the eighteenth century the Duke of Douglas had died childless, making the heir to his vast lands in Lanarkshire the eldest son of his sister Lady Jane Douglas. She unexpectedly gave birth to twins in Paris at the age of 50 and Archie Douglas the older of the two therefore became the heir. The Duke of Hamilton would be next in line to inherit, if Archie and his twin were not in fact Lady Jane's sons. He took legal action unsuccessfully and in my view quite wrongly, to try and prove this.

William Douglas-Home said that while this matter had been subject to debate, the child should always be given the benefit of the doubt, a sentiment and conclusion with which I was in total agreement. I would later see the play with my brother Hugh, in which Andrew Cruickshank of TV's *Dr Finlay's Casebook* played a leading role. When we were introduced to him afterwards as sons of the Duke of Hamilton, he was astonished that we had come to see the play and one of the other actors said it was all irrelevant anyway, as the State is going to inherit all the land eventually through death duties. This was not a sentiment which found favour with either me or Sir Alec Douglas-Home when I told him.

Soon after that eventful meeting at the Union, I found myself invited to another Junior Konigswinter Conference in West Berlin, where I was asked to Chair the Plenary Session, as Donald Dewar had done the year before. While in Berlin my mother wrote me a letter telling me that the demonstrations against the South African Ambassador were still provoking aftershocks. The Oxford University Disciplinary Officers, namely the Proctors, had become involved. The past President of the Union, Garth Pratt, the newly elected President, Eric Abrahams and Tariq Ali had apparently all left Oxford but had received a summons from the Vice Chancellor. It appeared that measures taken against Eric Abrahams, including "gating", might make it impossible for him to carry out his duties as President of the Union.

My mother was anxious that I should be left in no doubt about my father's strong views on the whole situation. "He thinks it is very important that anything you might feel inclined to do to help Eric or any of the others should not be done in any way that could be taken to imply that you were in favour of mobbing up ambassadors" she wrote.

It seemed to me that Eric Abrahams could do with some support, so that he could do justice to his term as President of the Oxford Union. Accordingly I arranged to put down a motion in his support at the first meeting of the Union in the Winter Term. The motion reaffirmed the right of all members of the University to take part in orderly peaceful demonstrations and condemned the banning in advance of student participation in demonstrations permitted by the city police. It also condemned the arbitrary decisions and punishments meted out by the Proctors in connection with the recent visit of the South African Ambassador.

The motion went through unanimously and a thoroughly interesting evening ensued. Eric Abrahams had persuaded Mrs Bandaranaike, Prime Minister of Sri Lanka to attend, and one of the speakers in the debate, whom I met, was the American Black

Power advocate, Malcolm X. When I spoke to him he replied pleasantly but his image was a potentially aggressive one when he spoke on a platform. When he addressed the students much of his speech was unexceptional, but the violence of his language when he referred to "white rapists" was such that it was possible to imagine him inciting large crowds. He too would be murdered, but in his lifetime he would not attract as big a cross section of support as Martin Luther King. Malcolm X's message was not as socially inclusive as that of Dr King's dream, of black and white Americans enjoying the same opportunities to achieve their potential in harmony with each other.

At the end of the evening I felt I had fulfilled all the obligations I had to the Oxford Union. It had been a fascinating place, which had provided a window on to world events for me. It had also been an excellent training ground for public speaking, which I had discovered could at times be as turbulent mentally as boxing had been physically.

CHAPTER 3

Cape to Cairo and a teach-in on Rhodesian UDI

In the autumn of 1964 I was due to start my law degree at Edinburgh University but before then there was a wonderful opportunity to take two months out and embark on a ten country tour of universities from Cape Town to Cairo. During this eventful odyssey I managed to fall foul of the apartheid regime in South Africa, was asked to leave the island of Zanzibar by the immigration authorities, and received five-star hospitality, from the Kabaka of Buganda. In Cairo I was told I could eat for a penny a day and having tried it ended up with stomach trouble by the time I reached Jerusalem.

I arrived in Johannesburg in early August and was fortunate to be welcomed by one of South Africa's foremost industrialists, Harry Oppenheimer, and his wife Bridget.

Apart from being morally wrong, it seemed to me that the policy of apartheid or separate development would certainly fail in the long term economically since the African Bantustans, covering some 13 per cent of the land area, were primarily agricultural, densely populated and lacking in industrial development. The wealth creating sector lay in white areas, whose separate identity was enforced by law.

Harry Oppenheimer was liberal in outlook and believed that growth of the economy would act as "the main agent for change," and he was in the forefront of those who wished to work for peaceful reform. Through him I had the opportunity to visit a diamond mine, which brought home to me the extent of Southern Africa's enormous mineral reserves.

From there I went to stay with Mrs Helen Suzman – for 13 years the solitary MP for the Progressive Party in the South African parliament who vigorously opposed the apartheid regime. Jeffrey Jowell, with whom I had worked closely in the Oxford Union, had married her daughter Francie.

Helen, who died at the beginning of 2009, aged 91, was a most remarkable person. Strong minded, courageous and forthright in her views, she had become "the conscience vote of South Africa," among white South Africans. I was allowed to borrow her car to go with an American student to visit Turfloop University in the north. Speaking to black students there it was clear that however well they did educationally, their ambitions were likely to be stifled by the restrictive apparatus of the State. There was, of course, strong resistance to Government policy, and those involved in plotting insurrection were sent to Robben Island, a kind of South African Alcatraz some miles from Cape Town.

Many years later I had cause to remember Helen Suzman's selfless and relentless stance against the forces of intolerance, when I visited the notorious prison with my wife. Along with more than 100 other tourists we saw Nelson Mandela's tiny cell, while Lionel Davies, a former internee, explained to us that when the guards were angry they would take away the prisoners' food. As punishment, prisoners were whipped, and on occasions buried up to their necks in the sand and left to roast in the sun.

41

Given the harsh treatment he endured, it is surprising that Mr Davies also insisted that in the new South Africa they had to have understanding, forgiveness and reconciliation. He then said something which made me sit bolt upright. In their darkest times when the African leader Robert Sobukwe was held in solitary confinement and Nelson Mandela was imprisoned with countless others, they were forgotten, by all but one person, Helen Suzman. She came to Robben Island to see Mr Mandela and Mr Sobukwe and others to do anything she could to help.

After Lionel Davies had finished speaking I told him that I was a friend of Mrs Suzman and she would be very grateful for his kind words. He replied "Tell Helen we remember her with pride." I passed on his message and it was appropriate that when a delegation of MSPs from the Scottish Parliament went to visit South Africa and Malawi I was able to arrange for them to meet this great lady.

I travelled next to Cape Town and there met Jonty Driver, who was president of the National Union of South African Students and his designated successor Maeder Osler, both of whom were strongly opposed to apartheid. The day after I lunched with Jonty he was arrested by the police. I was angry that a student leader was being victimised in this way for his views and I put out a statement for Maeder Osler to use:

It read: "As immediate past president of the Oxford Union Society, I should like to make it clear that members of Oxford University connected with the Oxford Union wish to convey their sympathy and support for the struggles of the National Union of South African Students against discriminatory and racialist legislation and in particular for its stand for academic

freedom in the face of increasing State control. We can assure
you that your voice will not go unheard."

I soon received a letter from Maeder Osler thanking me for my
message of support which together with many others must have
helped to put pressure on the Government. Jonty Driver was given
a one way ticket to Britain where in due course he became
headmaster of Wellington School.

Rhodesia was next on my schedule and I arrived there with an
American friend, Scott Thompson. Former Prime Minister
Garfield Todd, whom I had welcomed to the Oxford Union, had
invited us to stay at his ranch at Dadaya and his daughter Judith
met us and drove us there. We were taken down to the river where
we watched the hippos run into the water. I remember seeing a
very unusual four barrelled shotgun in the house which Mr Todd
assured us would only ever be used in self defence if he was charged
by a hippo.

Garfield Todd had arrived in Southern Rhodesia from New
Zealand as a Protestant missionary and had been elected to
parliament in 1943. Ten years later he was Prime Minister. While
in power he had tried to reform the education system and had
opposed any legislation prohibiting sexual relations between
Europeans and Africans. In 1958 his Cabinet had rebelled even
against his modest reforms and he was replaced by Sir Edgar
Whitehead. More extreme regimes followed culminating in the
rule of Ian Smith and his breakaway from Britain.

Having said farewell to the Todds, I moved on to meet Sir
Robert Tredgold, the former Chief Justice who had resigned in
protest against the law and order maintenance bill, which he
thought outraged almost every basic human right. Sir Robert took

me to Mana Pools, a game reserve, where he told me that buffaloes could be the most dangerous animals. That night while we were sleeping in tents surrounded by a lightly wired fence, an elephant came and trumpeted at the entrance to the encampment. Sir Robert emerged from his tent and repeatedly banged the steel butt of his rifle on the landrover believing that the metallic sound would scare away our uninvited guest.

We returned to our beds but I was woken again by a huge animal pressing against the wire fence next to my tent. Was it a buffalo or a lion I wondered and lay very still indeed. Eventually the beast, whatever it was, disappeared and I heaved a sigh of relief.

Soon I would make tracks to Zambia where I met President Kenneth Kaunda who had a high regard for Edinburgh University for having educated so many leading African politicians. Afterwards it was on to Tanzania where I met up again with my American friend, Scott Thompson. On 4 September we flew to Zanzibar, the exotic spice island, in the Indian Ocean, where a few months earlier there had been a bloody revolution during which hundreds of people had died. We were told that there was a Chinese military presence in the north.

We had not been given visas, so by going we had taken a calculated risk. On arrival we were stopped by the immigration authorities, and I told them that the British Consul was aware of my presence in Zanzibar as I had spoken to him on the telephone, Scott meanwhile said that the president's legal adviser would act as his referee and we were allowed to leave the airport. But trouble was just around the corner.

Both the British and American Consuls warned us to be extremely careful in the present atmosphere. I went on my own to have a chat with the local bank manager but my unease increased when it was clear he was very apprehensive. Things had happened which he did not wish to talk about.

Matters came to a head when I met Scott for a tense lunch at a local restaurant. We heard the sound of loud voices and turned a corner into the dining room where a large number of Chinese were eating and talking. My friend said "Good morning" to one of them who returned his greeting in English. Total silence followed although the eating went on. We felt we had intruded on a private gathering.

During lunch our nemesis arrived in the shape of the Chief Immigration Officer. He informed Scott that his supposed referee had not in fact given him the unqualified recommendation which he had anticipated and we were strongly advised to leave Zanzibar on the next available plane. I decided it was not worth arguing a point when you know you are not welcome and left the country for Kenya within the hour.

In Kenya we stayed with Sir Derek Erskine, whose brother Keith had founded the firm Securicor in Britain. He was a gracious host and had been one of the first Europeans to call for Jomo Kenyatta's release from prison. Through him we met (the by this time President) Kenyatta, whose name had previously been associated with the pre-independence Mau Mau Rebellion.

He was friendly and welcoming towards us – a marked contrast to my reception in Zanzibar. Meeting President Kenyatta made me realise that being imprisoned by the British is certainly not a disqualification from the highest office for an African Nationalist after Independence. In spite of his radical past, President Kenyatta was widely regarded in Kenya as an anchor for stability and good order.

I then flew on to Uganda. My father had been a friend of the Cambridge educated Kabaka or King of Buganda, and he had come to stay in Scotland. I telephoned his Private Secretary who said he would put me up in the Kabaka's lodge near the airport. The next day I was invited to the Palace, where I saw a most interesting ceremony.

Buganda was a historic and strategically important kingdom within Uganda and all the local Chiefs came to swear fealty to the Kabaka and to promise, if necessary, to die for him. After the ceremony the Kabaka or King Freddie as he was known in Britain welcomed me for a discussion, and asked me to sign the Visitor's Book, where he pointed out to me the signature of Sir Winston Churchill many years before.

It was a moving occasion, all the more so in retrospect, as some time later, in May 1966, tanks of the Ugandan Army under the command of Colonel Idi Amin attacked the Royal Palace. The Kabaka's men fought bravely but were overwhelmed, many of them being killed. Countless civilians were also mutilated, raped and tortured. The Kabaka escaped into the jungle, and on reaching Britain was treated in hospital for an injury to his leg.

I went to visit him, taking along some grapes. Beside his bed was a huge bodyguard, who invited me to eat a grape in case it had been tampered with in some way, which I did. I did not collapse immediately so I hope that King Freddie enjoyed the rest.

It was the last time I saw King Freddie but in years to come after his death, I would welcome his son Ronnie, the next Kabaka, on a number of occasions in the House of Commons. The monarchy was officially restored in 1993 and, long after the removal of the murderous General Amin, it was refreshing to learn that he and his Queen received rapturous and jubilant support at their Coronation in Buganda.

From Uganda I went to Ethiopia and the Sudan where I stayed in the Blue Nile Hostel in Khartoum and then on to Cairo in

Egypt, which brought with it an awareness of a great and ancient civilisation. Flying down the Nile at low level was fascinating. For hundreds of yards or more on both sides of the river the desert was driven back by the life giving qualities of the water and crops and greenery of all kinds sprouted alongside the massive river. It confirmed to me that conflicts in the future may one day be caused by disputes over water, and perhaps Scotland with its abundance of that commodity may one day take on a humanitarian role, when drought threatens to extinguish life.

Having visited Universities in ten African countries my thoughts were that whatever the demand for widening access to higher education, standards should not be sacrificed. There was a greater need for scientists, doctors, teachers, business people and technocrats than for students of Arts subjects. However applications for the latter were disproportionately high. African universities, would have to act as the cultural standard bearers for their countries and communities, focusing on the outstanding aspects of their heritage.

I had been told that in Cairo it was possible to eat for a penny a day and on arrival I thought I would take up this challenge. However the experiment was a misguided one and by the time I reached Jerusalem I was decidedly ill. After a day fighting a high temperature I flew on to the Eden Hotel in Rome where, after two months and what felt like a lifetime of experiences, I met up with my parents.

Back in Britain a few days later, I began studying Scots Law at Edinburgh University, but it would not be long before the lure of debating would attract me once more. On one occasion a lean, somewhat ascetic looking figure rose from the audience to put the points in support of my argument. His name was Malcolm Rifkind, and we began a life-long friendship.

In the summer term I was elected President of Debates unopposed. I immediately settled down to making up the programme and sent a letter to Lord Reith, founder of the BBC in the hope that he might participate in a debate on the Media. He had held a Commission in the Cameronians (Scottish Rifles) like myself and I thought that there was just a chance he might come to participate or to chair a debate on the Media or serve on a Panel. The terms of his refusal revealed what a powerful man he had been when the BBC was in its infancy. He wrote on 16 June 1965:

"I was much interested to hear that you were to camp at Shornecliffe with Cameronians; what fun. In my Territorial days we never got so far afield; it was always Barry or Stobs or Irvine, or places like that.

"I happened to be looking something up in my diary last weekend; and I came upon my Certificate B of 1910, and my Commission in the Cameronians of 1911. What a long wild stretch of years that is.

"Now as to your suggestion or requirement. I should be very glad to do something you asked me to do, and alternatively very sorry indeed not to feel able to do so. I do not think I could possibly be a member of a judgment panel, let alone Chairman thereof, in a matter where I am violently ex parte; where I could not be impartial; and where it would be morally wrong for me to be anything other than ex parte. I think the responsibility of the mass media is immensely serious, and a moral one; there are few people who, once involved in its operation, accept this point of view, or who implement it if, to any extent, they accept it.

"I made it quite clear from the beginning of the BBC that broadcasting was not going to 'give the people what it wanted', and with all that was therein involved. My attitude throughout my time was that we should be ahead of public taste, and should give people what they would come to like. This was derivative of the feeling of tremendous responsibility – intellectual and ethical.

"I am sure you will agree that, feeling as I do, I could not possibly do as you kindly suggest.

"As you will know, there is immense criticism of the BBC just now, and I think in almost every respect it has departed from the principles on which I conducted it. So far, for one reason or another I have not myself taken any part in the criticism of the BBC. It's better not to probably."

Lord Reith was not the only formidable figure of the twentieth century whom I would approach. I also wrote to Nobel Peace Prize winner and one of the greatest orators of his time, Dr Martin Luther King Jr, inviting him to Edinburgh, claiming that the students were "involved and enlightened".

The perhaps inevitable response came on 1 July 1965 from Martin Luther King Jr, President of the Southern Christian Leadership Conference, Atlanta, Georgia, USA:

"Let me say how deeply grateful I am to you for extending this invitation. Unfortunately because of the present temper of events in the Civil Rights struggle in this country, it is not possible for me to accept this gracious invitation ... Please know that I deeply regret my inability to serve you ..." Tragically Dr King would be assassinated just three years after he wrote this letter.

Soon after receiving his letter, I went to the Salzburg Seminar in American Studies on American Law and Legal Institutions. This seminar was set up in 1947 by graduates from Harvard who believed that there was a great need for influential Europeans to know more about American institutions.

There I was taught by the famous American Federal Judge, John Norman Minor Wisdom of the 5th Circuit Court of Appeal in New Orleans. He had been the Judge who had enabled George Meredith to become the first black student to enter the University of Mississippi, a milestone in the breaking down of racial discrimination in the Deep South of America.

Judge Wisdom was a most engaging and entertaining teacher who enthralled us with his collection of amusing legal folklore. He was particularly interesting on issues which involved conflict between Federal laws and States' Rights, some of which had to go to the Supreme Court of the USA for determination. We were impressed by his total commitment to human rights and to his conviction that the rule of law must prevail.

It was about this time that the idea of holding a televised Teach-In at Edinburgh University took root, if a topical subject could be found. On arrival back in Scotland I sought to make this a reality.

In July I had written to the Principal of the University outlining plans for a Teach-In on Rhodesia, as there was evidence available that Prime Minister Ian Smith intended to break away from Britain and issue a Unilateral Declaration of Independence in a bid to prevent African majority rule. The acting Principal Professor Michael Swann liked the idea of a Teach-In and pointed out that Professor Alan Thompson and other members of staff were proposing something comparable.

This suited all of us in the Debates Committee very well. I was ably supported by Stewart Hamilton, later to become a Professor of Accountancy, and by my friend Malcolm Rifkind, a future Foreign Secretary. Professor Alan Thompson would also give invaluable assistance. He had been Labour MP for Dunfermline and his knowledge of parliamentary matters meant that he would be a superb chairman acting with panache and gravitas.

The Teach-In concept had originated in the USA at the University of Michigan where students and staff discussed at length United States military involvement in the Vietnam War and the legitimacy or otherwise of the argument that if Vietnam became communist all the neighbouring countries would follow suit, tipping over like a line of dominoes.

The advantage of the Teach-In was that students and staff developed close working relationships in debating the political, economic and social consequences of policies. It was an exercise in analysis and participation which was popular among students and lecturers.

My friend Phillip Whitehead of BBC television told me that they would televise the Teach-in if I managed to secure the attendance of two African Prime Ministers. I thought that this would be an impossible hurdle to jump and my feeling was confirmed during my telephone call to the Private Office of the Prime Minister of Sierra Leone, where an angry official gave me the brush off.

"Are you seriously asking for the Prime Minister…The Prime Minister of all people…What did you say your name is?…Your request is absolutely out of the question…But I will tell the Prime Minister you telephoned" he said.

I went back to Phillip Whitehead and said that I was not going to be able to deliver African Prime Ministers, but there might be the possibility of getting former Prime Ministers of Britain and Rhodesia. Phillip Whitehead approached Sir Alec Douglas-Home with my support and I contacted Garfield Todd, and sure enough two telegrams of acceptance came in. But that was not quite enough for television to cover the proceedings. Even the acceptance of Cledwyn Hughes, a senior member of Harold Wilson's government as well as a large number of MPs from different parties including David Steel, Willie Hamilton, Teddy Taylor, Nigel Fisher and Humphrey Berkeley would not make them change their minds.

Then events took on a momentum of their own. On his way to attend the Teach-In in Edinburgh Garfield Todd was stopped by the Rhodesian police and put under house arrest. Immediately BBC TV became extremely interested. What was it that he had to say which Prime Minister Ian Smith wished to be suppressed? Meanwhile I made contact by telephone with his daughter Judith, then a student of journalism at Columbia University in Manhattan, New York. She agreed to speak in his place and it was clear in the current mood that she was going to be given a very favourable reception.

The occasion was staged on 20 October 1965 in a hall near the Students' Union and was attended by more than a thousand people who were overflowing outside. Three hours of Teach-In were televised live to the nation and some significant speeches were made. Judith Todd demanded that the British Government should suspend the Southern Rhodesian Constitution and do whatever was necessary to thwart UDI. Sir Alec Douglas-Home wanted the negotiation of a new internationally based treaty with more educational opportunities focussed on young Africans. Cledwyn Hughes gave warning that there could be serious consequences if

Ian Smith implemented UDI. All of this received considerable publicity especially as Ian Smith went ahead with his Declaration of Independence on 11 November.

The sequel to our efforts was that the Principal of the University, Michael Swann, wrote to congratulate the organising committee with its student and staff members on the success of the Teach-In. He did feel that there should be more academics participating and that such events should not be too frequent, since if they were "the sense of occasion is bound to disappear".

Sir Alec Douglas-Home commented on the "excellent arrangements". Judith Todd told me that the Teach-In had "sparked off a wave of anti-Smith feeling" and Garfield Todd wrote:

> "A few days ago I was taken under police escort from Hokonui ranch to government house in Salisbury and while there on what seemed to be neutral ground I was able to talk to Joshua Nkomo (the leader of the Zapu party) and others. I found that Joshua and his friends at Gonakudzingwa had tuned in direct to the BBC and had heard Judith's speech. I wish we had known and we could also have listened in. The Teach-In was certainly a great event and received world notice. You choose your subjects well and also the timing of your debates."

I received a Scottish reaction from none other than Donald Dewar. He had recently spoken at Edinburgh University in his usual polemical way, and I had put him up for the night. He wrote: "I enjoyed speaking in Edinburgh, but I am really writing to congratulate you on the success of the Teach-In. I agree that you are very lucky and owe a lot to Mr Smith, but at least you were the person with the initiative to capitalize on that luck. If I had been Convenor of Debates in Glasgow or anywhere else I would be in a frenzy of envy."

I recalled these events in early 2007, in the Scottish Parliament when Bill Gates of Microsoft visited to speak about a foundation he supported, engaged in improving literacy and health standards in Africa. He talked about how frustrating it was when his plans to reach out to help the African people were thwarted, as they had been by the Mugabe government in Zimbabwe. It is depressing to note that, more than forty years after our Rhodesian Teach-In, one form of extremism in Rhodesia has led to another in the renamed Zimbabwe. The abuse of human rights, lawlessness, and economic disintegration for many years under the government of President Robert Mugabe is a lamentable story.

CHAPTER 4

Rudolf Hess, MI5 and Albrecht's secrets

In my youth, I enjoyed all the usual Boy's Own adventure stories, but when I was young I remember being fascinated by a rather different tale. During a long car journey my father described an extraordinary episode which had taken place in his own life. It involved Rudolf Hess, Hitler's deputy, who flew to Scotland in 1941 and asked to see my father, after giving a false name to everyone else.

My father told me that Rudolf Hess had been very close to Hitler as a young man and that after the failure of the "Beerhall Putsch" in Munich in 1923, Hitler's bid for power in Bavaria, Hess had joined him in Landsberg Prison. There Hitler had dictated to Hess, who was acting as his secretary, the book *Mein Kampf* in which he set out his plans for establishing a German empire in Europe.

My father explained that the appearance of Hess in Scotland on 10 May 1941 came as a very great surprise. He was certain that the key to everything which had happened lay with a man called Professor Albrecht Haushofer, whom he had met at the Berlin Olympic Games in 1936.

In 1965 while I was attending the Salzburg Seminar in American Studies held in Schloss Leopoldskron, I was discussing the traumas of the Second World War with a German student when he asked me to tell him what I knew about Hess' Mission to Scotland. It was at that moment that I decided to get to the bottom of what had happened.

Why had this fanatical Nazi leader flown secretly to Britain on a solitary unauthorised peace mission? Why had he asked to speak to my father? Just what role had the brilliant but shadowy Professor Albrecht Haushofer played in this astonishing train of events?

Back in Britain I was introduced to the historian Sir Alan Bullock at Oxford University who had written the then standard work *Hitler: A Study in Tyranny*. He gave me his view that Hess was a rather boring fanatical Nazi, infatuated with Hitler, who really was not very interesting. It was well known, however, that General Professor Karl Haushofer, Albrecht's father, had regarded Hess as his favourite student. He suggested that if I could discover anything about the activities of Albrecht it might yield extremely interesting information.

He recommended that I study the captured German War Documents and other original material at the Wiener Library in London, an excellent centre for research which held a great deal of meticulously assembled information. I was sensitive to the fact that, while my questions were merely historical, others present might be making painful personal enquiries into what had happened to lost relatives during the Holocaust.

After completing my research there and at other venues, I wrote the first draft of a book while earning my living as a Scots Advocate, which I submitted to Sir Alan Bullock. He made a number of helpful recommendations and agreed to write the Foreword. My book *Motive for a Mission* was published in 1971 and I was delighted when it received the *Yorkshire Post* Book of the Year by a New Author award.

Since then a good deal of further information has come to light and in particular the MI5 records relating to Hess' arrival in Britain have been published which effectively corroborated my father's account of what had happened. These documents turned out to be of enormous significance and I will explain more about their contents later.

While writing the first edition of the book about Hess' mission, I was lucky to be on an inside track as far as the British side of the story was concerned. However it was what happened behind the scenes in Germany which was far more important, since the whole episode I discovered was a German-driven affair. I believed in the words of Albert Einstein that "those who know the truth have a duty to impart it".

Two of the most interesting men I met during my research in Germany and Austria were Dr Kurt von Schuschnigg and Fabian von Schlabrendorff. Schuschnigg had been Chancellor of Austria before the Anschluss, when the German Army had annexed Austria on 12 March 1938. He told me that if he had his life again he would never have gone to see Hitler at his mountain retreat in Berchtesgaden. While there, he had been subjected to blood curdling threats from the German dictator and had not been strong enough to withstand them.

Schlabrendorff, a lawyer turned army officer on the other hand had taken his life in his hands by putting a bomb in Hitler's aeroplane. Unfortunately it did not explode. After the failure of the later Stauffenberg bomb plot he was arrested and awaited what he believed would be his execution. Luckily before his SS guards were ready to act the American Army arrived and he was liberated. He became a judge in Wiesbaden, and he asserted that Hess' son Wolf Rudiger was "not very intelligent, just like his father."

He offered to put me in touch with the Hess family but I declined. However years later when I was an MP I had an interesting meeting with Wolf Rudiger Hess who came to Westminster to lobby support for the release of his father from Spandau Prison in West Berlin where he was the solitary inmate. I told him that I had supported his father's release on humanitarian grounds as he was no longer a danger to anyone and had been incarcerated for more than 30 years. He told me that his father had asked to see mine in the Second World War because the Duke had been the first man to fly over Mount Everest. This reminded me that Hess was an aviator himself and, in 1934, had won the first national air race to fly around the Zugspitze in the Bavarian Alps, the highest peak in Germany.

I said to his son later, at a press conference in the House of Commons, that I believed my father had never met his before the War. He said he would check with his mother and he later wrote to tell me that as far as she could remember the two men had never met prior to May 1941. Hess substantiated this in Spandau Prison to the commandant Colonel Eugene Bird, saying that he had not known the Duke of Hamilton and that it was the Haushofers who knew him – which was correct.

While researching my book, a visit to Hartschimmelhof, the home of Heinz Haushofer, Albrecht's brother, proved to be very helpful. His father General Professor Karl Haushofer had taught at Munich University where his favourite pupil had been Rudolf Hess, and his mother Martha had been of half Jewish origin. Hess on account of his friendship with the General Professor had issued letters of protection to Heinz and Albrecht, as Deputy Fuehrer in charge of the Nazi party so that the anti-semitic legislation would not apply to them. None of the Haushofer family would join the

58

Nazi Party, as they disagreed with its racial policy.

Heinz told me that in the days of Nazism if you were in a crowd and they were all saying "Heil Hitler" and giving the Nazi salute and you were not, there was a feeling of terrible loneliness. Heinz's son Martin reinforced that message saying that it was terrifying to live in a country in which whether one lived or died depended upon the whim of one man.

Heinz Haushofer told me that Dr Ursula Laack had completed a thesis on Albrecht Haushofer and had collected copies of all known documents by Albrecht which were attached to her thesis. I borrowed these documents from Kiel University, which was situated in what had been one of the largest torpedo factories of the Second World War. This evidence would be supplemented by information from the US National Archives, and material from the Public Record Office in London and archive centres in Germany.

I also learnt that the whole Nazi era attracted conspiracy theorists from those who forged Hitler's non-existent diaries to those who believed that Hess was not Hess, but an impostor sent in his place, or that Hitler had in fact authorised his flight to Britain. That last theory was particularly easy to disprove since the House of Commons had been burnt out with incendiary bombs on the very evening that Rudolf Hess had arrived in Scotland. If Hitler had wanted peace negotiations surely he would not have ordered the bombing of Whitehall and the British Parliament at that very moment.

Then there was a different far-fetched theory that the British Secret Service had lured Hess to Britain as part of a treacherous peace plot. This too was a ludicrous proposition, but the conspiracy theorists could argue that the British authorities had classified documents on Hess which had not been released. As I have already mentioned the MI5 documents have been made public since my book was published and they conclusively corroborated my father's account, which was that Albrecht Haushofer had indeed had a key role to play.

In 1936 my father who was a young MP for East Renfrew had gone to the Olympic Games in Berlin with some other members of Parliament. He attended a number of receptions and met a German official, Professor Albrecht Haushofer, a man of quite exceptional knowledge, who spoke English like an Englishman. My father was a person of interest to him as he was known to be the first pilot to have flown over Mount Everest in 1933, the year Hitler's regime came to power. Aviators at the cutting edge of new technology were of considerable interest to Nazi leaders like Goering and Hess as they placed great importance on the power of the Luftwaffe to achieve their expansionist plans.

It was this meeting and later contacts with Albrecht which were to involve my father in the whole Hess affair. Albrecht, an Anglophile who wanted cordial relations with Britain, had a dilemma in 1933. Should he emigrate and oppose Nazism from without or should he stay in Germany and try and moderate policies from within? If he were to oppose Nazism openly or leave the country, he would be endangering his mother, who was of half Jewish origin, at a time of intense anti-semitism. Open opposition would mean certain death and the option of rising through public service as an official appealed to him. In normal times he might have become Ambassador to Washington or London, or had a senior role in a University or the German Foreign Office

As it was he would be taken on as a personal adviser to Hess, would act as a special adviser to the Regime in the Ribbentrop

Bureau, and in 1936 would be sent as Hitler's envoy for secret discussions with President Benes of Czechoslovakia. On 26 June he warned Hitler against starting a world war by telling him exactly what would happen if he did. Haushofer's secret report stated:

"A German attempt to solve the Bohemian-Moravian question by a military attack would under present circumstances present for Britain (and British opinion also for France) a casus belli.

"In such a war the British Government would have the whole nation behind it. It would be conducted as a crusade for the liberation of Europe from German militarism. London is convinced that such a war would be won with the help of the USA (whose full participation, within days, not weeks, is anticipated) at the cost, of course, of an incalculable expansion of Bolshevism outside the Anglo-Saxon world."

This was not what Hitler and Ribbentrop wanted to hear, and as a result Albrecht fell into deep disfavour. By 6 May 1937 his existence had also come to the attention of MI5. In a secret memorandum he was identified as "a close associate of Hitler" and as "being on personal terms with most of the Nazi hierarchy". The MI5 officer who provided the information considered Albrecht, who he had met in Britain, was "probably employed in the collection of intelligence in the UK".

This was true, but Albrecht desperately wanted to prevent the Second World War and on 16 July 1939 wrote a very long and significant letter to my father warning him as to when war was likely to break out and giving him permission to show the letter to the Foreign Secretary, Lord Halifax, and to Rab Butler, who was also a minister. Albrecht ended the letter with the request that it be destroyed "most carefully".

My father showed the letter to Winston Churchill in his flat in London. Churchill, who emerged from his bath wearing a large towel, read it very carefully, took it's warning very seriously and declared "There is going to be war very soon." My father said "In that case I very much hope that you will be Prime Minister." Churchill's reply was "What a hell of a time to become Prime Minister!"

The contents of the letter were also made known to Neville Chamberlain via Lord Dunglass, (later Sir Alec Douglas-Home) although it is not certain whether the Prime Minister actually found time to read and absorb it. When my father showed the letter to Lord Halifax his response was that Hitler was out for world hegemony.

After the outbreak of war Albrecht had began to do some work with members of the Wednesday Club, which would later be known as part of the German Resistance to Hitler. Notwithstanding this fact Hess remained in touch with the Haushofer family. Hess had written, as Hitler's Secretary, in *Mein Kampf* that Germany must never again make the mistake of fighting a war on two fronts. Now that France had fallen he knew that war with Russia was fast approaching. It was therefore no coincidence that on 31 August 1940 Hess had an eight-hour meeting with General Professor Karl Haushofer. Hess was wondering whether a peace feeler to Britain could be made through a neutral country. He followed up this meeting by summoning Albrecht to Bad Godesberg on 8 September to raise this issue with him.

Albrecht explained to Hess that the British regarded Hitler as "Satan's representative on earth" who had to be fought. When pressed about the possibility of opening up a channel of communication with Britain, Albrecht crucially wrote down later: "As the final possibility I then mentioned that of a personal meeting on neutral soil with the young Duke of Hamilton who has access at all times to all important persons in London, even to Churchill and the King".

Hess then contacted General Professor Karl Haushofer saying he wished Albrecht to send a letter to Hamilton which could be delivered by a woman friend of the Haushofer family, a Mrs Violet Roberts. This mysterious missive would suggest a meeting in neutral Lisbon. Accordingly Albrecht drafted the letter dated 23 September, commenting to his father that "The whole thing is a fool's errand". Whatever his private view the letter which he drafted would electrify MI5, the Foreign Office and my father who were all fascinated as to what lay behind it. It ran:

B.Sept.23rd

My Dear Douglo,

Even if there is only a slight chance that this letter should reach you in good time, there is a chance and I am determined to make use of it.

First of all to give you a personal greeting. I am sure you know that my attachment to you remains unaltered and unalterable, whatever the circumstances may be. I have heard of your father's death. I do hope he did not suffer too much – after so long a life of permanent pain. I heard that your brother-in-law Northumberland lost his life near Dunkirk – even modern times must allow us to share grief across all boundaries.

But it is not only the story of death that should find its place in this letter. If you remember some of my last communications in July 1939, you – and your friends in high places – may find some significance in the fact that I am able to ask you whether you could find time to have a talk with me somewhere on the outskirts of Europe, perhaps in Portugal. I could reach Lisbon any time (and without any kind of difficulties) within a few days after receiving news from you. Of course I do not know whether you can make your authorities understand so much, that they give you leave...

But at least you may be able to answer my question. Letters will reach me (fairly quickly; they would take some four or five days from Lisbon on the utmost) in the following way: Double closed envelope: Inside address:- "Dr A. H." Nothing more!
Outside address:
'Minero Silricola Ltd.,
Rua do Cais de Santarem 32/1
Lisbon, Portugal'

My father and mother add their wishes for your personal welfare to my own...
Yours ever,
'A'.

The letter addressed to my father, which was intercepted by the British Censor had indeed been sent via a Mrs Violet Roberts. At this stage two problems arose as it appears that the original of the letter was lost, which delayed matters somewhat, although a photocopy of it still existed. Meanwhile MI5 wanted to find out who this Mrs Roberts was and where she lived and something of a saga followed. A scrutiny of the London telephone directory revealed a Mrs Roberts at 6 Hill Croft Crescent, Wembley and a memo mentions a proposal to put out a warrant for her arrest as someone who had been communicating with Germans in wartime. However MI5 had the sense to want to check, using Thomas Cook and Sons, to ascertain whether this was indeed the correct address for the woman to whom the letter had been sent.

Interestingly enough by 22 November MI5 had noted that the Dr AH who had sent the letter was probably Dr Albrecht Haushofer who they described as "the greatest authority in Germany on the British Empire." By 4 December it had been discovered that the correct address for the Mrs Roberts concerned was in fact 10 Wilberforce Road, Cambridge. It took until 14 May before a full report on Mrs Roberts was deposited in the files of MI5.

The Police were frank enough to admit they found it very hard to discover any information about this Mrs Roberts but eventually they did interview her as they wanted to find out if she was a German spy. She was not, but had been a friend of Mrs Martha Haushofer, mother of Albrecht, some years before the war. Mrs Roberts did not know the Duke of Hamilton, and was eliminated from the Police enquiries which, it has to be said, had taken longer than a highly efficient security service might have wished!

The RAF Intelligence Branch made contact with my father, with a view to discovering whether there might not be considerable value in making contact with Albrecht Haushofer, and whether he would be willing to respond to the letter. Since I wrote my book on the Hess flight, the statement made by my father arising out of these discussions on 11 March 1941 to the Provost Marshal's Department of the Air Ministry, has become available.

He said he had first met Haushofer in Berlin during the Olympic Games of 1936 where he had been introduced to him by his brother who was now Flight Lieutenant David Douglas-Hamilton. He went on "To my knowledge he was well known to the Nazi leaders and he introduced me to General Goering and several others of the significant men in Germany. In my opinion, while being a patriotic German, he did his utmost to exercise a restraining influence especially before Munich, on the Nazi leaders and I gather after the Munich agreement he was somewhat out of favour." In fact at that meeting Goering had instructed General Milch, chief of staff of the Luftwaffe, to organise visits to Luftwaffe stations for my father, a comparable itinerary to that laid on previously for the famous American aviator Charles Lindbergh. My father made the tour and then reported what he had seen to the military attaché at the British Embassy in Berlin.

In his statement he also referred to the letter Albrecht Haushofer had sent shortly before the outbreak of war and which Winston Churchill had read so carefully. He had not destroyed it as Albrecht had requested but had deposited it in his bank and had made it clear to the Intelligence Authorities that he would show it to them. In the meantime MI5 was considering a proposal that the Duke should go to Lisbon to find out anything he could from Albrecht Haushofer.

On 25 April Hamilton appeared at the air ministry to meet Group Captain DL Blackford. Also present was the famous Major "Tar" Robertson of MI5, Britain's master par excellence of double cross and disinformation and a man who would have many triumphs before the end of the War.

On 29 April 1941 "Tar" Robertson wrote an MI5 Report primarily about this meeting, which is now kept in the released file KV2/1685 at the Public Record Office at Kew. They had suggested to my father that he should go to Lisbon to see Albrecht Haushofer and he had seemed quite pleased with such a plan. However Robertson reported that Hamilton was not sure what would really be gained from it and had warned that while he could try to learn how Germany was weathering the war, he would probably be asked similar questions about Britain. Major Robertson said that they would write him a "script" and claimed rather astonishingly "we were always willing on matters affecting the civil population to tell the Germans the truth." Hamilton said he would think about the plan and let them know his decision as soon as possible. "Tar" Robertson ended his report with the following comments:

"Hamilton at the beginning of the war and still is a member of the community which sincerely believes that Great Britain will be willing to make peace with Germany provided the present regime in Germany were superseded by some reasonable form of government. This view, however, is tempered by the fact that he now considers that the only thing this country can do is to fight the war to the finish no matter what disaster and destruction befalls both countries. He is a slow witted man but at the same time gets there in the end; and I feel that if he is properly schooled before leaving for Lisbon he could do a very useful job of work".

However with regard to Albrecht's letter not even the quick-witted "Tar" Robertson or anyone else in Britain had spotted the possibility that Rudolf Hess, Hitler's Deputy, might be behind this German proposal and would be travelling to Lisbon with Haushofer. It later became obvious that this was indeed the plan which Hess had formulated, after he flew to Scotland with Albrecht Haushofer's visiting card in his pocket.

"Tar" Robertson's assessment of my father's political views corresponds with my own. Hamilton had wanted to fight Nazism and also to encourage a German resistance to Hitler. He had written in a letter to *The Times* at the outset of the war:

> "If Hitler is right when he claims that the whole of the German nation is with him in his cruelties and treacheries, both within Germany and without, then this war must be fought to the bitter end. It may well last for many years but the people of the British Empire will not falter in their determination to see it through."

The problem with opening up a channel some five months later was that too much time had been lost because Albrecht's original letter had been misplaced. In addition Archie Sinclair, Secretary of State for Air was very astute in expressing reservations about sending Hamilton to Lisbon. Group Captain Blackford wrote on the 3rd of May "Archie is apprehensive that action on the lines suggested might well be misunderstood at the present time."

He could not have been more right. If the RAF Intelligence Branch with the support of MI5 had sent a relatively senior RAF Officer to meet a German official in Lisbon, and Rudolf Hess had emerged out of the woodwork it would have led to a monumental row in the House of Commons. It would have been like sleep-walking into an ambush.

On 3 May, Group Captain Blackford wrote to Hamilton asking him to treat the matter as being in abeyance and three days later "Tar" Robertson also expressed doubts about a trip to Lisbon. Many years later Major Robertson spoke to me on the telephone about it and said that it would not have been possible to open up a channel of communication effectively, as too much time had elapsed from the time when Albrecht Haushofer's letter had been dispatched. For that reason, in his view, it could not have been used for disinformation or double-cross.

As for the Group Captain's letter, Hamilton responded on 10 May 1941, saying he believed the delay had jeopardised the opening of a channel of communication. He had earlier made it clear that he would only go if he had access to the British Ambassador in Lisbon and before leaving had a meeting with the Head of the Foreign Office. In any case, unknown to him, his letter was rapidly being overtaken by events, as later that day a lone Messerschmitt 110 was spotted making its way across the North Sea towards the Northumbrian shore. At the controls was Rudolf Hess who had lost patience with Albrecht's letter remaining unanswered and had set out on a desperate and ill-judged mission.

At this point it has to be acknowledged that conspiracy theorists have alleged that MI5 answered Albrecht's letter on my father's behalf, but without his knowledge, in an attempt to lure Hess to Britain. This was always wrong, and for a very obvious reason. Albrecht Haushofer in his letter had merely made a proposal for a meeting in Lisbon. Nobody in Britain had the faintest idea that Hess was in any way involved, as the MI5 records make abundantly clear. So any reply to Haushofer's proposal would have been a straight "Yes" or "No".

Certainly nobody in Britain had any interest whatever in inviting Albrecht Haushofer to Britain in the midst of the War. Whilst he could obtain permission to visit Lisbon, there was absolutely no suggestion that he or anybody else would have had permission or the means of conveyance to reach Britain, and no such thought was on the agenda.

Indeed there was nothing in his writing to imply that travel to Britain was even the remotest possibility. There could not have been, because Albrecht Haushofer had no inkling of the later change of plan by Hess to fly to Britain which Hess had formulated in strict secrecy. He made his decision, partly because he became frustrated that after many weeks Albrecht's letter was not answered. Apart from wishing to recover his dwindling influence on Hitler, Hess wanted to avoid an ever-expanding War on Two Fronts. He knew that Hitler was planning to invade Russia within an extremely short timescale and he had not forgotten the warning he had typed out in *Mein Kampf*, that Germany must never again make the mistake of fighting a War on Two Fronts. He might have come a long way, since being a prisoner with Hitler in Landsberg Prison, but his terrible dread of the War on Two Fronts, now impending, had never left him.

On the same evening that Hess' aircraft flew across the North Sea to Scotland during a heavy bombing attack on Whitehall, the House of Commons was gutted by incendiary bombs, leaving the Chamber a burnt out shell. This was nothing less than a symbolic attack on the very heart of British democracy and it was a thoroughly disastrous beginning for the most significant Nazi peace overture of the Second World War. Today the rebuilt Chamber has retained the broken stonework at its entrance to remind all visitors of the scars inflicted upon it during its prolonged struggle for freedom.

Meanwhile Hess parachuted from his ME110, upside down over Eaglesham Farm, south of Glasgow, leaving his aircraft to crash. He was taken in some pain with a chipped bone in his ankle into the nearby house of David McLean, and was soon collected by the Home Guard. Hess gave his name as Hauptmann Alfred Horn, and asked to see the Duke of Hamilton. Late that night my father received a phone call at his quarters near Turnhouse Aerodrome from Squadron Leader Hector MacLean to tell him of this unexpected request. The Squadron Leader recorded in his book *Fighters in Defence* that Hamilton was "just as taken aback by this strange development as I was".

On 11 May Hamilton arrived at Maryhill Barracks in Glasgow to see the mysterious Hauptmann Horn. Before going in he examined the prisoner's personal effects, which included the visiting card of Albrecht Haushofer, and then he went into the prisoner's room. To his astonishment the man said "I do not know if you recognise me, but I am Rudolf Hess....on a mission of humanity." He did not claim to have met my father at the Olympic Games but to have seen him there and he thought wrongly that my father had been present when the International Olympic Committee had lunched at his house. They had however attended the same receptions.

Hess, it emerged, was on a personal unauthorised mission to try to get Britain out of the war. He knew what Hitler's peace terms would be, and after a short conversation my father explained to him that there was now only one party in Britain and that he could hold out no hope for a peace agreement. This was because "Germany chose war in preference to peace at a time when we were most anxious to preserve peace." My father did not speak German and Hess spoke only broken English and my father used this as an excuse to break off the conversation so that he could return with an interpreter.

Later the same day my father flew to London and reported these extraordinary events personally to Prime Minister Winston Churchill, who at first refused to believe it, and then said "Well Hess or no Hess, I am going to see the Marx Brothers". Meanwhile Hess was treated as a prisoner of war, and after conviction as a war criminal at the Nuremberg War Trials, he eventually committed suicide in Spandau Prison on 17 August 1987.

Back in war-time Germany the situation for Albrecht Haushofer was dire. Opening up a peace feeler through a neutral country was one matter, but he had never imagined that Hess would fly into enemy hands. Under close arrest he was taken to Berchtesgaden and under armed guard, he had to write his report which he entitled "English Connections and the Possibility of Utilising them" for Hitler. When Albrecht wrote that report he was writing for his life.

Hitler was beside himself with anger. He feared that Hess' flight would have appalling consequences for the morale of German troops fighting at the Front, that the Axis Pact between Germany, Italy and Japan might disintegrate and that the plans to attack Russia might be given away. No one who saw Hitler at that time doubted the intensity of his anger. He said of Hess "If the man was not mad he would deserve to be shot."

However Albrecht was not executed at that time in case his great knowledge could be useful in future. Under the relentless watch of the Gestapo there was little he could do, but he did manage to write Peace Plans for the German Resistance to Hitler. After Colonel Claus Schenk von Stauffenberg's bomb failed to kill Hitler, Albrecht fled to Bavaria. He hoped the Americans might come forward, but the Gestapo found him first. He was brought to Berlin and, with the last remnants of the German Resistance to Hitler who had not been tried in court, he was incarcerated in Moabit Prison.

In these circumstances there was not one chance in a million that the Nazi leadership would allow Albrecht to survive the war. Hitler would have remembered that Albrecht had warned what would happen if Germany started the Second World War. He had been correct and Hitler wrong – that alone was sufficient reason for Hitler not wanting Albrecht to live. In addition Albrecht had written Peace Plans for the German Resistance and had gone into hiding after the bomb plot, which in Hitler's eyes made him a traitor.

Hitler would have known these secrets of Albrecht, but there was one secret Hitler never knew. Albrecht had given away to the British, including Churchill, the timing when Hitler would launch the Second World War. Albrecht had written my father a letter on 16 July 1939 giving his address as "Cruising the coast off western Norway." He wrote: " I am very much convinced that Germany can not win a short war and that she can not stand a long one – but I am thoroughly afraid that the terrific forms of modern war will make any reasonable peace impossible if they are allowed to go on for even a few months."

He had also written: "To the best of my knowledge there is not yet a definite timetable for the actual explosion, but any date after the middle of August may prove to be the fatal one." Albrecht was right. On 1 September 1939 German armed forces streamed into Poland.

More than fifty years later his nephew Martin Haushofer told me that he was appalled by this episode. I asked him if he thought that my father should have destroyed the letter as Albrecht had requested. He said no, but that it had been an incredibly dangerous thing to do, and any one in Germany sending a letter like that would have been executed. However Hitler had no inkling of its existence. Meawhile Albrecht had been arrested by the Gestapo but was still alive in Moabit Prison in the closing hours of the war.

He was writing poems which would be remembered as a memorial to the German Resistance to Hitler. He likened Hitler to the Pied Piper of Hamelin who had led the children of the town to destruction. There were times he said when madness ruled the land and then the best would be hanged. He felt like a man in a small boat being swept downstream towards the Niagara Falls. A last attempt to grasp the rudder had failed and he awaited his fate.

After the bomb had failed to kill Hitler, he had made a radio broadcast vowing to get even with the perpetrators "in the way to which we National Socialists are accustomed". This was a clear indication that he did not want any members of the so-called "Other Germany" to survive. However, amid the chaos of the crumbling Third Reich, Hitler's opponents languishing in Moabit Prison had not been tried or sentenced. Nonetheless there was to be no escape.

Hitler was preoccupied with sending the children and the frail elderly into battle in a vain and hopeless attempt to stem the Russians advancing into Berlin, but he could always rely on Josef Goebbels – that same Goebbels whom Albrecht had described to my father during the 1936 Olympic Games as "a poisonous little man, who will give you dinner one night and sign your death warrant the next morning". Goebbels may not have given the order but he let it be known that anyone who released those few prisoners in Moabit Prison would be executed.

In fact it was their colleague SS Gruppenfuehrer Mueller, Head of the Gestapo, another man who could always be relied upon to carry out the dirty work of Hitler, who gave the order. In Moabit Prison the sixteen were told that they would be freed. When they reached the Prison Yard they were given back their personal belongings, and when they arrived at the entrance they were met by 35 SS Sonder Commandos with machine pistols. They were taken to the bombed out Ulap Exhibition site, made to face a wall and were then mown down by shots fired through the back of the neck up through the skull. But one man was not dead. It was Herbert Kosney who had shared a cell with Albrecht.

The SS Obersturmbannfuehrer shot each man through the head and kicked Herbert saying that this "pig" has had enough and that they had more work to do. When they had gone Herbert, in great pain and agony, made his way to the flat of his wife in the Hagenauer Strasse, and through him the news of what had happened leaked out.

On 30 April, about one week later, Hitler and his wife, Eva Braun both killed themselves in their Berlin bunker. A few hours later Goebbels and his wife, having murdered all their children, committed suicide. On 7 May all German armed forces surrendered unconditionally and hostilities came to an end.

Heinz Haushofer one of the other prisoners in Moabit Prison was lucky enough to be freed by the Russians. He learnt from Herbert Kosney where he would find his brother Albrecht's body, and on 12 May he found him, at the place where he was murdered by the SS. Clutched in the hand of the dead man were scraps of paper, on which he had written *The Sonnets of Moabit*, the thirty eighth being called "Guilt". Yes, Albrecht considered himself to be guilty, but not as the Nazi Judge thought him guilty. He believed he had been right to plan for the future of the people but admitted that he should have condemned evil more sharply, having foreseen all too clearly the catastrophe which was about to overwhelm Europe and the civilised world. He had warned but his warnings had not been strong enough, and he therefore knew where his guilt lay.

In an extraordinary journey, his brother Heinz took Albrecht's body in a wheelbarrow and pushed it past the barracks where Stauffenberg had shouted "Long live sacred Germany" before being executed and on for miles through the ruins and wreckage of the city until he reached a churchyard. There he summoned up all his strength to bury Albrecht in a deep grave under the trees.

Years later, on what would have been the 100th birthday of Albrecht his former students unveiled a memorial to him for his part in the German Opposition to Hitler. One of those students was Rainer Hildebrandt, who had founded the Berlin Wall Museum next to Checkpoint Charlie, in a plea for more respect for human dignity at a time of totalitarian intolerance. He invited me to be present at the ceremony and told me that Albrecht had been an enlightened teacher.

How will history assess Albrecht? He is very likely to be remembered not just as a professor but as an official who was a special adviser to Hitler's regime and who warned very clearly against starting the Second World War, for which he fell into grave disfavour. He later unwittingly became implicated in the flight of Hess to Scotland, and then threw in his lot with the members of the German Resistance to Hitler. He failed as they failed. He and they did too little and too late. But they did do something. They were implicated in the plot to remove the Hitler regime, and they paid for their failure with their lives.

There was an unexpected postscript to my research when many years later, completely by accident, I met the sons of two of those who had been prominent in the German Resistance to Hitler, Manfred, the son of Field Marshal Erwin von Rommel, and Berthold the son of Count Claus von Stauffenberg.

I met Manfred Rommel in the Churchill Room of the House of Commons where he had been dining with David, Lord Montgomery, the son of Field Marshal Lord Montgomery of El Alamein, his father's old adversary. The younger Rommel, who was Mayor of Stuttgart, expressed much surprise and also gratitude that he had been singled out for a very significant British honour for playing an important part in improving relations between Germany and Britain. Watching them I felt that, had Hitler and Nazism not got in the way, the fathers of both these men might have got on well together too.

I also met, in the Scottish Borders, a most charming and delightful man who spoke such good English that I thought he was British. After a lengthy conversation I sensed that just possibly he might not be and I asked him what his name was. He replied "Major General Berthold von Stauffenberg." I asked him if he was the son of the famous Count, who had done his best to blow up Hitler in his headquarters in Eastern Poland. He confirmed that he was and that he was serving as German Military Attaché in London – a turn of events which would surely have enraged Hitler. When I asked him whether some of the older generals who had served under Hitler had shown any reservations towards him when he was a young German officer, he told me that he had sometimes been asked somewhat enigmatically "Are you your father's son?" to which he had replied simply "Yes."

The attempt to assassinate Hitler has been the subject of a recent film starring Tom Cruise as Stauffenberg and the event poses a fascinating question for students of history – how would it have affected the course of the war if Stauffenberg's bomb had indeed killed Hitler? My answer would be that the generals and officers associated with the July Plot would have tried to seize power and the SS and quite possibly some parts of the Armed Forces, all of whom had sworn an oath of loyalty to Hitler, would have resisted them. In any case by that time the Allies were fully committed to unconditional surrender of the German military and many of Hitler's outrages and crimes against humanity were being discovered. So there could have been no guarantee that the German resistance to Hitler would have succeeded in establishing a government, in either the short or long run. However the prospect of dissension and civil war in Germany after Hitler's demise, might have led to a much more rapid collapse of the Third Reich, which in turn would have saved countless lives.

CHAPTER 5

An advocate, a councillor, a married man and an MP

Sometimes the pace of life seems to quicken – President Abraham Lincoln once confessed that far from controlling events, events had controlled him. On a very different level I began to feel the same in the years before becoming a Member of Parliament.

After four years of legal training I was admitted to the Scottish Bar as an Advocate in December 1968 and hoped some criminal work would come my way. On my first day I received instructions from a solicitor named Mrs Winnie Ewing to take part in a divorce case. She had become the Member of Parliament for Hamilton the previous year and was the only member of the Scottish National Party in the House of Commons.

My first criminal case was sent to me by a friendly solicitor from Hamilton called Bob Gloyer, who had a great sense of humour. My client had been charged with attempted murder outside the mausoleum in the town where the Dukes of Hamilton had at one time been interred. I learned that the accused who had been refused entry to a local club had returned to challenge the bouncer to "have a square go" and, by the time they both arrived next to the mausoleum, the bouncer had allegedly been stabbed from behind.

My client claimed that the injured man had fallen on something jagged on the ground. Despite my efforts the evidence against him was strong enough that he was convicted and sentenced to nine years in prison. Afterwards I saw the accused in the cells and all he said to me somewhat forlornly was "It will be a long time away from Hamilton."

I am sometimes asked "How do you defend an accused person whom you know to be guilty?" The answer is that you do not know and you are not judge, jury or witness. On behalf of the defence it is your duty to put the accused's story to the jury and it is for them to decide what is true and what is not true.

A very short time later Bob Gloyer sent me another case, in which a man was charged with assault to severe injury by razor-slashing. In cross-examination the victim was unsure about the identity of his attacker, and the Advocate Depute did not call an extra witness, presumably because he was so confident of success. The jury unexpectedly returned a verdict of "Not Proven," and the judge who was about to make a prepared statement looked so unsettled by this turn of events that he almost forgot to thank the jury. When I met him a day or so later in the Advocates Library he told me I had got off a guilty man. My feeling however was that if the prosecutor had decided not to call the other witness, responsibility for what had happened lay with him rather than with me.

As luck would have it I soon got the opportunity to become a prosecutor myself when I was offered the job of interim Procurator-Fiscal in Dumfries during the Easter break in 1969. My chance came because all the other fiscals were busy prosecuting the Lord Lieutenant for some minor tax infringement!

I travelled down early and studied all the relevant papers. My first case involved a salmon poacher who had been caught red-handed with his fish by an off-duty police officer. Under some obscure legislative provision only one witness was needed to obtain a conviction for such an offence and a look of astonishment spread over the face of the accused when he was found guilty and fined £5. The salmon in question was in court, decomposing rapidly and emitting an unmistakable odour! I could not help feeling this was a shocking waste of a once splendid fish.

More intriguing cases followed. At a crossroads in Dumfries there were three banks. A young man was seen by a night watchman poking out the window at the back of one of the buildings, giving the impression that he was trying to get into the bank with a view to robbing it. The night watchman seized him, and in due course I prosecuted the alleged, would-be thief in court. The Sheriff, George Carmichael, looked somewhat puzzled by the defence of the accused which was that he had drunk so much that he did not know where he was, what he was doing or why he was doing it. He was convicted nonetheless and put on probation.

The most significant of the many cases I had to deal with related to a young man who had driven a car during a rally, and had apparently fallen asleep at the wheel. The car had crashed and his passenger had been killed. He was charged with driving without due care and attention. After a full day in court I returned to the not-at-all expensive lodging house where I was staying.

In those days advocates often were not paid until many months or even years after a case was concluded. As a result I was not staying at a five star hotel! Nor as it turned out was the accused. I came down to supper, sat down at a table, and there, as bold as brass, sitting opposite me was the man I had spent the day prosecuting. Very taken aback I asked him if we were indeed in the same case, and when he confirmed my worst fears, I excused myself and departed. Knowing that the prosecutor is not supposed to have any informal contact with an accused person in the middle of a case – and certainly not sharing supper with him or her – I made a swift phone call to my immediate boss, the chief prosecutor. Fortunately he was quite relaxed about what had happened, and said "Now you know how lonely it is to be a Procurator-Fiscal." Next day the driver was found guilty and was fined £25, a sentence which even in those days appeared somewhat lenient.

Back at the Scots Bar there was an enjoyable atmosphere, and what might be described as a pool of wisdom from which advocates drew strength. If one was known to be the greatest expert on a subject, he or she might be asked by a colleague what was the key point or points to address in any specialised or particularly complex area of the law. Often the answer, given sometimes in one sentence, would help point the young advocate in the right direction.

Not all cases were straightforward and one in particular worried me a great deal. It related to a seaman who had had an accident at sea, and had died. I was acting for the widow, on whose behalf damages were being sought. However it was not absolutely certain which law of which country applied, and the witnesses had either died or were virtually impossible to trace.

A Procedure Roll debate was fixed to decide on which law or laws would apply. The day before the debate, for the only time in my life, I worked on that case throughout the night. The legal arguments which could be put forward were clear but there were also strong counter-arguments and no guarantee of success.

I appeared in court ready for debate and a hand descended on my shoulder. It was my Senior Counsel, John McCluskey QC, who would become one of Scotland's best known judges. "Just you leave this to me" he said and proceeded to argue brilliantly before the judge, who sent the case to Avizandum, meaning he would give his judgement after full consideration.

Not long afterwards something really remarkable happened. I received an offer of damages which was ten times more than my estimate of the seaman's widow's claim. Within minutes I rushed in the acceptance and then went to tell my esteemed Senior Counsel what had happened. His response was that we must accept the offer immediately and I told him I had already done that. He then said that as soon as the other side acknowledged their mistake over the amount, we must do the honourable thing and give it all back! However from that day to this no mistake has ever been admitted.

Another complex case which came my way was an action of multiple poinding. This was an unusual form of action in which the court, after listening to the competing claims about the entitlement of people to certain rights or benefits, decides between them.

Many years before the case, a man, who through hard work had built up a fortune, under his will wished that his wealth should be of maximum benefit to his relatives. It was essential that distant family members from as far afield as Canada and Australia benefited correctly.

Succession law can be intricate and working on this case convinced me that advocates should be insured for all the written work they do in case any possible future happenings could have a bearing on the advice given. I was insured and happily no such claims would ever be made with regard to my written legal work, but I was aware that lawyers, however able and hardworking, are not necessarily infallible!

The Scots Bar is one of Scotland's great historic institutions, at which those who succeed are engaged in the pursuit of excellence.

At the time I practised there were just over 100 Advocates for the whole of Scotland – a tiny fraction of the numbers there now, nearly 40 years later. As a result most advocates had to give advice on a huge range of subjects. Specialisation was only for a few, but I do recall that two of the top commercial lawyers at the Bar were Angus Grossart and George Penrose. The former left to start up one of Scotland's best known merchant banks, Noble Grossart, and the latter, who was also a chartered accountant, became a judge, each of them having had huge practices.

There were many Advocates at the Scottish Bar, who aspired to go into politics. These included John Smith who would one day lead the Labour Party, Menzies Campbell, a future leader of the Liberal Democrats and for the Conservatives there was Malcolm Rifkind who would become Foreign Secretary, Peter Fraser, one day to be Lord Advocate, and Michael Ancram who went on to become a Scottish Office Minister and a Minister for Northern Ireland. There were others like Sheriff Alex Pollock and the inimitable Nicholas Fairbairn, who knew how to be both brilliant and highly controversial at the same time. He, along with Lionel Daiches, David Abbey and John Smith were some of the top defence counsel in criminal cases.

Each day we would meet in Parliament House in the heart of Edinburgh, where the old Scottish Parliament used to sit. We would wait there hopefully for instructions from solicitors. I remember on one occasion being approached by a young woman solicitor who asked me to take a criminal appeal before the High Court in a few minutes as no other counsel was available. I quickly read the papers and considered it a very weak case. I told her the chances of success were extremely remote, and that probably I would be out of the High Court within five minutes of being

1) The Crown of Scotland being borne to St Giles Cathedral to be presented to the Queen by the Duke of Hamilton, with the author and his brother.

2) The author acts as page to Her Majesty the Queen at the ceremony for the Knights of the Thistle in Edinburgh.

3) The author's father, a former Scottish middleweight champion, teaches his son to box on the sands of North Berwick in 1948.

4) The author defeats Cambridge boxing vice-captain Roger Houghton in 1962. Houghton had knocked out his Oxford opponent the year before.

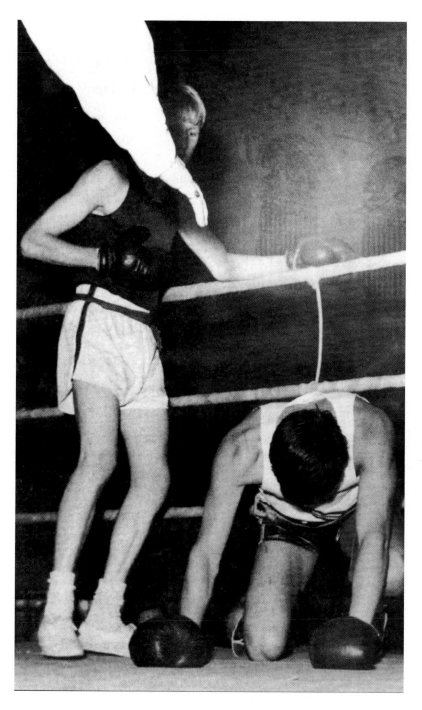

5) The referee rebukes the author for resting his glove on the ropes. Thereafter the opponent, from Loughborough, takes a count of ten, unable to rise.

6) The members of the Oxford Union shortly before the BBC televised the debate that Southern Rhodesia should not have independence before majority rule. Iain Macleod (seated on the author's left) and Garfield Todd (seated on the author's right) won the debate arguing in favour of the motion, 1964.

7) The author presides over the Oxford Union in session (on left, Jonathan Aitken, and on right, Tariq Ali) with Eric Abrahams reading the Minutes.

8) As a Cameronian officer taking part in the Edinburgh Military Tattoo in 1973 with Colonel Douglas Smith (centre) and Colonel George Soper OBE.

9) Engagement photograph of the author and Susie Buchan, 1974.

10) The family learn the skills of seamanship. (Left to right: Susie, Harry, Charles, Andrew, Jamie and the author.)

11) *Right*: The author with his sons (left to right: Jamie, Charles, Andrew and Harry) undertake their first official engagement, detonating a small charge to build a much needed tunnel through the rock of Edinburgh Castle.

12) Professor Dr Albrecht Haushofer (centre), a special adviser to Hess and author of peace plans for the German Resistance to Hitler, with Professor Hildebrandt (left) and Rainer Hildebrandt, the founder of the Berlin Wall Museum.

13) Geordie, 11th Earl of Selkirk, with a cigar, about to play diplomatic golf with the Prime Minister of Singapore, Lee Kuan Yew (left) in the early 1960s.

called. As fortune would have it I was rigorously cross-examined by Lord Wheatley for 40 minutes and when I emerged, somewhat battered, into the sunlight, the solicitor told me that I had been the eighteenth advocate whom she had approached! After that I was far more careful before I said yes to a last minute appeal for help.

I was instructed by more than 50 solicitors at one time or another, and was in the High Court for many high profile cases including at least 15 murders. On one occasion Ronnie King-Murray, who became a judge, asked me to assist with the prosecution of some youths who had been responsible for the death of a bus conductor. They were convicted on the evidence of their girlfriends. I actually felt moved when the girls howled with anguish after the judge pronounced that the youths should be "detained at Her Majesty's Pleasure", although I had not the slightest doubt that the girls had acted correctly.

But the most memorable case with which I was associated was the defence of a member of the Workers' Party of Scotland. The four accused were McPherson, Doran, Lygate and Lawson, My client was Lawson and my Senior Counsel was David Abbey, an exceptionally able QC. The accused had formed a small Maoist group of activists and allegedly they had decided to swell party funds through the novel approach of armed robbery of Glasgow's Banks, using at least one sawn-off shotgun.

Not surprisingly this had gone down very badly with the Banks, and had been seen as an extreme provocation by the City Police. At the end of the case McPherson, Doran and Lygate each received more than 20 years imprisonment, extremely heavy sentences by the standards of the time. Our client got six years.

Many years later as the Scottish Office Minister responsible for prisons, I visited the Barlinnie Special Unit. There the first person

I saw was none other than McPherson. When I reminded him I had acted as a defence counsel for his co-accused Lawson, we had a good chat. It seemed to me that he had come to terms with his sentence and was older and wiser. His last words to me were "Next time we meet I hope it will be in happier circumstances."

I later learnt that the case had given rise to a sad little ditty in some of the Glasgow pubs which the bank robbers may have frequented. The copyright is unknown but it seems clear where the author's sympathies lie. The facts may be less than 100 per cent accurate but here is the version which came to me.

> "Glasgow High Court was the stage,
> A relic of a bygone age,
> Children screamed and grown men wept,
> As Scotland's law few good men kept.
> Lygate for your politics
> You will go inside for 26
> I'm sorry I cannot make it more,
> As on your life I close the door.
> Doran for you the count is 24
> Because your politics I abhor.
> You are a threat to me and mine
> For you the cost is measured in time."

In the midst of all the human dramas contained in a stream of High Court cases, Malcolm Rifkind, who had become an Edinburgh Councillor, enlisted me to apply as a Conservative candidate for the ward of Murrayfield/Cramond, since the sitting member was resigning. Malcolm introduced me to Councillor Brian Meek, the leader of the Conservative Group. He was also a journalist and a person with a very incisive mind and a formidable wit. I decided to apply and was extremely pleased to be selected.

In the by-election which followed in the autumn of 1972, the major issue was the future of Edinburgh's selective fee-paying schools, one of which was the Royal High School, prominently situated in the middle of the ward. The ruling Labour administration had the majority of votes but many of the electors were outraged that the Royal High and the Merchant Company schools and some elements of selectivity were under threat for abolition.

Apart from supporting the Royal High I made it clear that I would give a high priority to conservation issues and to the views of community bodies like the Corstorphine Trust and the Cramond Association. I would campaign for a community centre of Drumbrae and for improved safety for school children.

On the night of the election my father appeared, and he was allowed in to the counting of the votes at the City Chambers. He had been a Scottish Conservative MP for ten years from 1930-1940 for East Renfrewshire and although he did not live to see me reach the House of Commons, he was very pleased to be present to see me elected with a decisive majority.

On the council I joined a number of former Edinburgh University students. In addition to Malcolm, there were Robin Cook, a future Labour Foreign Secretary and George Foulkes, who became a Labour minister, a Life Peer and currently an adornment to the Scottish Parliament! The latter had asked me to second him as Rector's Assessor for Edinburgh University and I did so but at my first council meeting he did not return the compliment. When it was proposed that I should go on the same committees as my predecessor, Councillor Foulkes said that in view of my total lack of experience it was hardly appropriate for me to be considered for such illustrious duties. So before I had even uttered a word, the vote went against me and membership was denied.

In spite of this I found myself exchanging banter with George over lunch later that day. I was sitting next to the Labour Councillor Donald Renton who had fought for the Republican side with the International Brigade in the Spanish Civil War. I remember he had one great passionate speech on what it was like to man the barricades against fascism, with which he would periodically entertain and enthral the other Councillors.

On this occasion the old campaigner was rather silent at first, until suddenly he said "I never thought I would see the day when I would sit next to a scion of the House of Hamilton!" To this George Foulkes replied "Well, Donald that is local democracy for you."

Work as a Councillor took up much of my time when I was not in court. The political parties had gradually taken over from most of the Independents and the Progressives. The voters liked to be kept informed about services from the council and local planning and environmental issues through regular newsletters. To be re-elected a Tory Councillor you not only had to work hard but be seen to work hard.

There was also my service with the Territorial Army, as an officer with the Cameronians Scottish Rifles. In 1972 I had passed the Lieutenant to Captain's course at Warminster, and had acted as the Army ADC to the Lord High Commissioner to the General Assembly of the Church of Scotland, Lord Clydesmuir. I began to feel that work as an advocate supplemented by work as a Councillor and as a TA officer was enough for the moment, and that it was important not to become over committed.

This was to be a relevant consideration when I received a letter from a senior solicitor instructing me to act in a number of substantial cases. He wanted me to become a trustee of his favourite charity, but reading between the lines it seemed to me that what he really meant was that, if I wanted to receive any more cases from him, such charity work was obligatory! I had enough on my plate already, so I sent him a £5 donation for the charity and what I hoped was a diplomatic refusal from getting further involved. As I had anticipated, no more cases from him were forthcoming.

Later that year I was asked by an old school friend, Alexander Macmillan, to stay at Birchgrove, the home in Sussex of his grandfather, the former Prime Minister Harold Macmillan. Their firm of publishers had brought out my recent book on the story behind Hess' wartime flight to Britain, and this was an opportunity not to be missed. I had admired the PM's famous "Wind of Change" speech to the South African Parliament in 1960 and had not forgotten that during his premiership in the 1950s Scotland had a majority of Conservative MPs.

I accepted Alexander's invitation which included attendance at a pheasant shoot on the estate. A rumour had reached me that on such occasions, if the former Prime Minister thought somebody was not particularly good at shooting, he would position himself behind the unfortunate individual, aiming for whatever pheasants that person had missed. Sure enough on the day in question, in the late morning, I sensed the presence of a shadowy figure sitting on a shooting stick someway behind me. I turned and there indeed was Harold Macmillan and what was more he did shoot any birds that I had missed!

The grand old man was extremely interesting to talk to and recalled for me the memorable occasion at the United Nations in

New York when he was addressing the General Assembly. During his speech the Soviet leader, Mr Khrushchev, had interrupted him by shouting and pounding on his desk. In the midst of this uproar Harold Macmillan had said that if the Soviet Premier was going to continue, he wanted a translation, which gave rise to a great deal of merriment and was interpreted as an extremely effective British put-down. In fact "Supermac", as he was nicknamed, told me that he had actually thought that Mr Khrushchev might be saying something important and he genuinely wanted to know what it was. Hence his call for a translation.

Harold Macmillan also spoke to me about his African "Wind of Change" speech and when asked whether he knew how great the impact would be, replied that he had thought "it was all happening anyway". One story he told amused me greatly, it was about a visit he made to North Africa with Winston Churchill during the Second World War. In the early hours of the morning he felt exhausted and was much in need of some sleep, however, the Prime Minister chose that moment to launch into a tremendous tirade against the wickedness of Hitler. Eventually Macmillan sought to bring this to an end by saying that there must be something to be said for Hitler, whereupon Churchill asked him to explain himself. Macmillan rather daringly said "If it was not for Hitler you would not be Prime Minister." Churchill agreed that he might have a point about that and this was the signal for them to get a little sleep at last. I sensed that you had to be Harold Macmillan in order to get away with a joke like that with Churchill.

Back in Scotland in the spring of 1973 our family was shocked and saddened by my father's unexpected death after a routine operation. When I was young I had been aware of his celebrity status as Middleweight Boxing Champion of Scotland and the first man in the world to fly over Mount Everest in 1933. With the other pilot, David McIntyre, he later established an aviation industry in Scotland which still employs many hundreds of people. They also went on to develop Prestwick Airport with my father as Chairman and David McIntyre as Chief Executive of Scottish Aviation Limited.

In those days the early aviators were held in much the same regard as astronauts were by a later generation. Perhaps it was this which caused the well-known writer and actress from Glasgow, Molly Weir, to tell me in a letter "He was a very fine character and truly the stuff that heroes are made of …."

My father had many responsibilities and was associated with a host of Scottish charitable projects, including being Chairman of the successful Restoration Appeal for St Columba's Abbey on the island of Iona and, as chancellor of St Andrew's University, participating in a very effective fundraising tour of North America. He had also been Lord High Commissioner to the General Assembly of the Church of Scotland four times – more often than anyone else in the twentieth century.

Immediately following my father's death I received well over 100 letters of condolence from people ranging from Harold Macmillan to Mrs Winnie Ewing. Menzies Campbell referred to his "warm hearted hospitality and kindness," and the senior Scottish judge Lord Migdale was of the view that "For all his great achievements, he was always so modest and self-effacing." This was a quality endorsed by Mrs Ewing. She wrote:

"I had an affection for your father based on just a number of meetings. For my part I really liked him. He was a fine mixture of modesty and ability which always is appealing to some of us who saw so many less attractive persons in the mean art of politics… If you follow in your father's footsteps you will be a fortunate man deservedly surrounded by friends."

On the 40th anniversary of his flight over Everest, his ashes were scattered from the air by my brother Angus and myself over the "Politicians Walk" at Lennoxlove, which had been his home for a quarter of a century. For me he had been a good friend as well as a father, and his loss was a little bit like the fall of a great oak tree which leaves a large hole in the forest.

I hoped that one day I would follow my father's example and become a Scottish Member of Parliament. In the meantime, though, I would have to face re-election as a Councillor. I also kept up my service with the TA, commanding the Edinburgh Castle Guard for about ten nights, taking part in the Military Tattoo with Cameronian soldiers and passing the Company Commander's course at Warminster.

The opportunity to fight for a seat in the United Kingdom Parliament came early in 1974 with the so-called "Miners' Election" called by Edward Heath after the miners went on strike. I found myself being selected as the Conservative candidate for Hamilton in Lanarkshire where the Tories had lost their deposit in the previous poll.

During the campaign Baroness Elliot of Harewood, the first woman to take her seat as a Baroness in the House of Lords, came to speak for me in the Hamilton Bingo Hall. The players listened to her for all of three minutes, and then went back to discussing the finer points of their game among themselves, much to her displeasure.

The sitting Labour MP, Alex Wilson, had earlier been defeated in a by-election in 1967 by Mrs Winnie Ewing but had won back the seat at the next General Election. He was concerned that Conservative supporters instead of voting Conservative might switch to the SNP as they had done in the by-election. This did not happen owing to a vigorously fought campaign in which the Hamilton Conservatives and I managed to double the Tory percentage of the vote. We did not win but the party considered it to have been a creditable performance.

Oddly, one issue which hovered in the background at the time of the campaign was what my attitude might be to the small matter of an Egyptian Sarcophagus. This rather macabre matter had all the elements of a black comedy. Its main player was one of the former Dukes of Hamilton, the 10th holder of the title, who had been ambassador to Moscow at the time of the Napoleonic Wars. He had struck up a friendship with Napoleon's sister, Princess Pauline Borghese, who left him her Travelling Service, a magnificent set of dressing table accessories, in her will, "as a mark of my friendship". It is now in the National Museums of Scotland.

This same Duke, a somewhat grand figure, arranged for a huge Mausoleum to be built, with instructions in his will that on his death he was to be laid to rest in a black Sarcophagus in the building. After he died this was done, but rather ghoulishly – they had to break his legs to get him into the ancient coffin as he was too tall to fit it.

However, during the early twentieth century much of the area was mined for coal, causing the Mausoleum to subside and to list slightly to one side. The Hamilton Trustees, whose chairman was then Admiral of the Fleet Lord Fisher of Kilverstone, were concerned that flooding might adversely affect the vaults of the Mausoleum and a decision was made to move the Sarcophagus and all the other coffins to graves in the Bent Cemetery of Hamilton, alongside many graves of Scottish miners.

And there the matter would have rested, so to speak, if it had not been for the fact that shortly before his death my father had expressed the view that the 10th Duke's wishes to rest in the Mausoleum should be respected. This was easier said than done, as no one knew exactly where the Sarcophagus was now buried. My brother Angus and I were asked to sign a document saying we had no objection to the 10th Duke being disinterred.

Actually the prospect of digging up a grave filled me with a total lack of enthusiasm. I was not descended from the 10th Duke but from the 4th incumbent. My grandfather had been a Lieutenant in the Royal Navy and a friend and shipmate of Admiral "Jacky" Fisher. He succeeded to the title of Duke of Hamilton after the 12th Duke died, although he was only a fourth cousin. My grandfather Alfred came from a line of naval officers. His great grandfather had been Admiral Charles Douglas-Hamilton and he had carried the medals of Admiral Horatio, Lord Nelson at the latter's funeral service. To be frank I related more readily to the military traditions which his family had represented rather than that of the Dukes, who had possessed extensive lands in the nineteenth century.

So it was difficult for me to understand why any Scot, let alone a relative, could have wished to be interred in an Egyptian Sarcophagus, but I was informed that the 10th Duke had been a proud and powerful man. I learnt from Cyril Aldred, Keeper of the Royal Scottish Museum, that a rubbing taken from the inscription on the Sarcophagus indicated that it belonged to ITHOROS, daughter of TANID. He thought that the carving was of the highest order, suggesting work of the Ptolemaic period, probably in the 3rd Century BC.

I dreaded this delicate subject coming up during the General Election campaign but happily it did not as the sarcophagus could not be found. All I had to put up with were a few wry comments from the press that I was not only standing for Hamilton, but had quite a number of my ancestors buried there!

After the election I returned home to join my mother in welcoming Harold Macmillan who was about to give the annual tribute, organised by the Sir Walter Scott Club, to the renowned author. I had invited the former Prime Minister to stay at Lennoxlove and he had accepted. Harold Wilson was about to form a Labour Government, after a narrow victory in seats over the Tory leader Edward Heath, but the Tories had won a majority of the popular vote. Harold Macmillan's view was that after a close election it was much easier for a Conservative Government to offer a coalition deal from a position of strength, than for a Labour Government, and that in this case it would not happen.

He sent me a very friendly letter of thanks for his stay with us saying "It was great fun and it was made all the more interesting by taking place at such a dramatic moment in the life of Britain. Incidentally may I congratulate you again on your good fight at Hamilton." This gave me hope of getting into Parliament since if that was his view it might be possible to be selected for a winnable seat before too long.

During my search for a seat before being selected for Hamilton, I learnt that Colonel Colin Mitchell, MP for West Aberdeenshire and nicknamed "Mad Mitch" as a result of his military exploits, had decided not to stand for re-election, so I went up to study the constituency in the hope that I might be interviewed. One of my sponsors for the Candidates List had been Lady Tweedsmuir, who offered to put me up. She had been one of the first women to sit in the House of Commons, and had been MP for South Aberdeen for 20 years, as well as serving as a Minister of State in both the Scottish Office and the Foreign Office. She had been defeated by Donald Dewar in 1966, and had been made a member of the House of Lords in 1970.

While staying with her, I met her daughter Susan, who was working for the publishers John Murray in London. Very attractive, blonde and sparky, she happened to be at home recovering from an appendectomy, otherwise we might never have got together. I left West Aberdeenshire without even an interview but invited Susie, after her return to London, to come up to Scotland to visit me. Events moved swiftly and I proposed to her in the woods at Potterton near Aberdeen, she accepted and we were married within six months. As she would be leaving her employment in London, we held our engagement party there and were delighted that Harold Macmillan was able to come, full of good humour and with that special touch of panache as ever. The party was also attended by a number of Buchans, since Susie's grandfather, as previously mentioned, had been John Buchan, the well-known Scottish author of *The Thirty-Nine Steps*.

It was almost immediately after this that Tony Stodart, MP for West Edinburgh for the last 15 years, gave notice that he would not be standing again. I let my name go forward and the Crossbencher Column of the *Sunday Express* tipped me as the most likely candidate to emerge to join such other lawyers as Malcolm Rifkind, Michael Ancram and Nicky Fairbairn at Westminster. The final round was highly competitive and Susie came along as my fiancée. The partner of each candidate had to sit at the top table but was not cross-examined. The outcome proved to be relatively close with Professor Ross Harper allegedly receiving 22 votes and myself 29. He went on to develop a very prosperous and outstandingly successful legal practice.

The General Election was almost upon us, but there would be time to get married. On the day of the wedding, unbeknown to us, there had been a hoax telephone call to the *Edinburgh Evening News* saying that there was a bomb in the Canongate Church where our wedding was to be held. Fortunately there was no bomb, but the threat accounted for the presence of large men in tailcoats at the reception later, whose boots gave them away as police officers.

I walked down the Royal Mile with my best man, Ian Forrester, who went on the become an Attorney for Microsoft in Europe. I had travelled with him in 1966 when we were selected by the English Speaking Union to take part in a debating tour of 29 Canadian Universities, sponsored by the British Information Services. At the church the Minister, the Very Reverend Dr Ronald Selby Wright, known as "the Radio Padre" in the Second World War, addressed Susie and I in inspiring language. He said:

"Though you are beginning your married life in anxious and troubled times, be strong and of good courage. Faith and hope and a brave heart, a sense of humour that will prevent you from taking yourselves too seriously, a sympathy that is wide enough to embrace not only yourselves but others, forbearance, a mutual desire to give and take, a glad buoyancy of spirit that keeps the heart young, a simple faith in God, which inspires the high ambition to make of life a thing of honour and of beauty, these are the things that will give you victory over the world, and holding to these, you can go on your way rejoicing for you need not be afraid of anything, either of life or death."

The reception was held at Lennoxlove in a marquee in the grounds. In a very short speech I thanked the best man for getting me to the Church in good order, together with the ring, and at least one spare ring. I ended by saying "This is the most enjoyable wedding I have ever attended, and I hope you have enjoyed it as well!"

We departed for our honeymoon which was to be at the Sandy Lane Hotel in Barbados. On the way there, landing at Antigua, an odd incident occurred. A rather swarthy looking man put down a large bag on the vacant seat beside me and then went to sit a long way down the aircraft. Susie was suspicious about his actions and wanted to know why he had abandoned his bag, so I went up to him and asked him to remove it. He picked it up and walked straight off the aircraft before we took off. I have often wondered what he had in it and suspected it might have been full of drugs.

Back in Britain the election was called as soon as we returned. I felt a pang of sadness as I hung up my wig and gown but recalled the farsighted words of David Edward QC to whom I had devilled before becoming an advocate. He had written to me: "You may find that the Bar is not your career. You seem to be looking for an excitement, and an opportunity to help the underdog, which rarely if ever presents itself to the practising advocate, and may even at times be a positive disadvantage to him if he is to do his job properly." Certainly there was no turning back and in the election campaign my wife's mother came to speak for me. Priscilla Tweedsmuir had a natural authority, a clarity of mind and a strong speaking voice. Her presence amidst the Conservatives' spirited campaign was of considerable assistance and within a few weeks I had the honour to be elected as Member of Parliament for Edinburgh West.

It had been just a month after Susie and I became engaged that I was selected as a House of Commons candidate. Having been brought up in a political family, she knew what to expect and some years later she wrote about the ups and downs of being an MP's wife in the local Conservative newspaper. "My husband leaves on Monday mornings and gets home sometimes on Thursday evenings or Friday mornings. He usually spends a good deal of Friday in the constituency and holds surgeries on Friday evenings several times a month. Before the arrival of our four sons, I used to help with some of the surgeries and I think that it is one of the most rewarding aspects of his job helping to resolve real problems." The children, she said, having never known a different way of life seemed to accept it when their father left early on Monday and did not return until Friday.

But despite the separations, there were some exciting compensations and recalling some of the invitations we had received Susie chose to highlight the chance to have lunch with the Prime Minister, Mrs Thatcher, at Chequers. "She met us at the door and after lunch showed us around the whole house and garden with her husband and son, Mark. This was greatly appreciated as it was a Sunday" she wrote. There were also invitations to dine with the American, French and Italian ambassadors at their embassies or residences and she recalled the "great occasion" of a dinner with the then Speaker of the House of Commons, George Thomas.

Back at Westminster in October 1974, as a new MP one of my first duties was to deal with the mail which had been building up and eventually contained more than 100 letters. Some 30 or 40 related to the Edinburgh West constituency and local issues, while a good deal of the remainder referred to the work of Standing,

Select and All Party Committees. Some of the rest raised bizarre matters such as the claimed arrival of flying saucers or called for the search for the Loch Ness Monster to be stepped up!

I made it a practice to obtain tickets to the Visitors Gallery for any constituents who arrived from Edinburgh and in this connection the Edinburgh Conservative MPs would help each other out. The House of Commons was a convivial place and MPs and Ministers were accustomed to addressing each other in correspondence using their first names, giving a glimpse of the informality which can exist between Parliamentarians of different parties.

The Scottish Conservative Group which was 16 strong at that time, worked together as a team, seeking to cover every significant subject that might come up in Oral Questions or debate. I was asked to work with Teddy Taylor, the Shadow Minister of State with responsibilities for Housing and Local Government.

Entering the chamber in order to listen to the Queen's speech debate, I deliberately chose what I thought was an unobtrusive seat. Then I discovered I was sitting right behind the Reverend Ian Paisley and Enoch Powell – not the best place if you are trying to keep a low profile! Then it came home to me that I was now one of more than 600 hundred men and women charged with considering the great issues and controversies which might come before the nation. I felt a sense of belonging and wished my father could have been looking down from the gallery.

CHAPTER 6

The House of Commons and the fall of a Labour Government

The House of Commons was a highly charged place during my first few years on the green leather benches. After the second poll in October Labour had an overall majority of only four and in 1976 came Harold Wilson's shock resignation. In order to stay in power Labour made a pact with the Liberals after Jim Callaghan became Prime Minister.

At first in spite of such a slender numerical advantage, Prime Minister Harold Wilson had command over the House at question time and in debates. He had a very quick mind and he seemed like a gifted piano player who knew exactly which note to strike to delight the audience. On one occasion Andrew Faulds, the actor turned Labour MP, asked him a critical question to which the Prime Minister replied that if he could not think of a better question than that he should change his speech writer. Andrew Faulds, on a point of order insisted that he always wrote his own speeches. Harold Wilson retorted – that was WHY he should get a new speech writer! This kind of exchange always delighted the House of Commons, and made MPs think twice before they crossed swords with the Prime Minister.

For a new Member of Parliament the first tricky hurdle is the maiden speech and I took my time before leaping in. By tradition an MP's first utterance is supposed to be fairly non-controversial and should contain praise for the constituency and usually the member's predecessor. It is also normally heard in silence. The Scots Tory Whip Hamish Gray, or "Highland Hamish" as the press liked to call him, gave me what he thought would be helpful advice. Whatever I did, I should not speak against the death penalty he said, as this might not go down well with the electorate in Edinburgh West. The trouble was I had been thinking about doing just that in a forthcoming debate on whether capital punishment should be brought back for murders committed by terrorists and I felt honour bound to admit it. Emotions were running high on this sensitive topic as my speech was being given not long after the IRA had left explosive devices in pubs on the British mainland which when detonated had killed 21 people.

At that time while I was opposed to the general reintroduction of capital punishment I was not against imposing the death penalty for the premeditated murder of prison and police officers, although in later years I came to believe that the time for even that had passed.

When I made my intentions known, a look of grave concern spread over Hamish's face, but he was a good and loyal friend. On the day the maiden speech was to be made, he came to sit next to me to offer some moral support, even if he was alarmed by my choice of subject matter and was going to vote in a different way. When I rose to speak to a relatively full House, I advanced the argument that terrorism must be dealt with in the most effective way possible but to condemn the perpetrators to death could be counter productive as it could create "the cult of martyrdom on the brooding consciousness of the Irish mind".

I put forward a number of reasons as to why I was against the death penalty for terrorist murders. They included the possibility of the wrong person being convicted, perhaps through misidentification when feelings were running high. I said "It is hardly necessary for me to mention to the House that the execution of a man convicted of murder by terrorism, who, had in fact not committed murder but had been in the wrong place, at the wrong time, with the wrong accent might lead to appalling repercussions."

Finally I drew the conclusion that hanging supporters of Sinn Fein after the 1916 Easter Rising had not deterred further acts of terrorism and the gist of my argument was that we did not need a knee-jerk reaction to the terrible events in Birmingham but a well thought out position on how to deal with such terrorist outrages, that could stand the test of time. The alternative I proposed was to implement the Emslie Report which had recommended that judges should be able to specify the minimum number of years a convicted murderer should serve in prison. This in practice would mean much longer sentences for premeditated murder. Any argument that bringing back the death penalty would lead to a net saving of life remained in my opinion "not proven".

To my surprise I received praise from both sides of the House. The Home Secretary, Roy Jenkins, in his summing up speech for the debate referred to my contribution as "brave and lucid." The MP sitting next to me said that "lucid" was the real compliment, because "brave" merely meant that he agreed with me. Perhaps I valued most of all a letter from the Deputy Speaker, George Thomas, just before his election to the Speaker's chair. He wrote "My warmest congratulations on a superb maiden speech. I am glad I was here to hear you. It is clear that you are going to play a great part in this House."

On a free vote, the House rejected the reintroduction of the death penalty by a considerable majority.

At this time the Scots Labour MPs were led by the gruff and formidable Willie Ross, one of Scotland's most powerful Secretaries of State. I knew him a little as my father had to entertain representatives of foreign governments in his role as Lord Steward and as Hereditary Keeper of Holyrood Palace. Willie Ross had always been very helpful and had played a key role at such gatherings.

At the Despatch Box he was a tough and forceful performer and as a new MP I was perhaps a little bit in awe of him. Tiptoeing past him in the Smoking Room one morning, I heard a deep voice saying "James Douglas-Hamilton has chosen not to notice me this morning." That was in fact my invitation to sit down and have a cup of coffee with him. Such informal chats always proved both entertaining and informative.

My first brush with Prime Ministerial authority came shortly after I was elected Group Secretary by my fellow Scottish Tory MPs. I was asked to request a meeting on their behalf with the Prime Minister, Harold Wilson, to protest about a fresh round of pay rises to senior local authority officials when they had already received substantial increases in the past year.

I was far from convinced that this would be well received but went ahead. The reply from No 10 Downing Street came swiftly and was dismissive. Mr Wilson did not feel "that any useful purpose" would be served by a meeting with us and he was "surprised" that Conservatives who had previously argued in favour of reducing controls on local government should now feel free to urge the Government to intervene over officials' salaries.

I had remembered my father's previous advice always to keep letters to Prime Ministers confined to one sheet of paper but the reply showed me that leaders of the nation do not wish to be too readily accessible to direct arguments over policy points.

In 1975 a Referendum on whether or not Britain should remain within the European Economic Community was called by the Prime Minister who allowed his Cabinet colleagues a dispensation to vote as they thought best. Both Labour and the Conservatives were split on this issue. I was in the "Yes" camp on grounds of collective security and because I believed that staying in would safeguard and help develop Scotland's trade as part of a larger market. The same sort of arguments I might have put forward on behalf of the proposed Union between Scotland and England if I had been around in 1707.

Another big constitutional issue was that of devolution. The issue of Home Rule for Scotland had rumbled on for many years and both former Conservative Prime Ministers Sir Alec Douglas-Home and Ted Heath had supported the creation of a directly elected Assembly without a separate Executive. Later both men (Ted Heath in particular) wanted to go further, but I personally supported the original scheme put forward by Sir Alec. The difficulty with it was that it went too far for most Tory MPs and not far enough for the other parties. As a result it was not going to get through the House of Commons.

When the Labour Government's Scotland and Wales Bill had its Second Reading Debate, a considerable rebellion against the Conservative Shadow Cabinet policy emerged. Margaret Thatcher had defeated Ted Heath for the leadership of the party, and her Shadow Cabinet did not feel compelled to stand by his former commitment to an elected Assembly. My own view was that the bill should be considered by Parliament before being rejected, and along with some 30 other Tory MPs, including Ted Heath, for the only time in my political life I defied a three line whip and abstained.

The pro-devolution Shadow Secretary of State for Scotland, Alick Buchanan-Smith, and the Shadow spokesmen, Hamish Gray and Malcolm Rifkind, all resigned as they were not prepared to vote against the bill. John Corrie, the Scottish Conservative Whip, also rebelled and had to resign. Although I had defied orders to vote down the bill, some time later I was invited to join the Whips' Office.

The Whips' main function is to act as the eyes and ears of the Leader and a part of their role is to enforce discipline among backbenchers. They have gained a somewhat sinister reputation especially since Scots actor Ian Richardson's award-winning portrayal of Francis Urquhart as the embittered, malevolent and ultimately murderous Tory Chief Whip in BBC TV's *House of Cards*. The Whips of all parties may know where the "bodies" are buried in terms of what MPs get up to but I am glad to say their activities are nothing like as draconian as Urquhart's were!

The Tory Chief Whip at the time, the tall, suave Humphrey Atkins had to let Mrs Thatcher know the views of all members on issues of controversy, so that the leader would always be aware which policies would receive the support of Tory backbenchers. The Chief Whip had to act as the principal channel of communication with his own side and with the other parties.

In my position as the Scottish Conservative Whip I was invited to make contact with my opposite number, the Scottish Labour Whip, Jimmy Hamilton MP for Bothwell. I wrote to him on 2 February 1977 signing the letter "from the other Jimmy

Hamilton". Soon the two of us would be enjoying a cup of coffee, but when Willie Ross saw me pay for both cups his wry comment to Jimmy Hamilton was "Beware of Greeks bearing gifts."

By this time the future of the Labour Government looked precarious, and they depended on the Lib-Lab pact to secure a majority. However I realised that on certain issues Labour could be defeated and two of them related to my own constituency. One concerned whether Dunfermline College of Physical Education for Women in Cramond should be merged with another institution namely Dundee College.

Dunfermline College, with its purpose-built facilities, was doing a very good job and had a most formidable principal, namely Miss Molly Abbott. The Secretary of State at that time, Bruce Millan, had indicated his intention to close several colleges in order to deal with surplus capacity. However, it seemed to me that the small popular colleges were to be victimised to benefit larger, less popular institutions.

After putting down more than 50 Parliamentary Questions on this issue, I discovered that the particular proposal to remove the women students from Cramond to Dundee would seriously disadvantage them with regard to facilities compared to what was available to their male counterparts attending Jordanhill College in Glasgow.

A way to help Dunfermline College, and incidentally to embarrass the Labour Government, suddenly occurred to me and I immediately reported Bruce Millan to the newly-created Equal Opportunities Commission, a move which Donald Dewar told me later intensely annoyed the Scottish Secretary.

The Commission's head, Betty Lockwood, replied that she was both "interested and concerned" to read what I had to say and appreciated the "very helpful detail" in my letter. Three days later I stepped up the pressure with a letter to the Prime Minister, Jim Callaghan. I warned him of the seriousness of discriminating against women student teachers of physical education and claimed it would surely be "quite improper" for Bruce Millan to remove the college from its specialist facilities before the Equal Opportunities Commission had investigated the matter. Then I hinted this was an issue on which Labour could be defeated on the floor of the House of Commons.

This time I learned that the campaign had been effective. The Government's plans were abandoned and when I appeared at Molly Abbott's victory party the students cheered me like some kind of pop star. However I had no illusions, it was Molly's victory and while it was a worthy cause, at the same time I hoped the good feelings towards me would eventually be translated into votes.

Another campaign involved the Department of Trade's plans to take over the running of the Highlands and Islands airports from the Civil Aviation Authority giving responsibility for them to the British Airports Authority. This would have resulted in my constituents, who worked at the headquarters of the CAA in West Edinburgh, losing their jobs and I managed to persuade the SNP and Liberal Democrat MPs who had Highlands and Islands airports that this empire building would put the future employment of their constituents under threat.

A debate on the Consolidated Fund, which did not involve a vote, was held on the Government's plans, after midnight, in the House of Commons on 15 December 1977. During its progress it became clear that if members had been able to vote the Government would have faced defeat.

As a result on 1 February the Government gave in and in a letter the Trade Minister, Stanley Clinton Davis, outlined the terms of the surrender. He wrote "In view of the strong feelings in Scotland about this issue, it was most appropriate that the matter should be decided there by the Scottish Assembly which will have the right to determine the future role of all Scottish airports. Accordingly we opted to maintain the status quo."

Meanwhile the future of the proposed Scottish Assembly still hung in the balance. In 1979 Scotland and Wales both had a referendum after Labour's devolution bill was passed by Parliament. Wales voted against and the vote in Scotland produced a narrow majority in favour but it was insufficient to meet the 40 per cent test incorporated into the Act, as a result of the efforts of the Labour MP George Cunningham, a Scot who sat for an English constituency.

Back at Westminster the Prime Minister refused to try and implement the terms of the Scotland Act and I reported to the Tory Chief Whip that not surprisingly the eleven SNP members were extremely annoyed with him. As a result they would support a Motion of No Confidence in the Labour Government.

The Chief Whip believed we might have a chance of bringing down the Government and forcing an election. Such an event had not happened since October 1924 when the Labour Prime Minister Ramsay MacDonald was compelled to go to the country after losing a Confidence Vote in the House of Commons. However Humphrey Atkins thought we should not make our move, until we could be absolutely sure of maximising the vote. After the miserable "Winter of Discontent" when strikes had seriously disrupted a variety of public services, there was a strong mood in the country for change.

Eventually in a move which Jim Callaghan derided as "turkeys voting for an early Christmas", the SNP members put down a Motion of No Confidence and immediately the Conservative Whips' Office called on every single Tory MP to be present for this critical vote on 28 March 1979.

It was a day of high drama at Westminster and in fact turned out to be one of the most exciting and nerve-wracking evenings of my life. Labour thought they might just scrape home and in desperation they persuaded the sole Independent Irish MP, Frank Maguire, a publican who represented Fermanagh and South Tyrone, to come to the House of Commons. After his arrival however he came under sustained verbal attack in the chamber from Gerry Fitt, the SDLP leader. Despite all Labour's blandishments, Mr Maguire also allegedly influenced by his wife, decided to abstain and to make the outcome even more uncertain, two Ulster Unionists, John Carson and Harold McCusker, voted with Labour.

I had my own problems. One of the Scottish Conservative members, the colourful and unpredictable Nicholas Fairbairn had a lecture to give in Oxford that day. I implored him to cancel the engagement as he might not be back in time for the vote. To my dismay he flatly refused. When he re-appeared only forty five minutes before decision time my heart was in my mouth and I remember thinking that one day his luck would run out.

The debate reached a noisy climax at 10pm and when the division was finally called it was clear that this might be the closest and most fateful vote in which most MPs would ever participate. Even a draw would have been hugely significant as the Speaker by convention would have given his casting vote for the status quo and the Government would have survived a few more months, when its electoral chances might have been a lot better.

Before the vote was formally announced, I still did not know who had won but knew the result was desperately close. Jimmy Hamilton the Scots Labour Whip thought that his side had triumphed and he gave the thumbs up sign to the Labour benches. The Labour MPs began to wave their order papers jubilantly in the air, assuming victory and Margaret Thatcher, the Tory leader and Francis Pym sitting next to her, looked at their feet disconsolately.

Then amidst enormous excitement the Whips, who had acted as tellers in the division lobbies, arrived. The Conservative tellers, Spencer Le Marchant and Tony Berry, lined up on the right in front of the Speaker's chair, a sure sign that their party had won, and all of a sudden it was the Tory MPs who were waving their order papers and Mrs Thatcher's eyes sparkled.

Spencer Le Marchant's powerful voice resounded around the chamber announcing the success by one vote of the No Confidence Motion in Her Majesty's Government. The whole House of Commons burst into life with "Hear Hears" echoing across the floor. At this point the Left Wing Labour MP Eric Heffer rose in his seat, and led a number of his colleagues in singing "The Red Flag." I felt the impending General Election campaign had begun.

On the next day the Chief Whip wished us all the largest majority of our lives in our own seats and presented each of us with a document which we had all signed, detailing the momentous result, which was 311 for the Motion of No Confidence and 310 for the Labour Government. It had been a historic occasion and every Conservative MP had responded to the call of duty. In addition 13 Liberals, the 11 Scottish Nationalists and 8 Ulster Unionists all voted against the Government.

The absence of one Labour MP, Sir Alfred Broughton, who represented Batley and Morley was also highly significant. He was very ill and some consideration was given to the possibility of bringing him into the precincts of Parliament in an ambulance where his vote would have counted. Whatever the nature of the private discussions in the Labour Whips' office as to whether or not he should be brought from Yorkshire to London, this did not happen. As a result Labour lost by one vote and Prime Minister Jim Callaghan was forced, as he put it, to take Labour's case to the country.

Talking of miniscule majorities there is an engaging story that on one occasion, Ted Heath, as Conservative Chief Whip, summoned Prime Minister Winston Churchill to return from a posh dinner in the Savoy Hotel for a close vote and the Government scraped through with a majority of three. Afterwards Ted Heath followed the Prime Minister down to his car to say how sorry he was that the dinner in the Savoy had been interrupted, explaining that the prospect of such a close vote had made him feel his return really had been necessary. Sir Winston's reply would have recommended itself to Mrs Thatcher on the evening the Labour Government fell. He told Ted Heath not to worry about interrupting his dinner and added "But one is always enough!"

The evening of the No Confidence vote in 1979 had not been the only cliff hanger during this Parliamentary session. The nationalisation of ship building had scraped through by one vote but the fall of the Labour government was such an unusual event that the Conservatives entered the subsequent five week general election campaign full of confidence, bounce and vitality. In addition we were all conscious that Britain stood on the verge of gaining its first woman Prime Minister.

CHAPTER 7

Dominica, the Falklands and the smallest majority in Scotland

After the Conservative victory in the General Election I received an invitation to serve as a Government Whip and a Lord Commissioner of the Treasury, which meant that I would have to sign Treasury Orders, cheques and warrants, so as to relieve the Chancellor of the Exchequer from routine paperwork.

The Chief Whip was Michael Jopling, assisted by his Deputy, John Stradling-Thomas, the Pairing Whip and Regional Whips. In Government the job of a Whip is more demanding than in Opposition, since the Whips' Office is responsible for ensuring that there is a majority at all times in votes on Government business in Committee or on the Floor of the House.

In Government the Chief Whip in particular is extremely powerful. He or she is consulted by and advises the Prime Minister on appointments and a range of other subjects including Parliamentary strategy and tactics, with a view to making the best use of Parliamentary time.

Those of us who were Whips would have at least one meeting a week in No 12 Downing Street, and there I was thrilled to see in the ante-room the print of the only meeting between the Duke of

Wellington and Admiral Lord Nelson. Within six weeks of that meeting Nelson would be dead at the Battle of Trafalgar and I could not help reflecting that some time before that my great, great grandfather had served as Flag Midshipman on Nelson's Flagship the *HMS Victory*.

It was therefore altogether appropriate that Michael Jopling on behalf of the Whips' Office at a dinner in Downing Street presented the Prime Minister, Mrs Thatcher, with a splendid figure of Wellington, or the Iron Duke as he was popularly known then. Of course it would not be long before she gained the nickname of the Iron Lady which would mark her out as the most decisive peace-time Prime Minister of the twentieth century.

The Whips' office was a most interesting place, often privy to what might happen before it actually happened. Two of the Whips, Bob Boscawen and Carol Mather, had a special authority about them. They were holders of the Military Cross. Bob, after countless engagements following D-Day, had received his for leading his tanks in a pitched battle repulsing and driving back an enemy attack in an orchard not far from the German border. Carol had been one of the first SAS officers in the North African desert, and Field Marshal Montgomery had recommended him for the MC for conveying a message of critical importance at about the time that the town of Nijmegen was taken.

One of the greatest experts connected with the Whips' office was Murdo (later Sir Murdo) Maclean, who was the senior civil servant in charge of Government business. Working with the Chief Whip and the Leader of the House of Commons, he was accustomed to dealing with approaches from Opposition parties over the management of Parliamentary business, as well as the intricate protocol for State occasions. What he did not know about negotiations in the corridors of power was not worth knowing.

He was from the Western Isles and had the virtue of being intensely loyal to his roots. I enjoyed discussions with him about the special infrastructure needs of the islands and I remembered what he had said later when I was in the Scottish Office and responsible for transport and construction.

One day the Chief Whip invited me into his office and asked me to lead a deputation to St Lucia and Dominica in the Caribbean along with a Labour Opposition, Whip Joe Dean, to present gifts on behalf of the House of Commons as part of their Independence celebrations. Little did I know that what seemed like a pleasant trip to sunlit climes would plunge me into controversy.

At first all went well. On arrival in St Lucia we presented a clock and gavel set to the Speaker of the Parliament and we found that the islanders had been coping effectively with the damaging aftermath of a recent hurricane. While there I received a special request of a very unusual nature.

The President of the St Lucia Parliament told me that it would be a great help to him if the Lord Chancellor, Lord Hailsham, back in Westminster could send him his spare gown, so that he could act in a way which was commensurate with the dignity of his office. I did convey this request to Lord Hailsham and received a remarkable response from him.

Apparently a naked man had swum across the Thames and had managed to enter the Lord Chancellor's lodgings, where he covered himself in his Lordship's spare gown. The person concerned was assisted out of the lodgings when he was discovered, but by that time the spare gown regrettably was no longer in a usable condition for anyone. Whether the President in St Lucia was satisfied with that explanation I do not know, but I was not pursued by him on that point.

Dominica was a very different matter. There was no British representative on the Island, and the British Foreign Office was not even aware of the names of the Government Ministers, other than the Prime Minister, Miss Eugenia Charles, Leader of the Freedom Party. We learned that Dominica had recently been ravaged by hurricanes "David" and "Allen" after an absence of such storms for many years.

The island was heavily dependent on Britain as 90 per cent of its produce, namely bananas, were exported there. On arrival we were warmly welcomed by the Prime Minister herself, and from her we found out to our considerable dismay that the Speaker's Chair which we had come to present had not arrived.

We discovered that the Parliamentary authorities in Britain in a bid to restrict public expenditure had sent the Chair as freight by ship via the St Lawrence River in Canada as the cheapest way to forward it to Dominica. Unfortunately the St Lawrence had iced up and the Chair had been held up on the frozen river and was now somewhere between Canada and Dominica being transported by air freight. The indications were that it would not arrive in time for the ceremony.

The Prime Minister agreed that we should go ahead with a symbolic presentation. However, when we were asked about the separate Independence gift from the British Government, whose nature still remains unknown to me, we were further embarrassed. It too had not reached Dominica having apparently been stolen in transit. All that the Foreign Office would say was that "the gift went astray." By this time I felt the situation could scarcely get worse but more drama was in store!

On the day of the ceremony the entire Parliament was assembled. The Prime Minister, the Members of Parliament, the Civil Service, the Police and members of the general public were all there. But there was still no Chair. We made our speeches as well as we could, considering that the main reason that we were there was to present a gift which was nowhere to be seen. By the time we had finished, we felt that we had made the best of a very difficult job.

It was at this point that the row occurred. The former Leader of the Opposition attacked the Government of Dominica, and by inference ourselves, on the grounds that the £10 million of British Aid that had been promised many years before had not materialised, but he was quickly dealt with by the Prime Minister in the debate that ensued.

It appeared that Aid had been given, but that a good deal of it had not got through as desired and substantial allegations of corruption had been made against the former Government. On hearing all this I thought it might have been better if agreed contracts for specific projects had been used with regard to the channelling of Aid funding.

In the late afternoon the Speaker's Chair at last arrived, much to our relief, and we took part in an evening ceremony attended by the Prime Minister and her Cabinet, which this time was entirely successful. On close examination it certainly was a magnificent piece of furniture.

Later the Prime Minister gave us a large parcel which contained a gift of a wooden model boat for the Speaker of the House of Commons and she threw a tremendous party for all MPs and Ministers in her home. It was then that I realised what a formidable leader she was. When the howling winds of the hurricanes had flattened so many dwellings, she had put up about 150 homeless individuals in her own house and she had done this when concentrated gusts of up to 200 mph winds had left the land looking as if it had been scorched with a blowlamp. After the hurricane had passed, with the help of the Royal Engineers, she had used her organisational skills to regenerate the Island.

The difficulties which had beset our trip however were not quite over. The next morning we learnt that we were stranded on the Island by a British Airways strike. No less a person than Miss Eugenia Charles made arrangements for us to return to the UK via Guadeloupe and Paris. But there was one last obstacle to overcome. The police car taking us to the airstrip developed a puncture on the way and I was given the opportunity to change the wheel for them as it was quickly clear that I was more familiar with that activity than the local constabulary. We caught the flight and were able to spend some time in Guadeloupe, which proved to be very interesting, resembling as it did mainland France.

Unlike the British, the French sought to integrate totally their former colonies, and, while their Empire was infinitely smaller, they had poured massive resources into islands such as Guadeloupe. Britain with its very much larger Empire had not been able to deliver equivalent support to all of its far flung colonies.

On return I sent a Report to the Prime Minister, copied to the Foreign Secretary, as it seemed to me that the Foreign Office was paying insufficient attention to the needs of Dominica and in particular to the misappropriation of Aid. I also drew Mrs Thatcher's attention to the fact that there was not a single representative of the British Government on the island.

The PM in her reply confirmed that she hoped to be able to see Miss Eugenia Charles when she next came to the United

Kingdom. The Foreign Secretary, Lord Carrington, told me that were it not for public spending restraints he would "quite like" to have a resident representative on the island but added that perhaps it would be better to spend the money on Dominica rather than on supporting a representative there. As it happened Miss Charles would soon be photographed beside President Reagan after the US invaded Grenada in a bid to restore democracy there.

This was not quite the end of the saga. The Clerk in the House of Commons who had accompanied us, who was called John Sweetman, told me later that my whistle-blowing letter had caused Margaret Thatcher to demand an explanation about the aid situation with regard to Dominica from the Minister for Overseas Aid, Neil Martin. I was left with the feeling that in future support for Dominica would be more likely to reach those for whom it was intended. John Sweetman did, however, give me the impression that it might be some time before I was asked to go on another such delegation, as it had not been anticipated that if I had concerns about the situation on the ground, I might directly alert the Prime Minister!

After my eventful journey abroad, I found myself chatting to the Scottish Labour MP and formidable backbencher Tam Dalyell. His view was that if you visit parts of the Commonwealth on behalf of the House of Commons you are left with a moral obligation towards them in years to come. I agreed with that comment but I also felt that I had already discharged my moral obligation to Dominica by alerting the Iron Lady.

By September 1981 I had been a Whip for four and a half years and a reshuffle was in the air. I was informed by the Chief Whip that he wished to bring on the 1979 intake of MPs. Although I would be leaving the Whips' Office and another post was not on offer, I knew that a massive redistribution of parliamentary boundaries in my constituency was on the cards and that if it went through I would be facing the fight of my life. I would need to focus all my efforts on holding onto the seat and it would be a relief to be able to speak out again from the backbenches on behalf of my constituents.

I received a generous letter from the Prime Minister saying "throughout your years in the Whips' Office we have had not only a happy Office, but also a happy Parliamentary Party. You have contributed greatly to that success."

The Secretary of State for Scotland, George Younger, wrote "you stepped into the job at a most difficult time, and the way you got all our Members working together since then has been a great achievement. The Scots Tory Members have never functioned better than they have over the past few years, and a lot of this is due to your skill and hard work ... and your successor will be hard put to it to equal your record of getting highly controversial legislation through the Scottish Committee, let alone to surpass it."

The boundaries issue now hung over my head like the Sword of Damocles. Edinburgh West was about to be emasculated and in the process Murrayfield, which contained a huge number of Tory supporters, would be removed from the Constituency, converting it into the most marginal seat in Scotland. It felt like losing my right arm, and whether or not I could survive as a Scottish Member of Parliament was extremely uncertain. My future as an elected representative was hanging on a very shoogly nail.

That autumn another chance to travel abroad came my way when the Chief Whip contacted me to say that a vacancy had arisen at short notice on a delegation of MPs going to Japan. This turned out to be the opportunity of a lifetime, although it was important for me to return a day or so early to host an annual party for my constituency activists.

At that time Japan was still a faraway destination which few Britons ever reached. I arrived there, full of anticipation, on 10 November 1981. By the end of the first day I had already gained the impression that the Japanese were extremely hard-working. They depended on exports to balance their trade budget, as the country produced little more than 50 per cent of its food supply.

By the end of the second day I had discovered that there was a considerable pressure for housing as there was relatively little space for the 110 million inhabitants on the country's crowded islands. Most of the houses were very small and few Japanese possessed gardens.

Japan spent less on Defence and Overseas Aid than Britain, enabling the country to invest far more heavily in industry. We were told that Japanese investment in Britain, as in the case of the Nissan car company, depended on Britain staying within the Common Market, as Japan wished to use Britain as its launching pad to Europe.

That evening I searched for Christmas presents for Susie, finding a beautiful silk jacket, and a pearl necklace with soda lighting. It seemed a pity to travel so far without bringing back some Japanese splendour.

Some time later during the visit, the leader of the delegation, Sir Julian Ridsdale, revealed that he had worked in Intelligence in the Second World War before the Japanese attacked the American Pacific Fleet in Pearl Harbour. He told us that the British High Command had been correctly informed about Japanese moves, and believed they were making preparations to attack, although the location was not known. This information had been passed to the USA without revealing its source.

He also said that when the Japanese attacked Pearl Harbour, they did not fully comprehend the kind of adversary they were taking on nor the massive industrial potential of the USA, as virtually none of the Japanese political leaders had visited America.

During the visit certain events showed me that some aspects of Japanese culture were very different from what happened at home. For example I was invited to play golf with the Justice Minister, Mr Ikumo, and with an industrialist called Mr Kaga at the prestigious Hodogaya Country Club near Yokohama in sight of Mount Fuji. To my surprise the caddies who appeared were Japanese women but I preferred as usual to carry my own clubs. What was more unusual was the invitation to go and have a Roman bath after the match.

I was invited into a bath house at the club and sitting side by side on stone slabs we all set about washing ourselves using hoses and soap. Then for the finale we discarded our towels and submerged ourselves completely naked in a huge communal Roman style bath, which was hot enough to make us flinch.

On 15 November we saw the Temple at Nikko which was beautifully laid out among ancient cedar trees. There we were able to have our fortunes told, and we were informed that if we did not like what was claimed to be in store for us we could tie the piece of paper on a tree when leaving. My fortune advised me that everything in my life would work out, but I must not be in too much of a hurry, which amused me.

I remember we also visited the Fujitsu Fanuc Limited factory, where we witnessed the extraordinary sight of robots making robots, which resembled a scene from a science fiction movie – thankfully the whole process still had to be overseen by humans! A day or so later we got up early to see the Tokyo fish market which in contrast employed many thousands of people.

On 19 November we paid a courtesy call on the Prime Minister, at which Julian Ridsdale and Harold Walker said how much we had appreciated the welcome, what an honour it had been and how great our problems in the UK were with rapidly rising unemployment. Mr. Suzuki, the Japanese Prime Minister, welcomed us, wished us good health and said that with regard to trade between our two countries, tariffs and non-tariff restrictions would be reduced and that Japan would exercise voluntary restraint in the field of light commercial vehicles. He made it clear that his Government wished to have close and friendly relations with Britain and he claimed that the position of the Japanese Government was very close to that of Britain on foreign policy issues.

I had to return to Scotland early and was sorry to miss the delegation's visit to Hiroshima. I had wished to see the memorial to those who lost their lives when the atom bomb was dropped by the United States aircraft *Enola Gay* in August 1945. The inscription on the memorial contains the words "let the souls rest in peace for the mistake will not be repeated."

I had come away with the impression from my brief period spent in Japan that this was a country of quite enormous economic strength. She relied on other nations for fuel, and in her current mood she would want to invest more abroad. Modern Japan in 1981 was a country which we could not afford to ignore.

A few months after I returned from the Far East, the British Government was stung into action when troops of the Argentine Junta under General Galtieri invaded the Falkland Islands. From the beginning I was convinced that such Fascist dictators only give way when they are faced with armed forces of overwhelming superiority. The House of Commons was recalled and we were informed that a powerful Naval Task Force would leave with all possible speed for the South Atlantic to free the islands.

In the ensuing debates, MPs were called in order of seniority, and by that yardstick I had to prepare again and again without having the chance to speak. Suddenly in June 1982 I heard my name called by the Speaker. It felt a little bit like falling off a cliff into the sea and realising one either had to sink or swim!

Once on my feet, I made a strong appeal to the Government of the U.S.A. to give support to Britain and emphasised that a dictator who was capable of making his opponents disappear without trace could not be trusted in any way.

I ended by saying "I believe that the Americans will eventually come off their neutral stance… and support us wholeheartedly…. the Falkland islanders have rights that cannot and must not be overridden by the most powerful dictatorship in South America. I believe that the Americans will come out in our favour, because they are aware that hundreds of thousands of their countrymen fought, so that in Lincoln's words 'Government of the people, by the people, and for the people shall not perish from the earth.'"

Within hours, I am delighted to say, the Americans did abandon their neutrality. I could not claim to have influenced President Reagan in the White House but at least the speech was well-timed.

Not long afterwards, to my surprise my uncle Geordie Selkirk came up to me one day and said "What have you been up to? Admiral of the Fleet Lord Hill-Norton tells me that you are good news!" I looked at my uncle in astonishment. I had never spoken to the Admiral and I could not imagine what could have made him say such a thing.

Then I remembered. I had done something, although I had not attributed any importance to it at the time. In Prime Minister's

Questions, which that day had been answered by William Whitelaw, I had asked whether in view of the great importance to the Falklands Task Force of the British aircraft carrier "Invincible" consideration would be given to cancelling its proposed sale to Australia. My belief was that Britain needed to have two aircraft carriers operational at any given time.

This question elicited growls of approval and many "hear hears" from MPs and Willie Whitelaw, who was clearly buying time, replied to the effect that the Government was grateful to Australia for the offer to buy the carrier and added that it "will be most carefully considered".

Evidently I had only put a point about "Invincible" that the Admirals had expressed on many previous occasions to ministers. Other MPs had also raised the matter but the timing of my question clearly illustrated the mood of the House and the case for disposing of the much-needed aircraft carrier evaporated. Within days the sale had been cancelled and it was refreshing to learn that Lord Hill-Norton thought that my question actually had made a difference.

The Falkland Islands were going to be recovered and nothing signalled the outcome more starkly than the victory of the Parachute Regiment at Goose Green, where they took the surrender of many hundreds of Argentine soldiers. Sadly, at the height of the struggle Colonel H. Jones, the Commanding Officer was killed.

I heard that some of the Ministry of Defence officials, who had never been in battle, had been saying that he should not get the Victoria Cross, since it was the job of a commanding officer to take overall charge of the battle and not to lead an individual attack. Having served for just on 10 years with the Territorial

Army, I took a very different view, believing, that Colonel "H" had not only made the ultimate sacrifice, but had turned the tide of battle by his example.

As fortune would have it, my grandfather's cousin, Acting Colonel Angus Douglas-Hamilton, had been awarded the VC posthumously for comparable conduct during the Battle of Loos on Hill70 in 1915. His widow had received a glowing citation "For most conspicuous bravery and devotion to duty," which accompanied the medal. I wrote to the Secretary of State for Defence, John Nott, pointing out the striking similarities and suggesting that if a similar posthumous award was to be made for Colonel "H" at the appropriate moment, "it would be regarded as being extremely well deserved as well as being a great honour for and tribute to the Parachute Regiment."

The Minister of State for the Armed Forces, Peter Blaker, replied on 22 June that while he could not forecast what awards might be made, he agreed that Colonel Jones had "behaved in the finest traditions of his Regiment, the British Army and the nation". Happily the weight of informed opinion did lead to Colonel H's posthumous award of the VC and well-deserved awards for others who had fought so bravely to win back the Falklands.

Back in Edinburgh my constituents in the Ferranti factories who were engaged on defence contracts, had been working round the clock. As a result of their activities, RAF Harrier aircraft were given the capability to fly off Royal Naval carriers. Ferranti had also devised a machine whereby if it was turned on at the right moment by a serviceman on the ground, a bomb from a Harrier could fly down a laser beam to the target with pinpoint accuracy. This ingenious device would play an important role in the hostilities shortly before the Argentine surrender.

After the end of the conflict, I watched the return of the Task Force amid much celebration with mixed emotions, great pride in the professionalism and dedication of all who had served and great sadness that so many had not returned. At least MPs could be thankful that unprovoked aggression had not paid and the Falkland islanders were free once again. It had been a huge triumph for the Prime Minister, Margaret Thatcher, who had kept her nerve and confounded her critics.

During the next month I initiated an unusual debate at Westminster on the subject of a hero of the twentieth century, Raoul Wallenberg, the Swedish diplomat who had saved the lives of around 100,000 people of Jewish origin during the Second World War. I told the House that humanity owed him "an enormous debt".

The debate was entitled "Government enquiries concerning the fate of Raoul Wallenberg," and was due to be answered by my friend Malcolm Rifkind who was now Minister of State at the Foreign Office.

The facts were indisputable. The famous Swede had saved countless people of Jewish origin from being sent to Auschwitz concentration camp, by issuing them with Swedish passports at the station in Hungary. He had warned the German commander in Budapest that he would be prosecuted as a war criminal if he turned his whole army against Jewish civilians. At the end of the war and as a result of Wallenberg's efforts, the city contained the largest Jewish community remaining in Eastern Europe.

On 17 January 1945 Wallenberg was taken into custody by the Russian authorities and was never released. Reports of sightings of him were persistent but there was no satisfactory explanation from the Russians of what had happened to him. Two years later the

Deputy Foreign Minister of Russia, Vyshinski, claimed he had probably died in Budapest in 1945 and then in 1957 the Soviet Deputy Foreign Minister, Andrei Gromyko, suggested Wallenberg had died in prison in 1947.

I ended my speech in Parliament by saying "The forces of totalitarian injustice must be reminded that, try as they may, the individuals who suffer at their hands will not be forgotten."

In response Malcolm Rifkind confirmed that the Russians had not consistently told the truth about this matter. He would later be told in direct discussions with the Soviet Government that Raoul Wallenberg was no longer alive and had indeed died in prison – a sad end to a truly heroic and selfless career.

While continuing with my constituency work in Edinburgh West, I learnt that a Commonwealth Parliamentary Association delegation was to leave for India later that year. There was much competition to join the visit and I was lucky to be selected, along with John Smith, the future Labour leader. Heading the delegation was Peter Thomas, a former Tory Secretary of State for Wales.

After we took off on the morning of 22 November the Captain of our Air India jumbo jet announced with evocative simplicity "We are now rolling towards the East." By late afternoon as we flew over the mountains of Afghanistan, I could not help reflecting that my father's first flight over Mount Everest nearly 50 years before had only just been technically possible. It was extraordinary to think we could now travel non-stop from London to Delhi, a journey by air which would have been well beyond the capabilities of the early pioneers.

India is the world's largest democracy with a population of over 700 million, exceeding the entire population of the continent of Africa, and containing three quarters of the citizens of the

128

Commonwealth. We were all aware that we would witness the effects of poverty but none of us were familiar with the tremendous advances made to provide India with some of the most modern industries in the world.

Shortly after our arrival we were warmly welcomed by the Prime Minister, Mrs Indira Gandhi, and I conveyed to her the best wishes of the Edinburgh India Association which would be celebrating its centenary in 1983. She asked me to pass on her best wishes and wanted to know what form the celebrations might take.

She discussed many issues frankly and directly with us, including the Soviet presence in Afghanistan. She wanted foreign troops to withdraw from that country, and it had not escaped her notice that the Soviet regime was supporting her Communist opposition, a fact which she had noted with displeasure. Above all she was totally committed to the rapid modernisation of India.

We learnt that the country had the technology and capability to make turbines, generators, transformers, machine tools, vehicles, machinery of all kinds and power stations. She had one huge advantage over Western nations – wage rates were very low, meaning some British industries could not compete, as for example in the production of sewing machines.

There was considerable interest in the ways in which British industry might make a contribution in India in areas such as engineering, plastics, chemicals and housing. The Indian industrialists liked to have contracts which allowed them to make use of British technology under licence. Of course after the expiry of the licence in five or seven years the Indian company owned that technology and would be in a position to sell this to Third World countries.

It seemed to me that for Britain to obtain maximum benefit for the transfer of technology, a joint venture was a good way to proceed.

This would retain an involvement in operations over a much longer timescale than would be the position with a licensing project.

We were particularly impressed by the experimental nuclear power station near Mumbai and I remember my Labour colleague John Smith asking the director how he justified such huge expenditure when a great many Indians were living in slum conditions nearby. The director paused before replying and then said "It takes time." He meant that the huge problems of India's homelessness and inadequate housing in shanty towns would take literally years to address.

On a personal level one of the highlights of the visit was to meet an old friend Girish Karnad, who had been a President of the Oxford Union a year and a half before me. He was a completely self-made man with a charismatic presence. Girish had become well known as an Indian producer of films, and indeed very famous as a film actor. He was also a playwright and a poet.

I asked what film had made him a star, and I was told it was *Sanskara*. He had played the part of a Brahmin chief priest in a village where a man of low caste and uncertain reputation had died. The chief priest refused to allow him to be buried with full religious rites, considering that he did not merit it. The village was split down the middle on the appropriateness of this decision. After appeals from the dead man's girlfriend, the chief priest relented and the religious ceremonies went ahead.

This film was very controversial as it was seen by many as being critical of the Indian caste system. It seemed to me that Girish Karnad was trying to focus Indian thinking on what were current social issues in his country. Through his films he was making appeals to modern India to exercise compassion and humanity in a world where such virtues had not always existed in the past.

We flew on to Pune to see a factory making pumps and John Smith and I learnt that Girish Karnad was starring in a film being shot nearby and decided to visit him. After driving through the streets, which were densely crowded with men, women, children, bicycles, rickshaws and even cows, we emerged out of the dust of the Indian plains at a modest house. There, a crowd of more than 100 villagers watched in respectful silence while the filming took place. Girish was playing the part of a taxi driver who had been disabled in an accident and was coming to terms with the painful reality.

We were introduced to those working on the set and Girish explained that the purpose of this educational film was to help prevent road casualties. As we talked he stressed that Britain and India had many lasting ties including a common language and a passionate belief in parliamentary democracy.

On the return flight home I sat next to John Smith who told me he had detected political currents in India which were not always obvious to outside observers. In particular he thought that Mrs Gandhi's daughter-in-law Sonia would have an extremely important future role to play alongside her husband Rajiv. He had particularly valued the chance to come, he said, since the government of Prime Minister Nehru had got on extremely well with the post-war Labour Government of Clement Attlee.

We discussed the forthcoming British General Election, and he warned me that while he was against tactical voting, it was increasingly being used. This was a serious concern for me in Edinburgh since if Labour voters thought that a Liberal candidate was the main challenger to a Conservative they might decide to vote for him or her. This was because over the years the Liberals had worked more closely with the Labour Party than had the

Conservatives, whom Labour saw as their traditional opponents. If I wanted to be re-elected I might have a steep hill to climb.

As it was, before the election came in the summer of 1983 my worst fears were confirmed. The boundary changes in Edinburgh West removed the largely Tory supporting area of Murrayfield and in return Stenhouse/Moat, which was mainly Labour territory, came into the constituency. This change was not lost on the Liberal Party who saw the newly designated seat as their top target in Scotland. My Liberal opponent, a young man called Derek King had recently won a council seat in the area and was a skilled exponent of community politics. His claim was that it was neck and neck between the Conservatives and the Liberals and his supporters were bombarding the voters with leaflets on a multitude of local issues.

By the last weekend of the campaign I sensed that I was fractionally behind. All the stops were pulled out and every possible effort was made by the Conservative team. At public meetings I felt I had the advantage but I had been told that Liberal activists had been flooding into the constituency from all over the south of Scotland.

The night that the votes were counted at Meadowbank Stadium could not have been more dramatic. Wherever I looked it appeared that the electorate had given more or less equal support to myself and my Liberal opponent, and knowing that there was now nothing I could do, I stood by feeling utterly powerless while my fate was being decided.

My friend Mo Rizvi, the first councillor in Scotland of Muslim Asian origin, who held a seat in Corstorphine in West Edinburgh, was a marvellous support. Throughout the evening he kept appearing at my side saying he had seen piles of voting papers on the counting tables in which I was ahead by six votes or eleven votes or four votes, but definitely ahead.

By the end of the night I had been re-elected by the smallest margin in Scotland. The Conservatives had a majority of 498 over the Liberals in Edinburgh West which for me had been far too close for comfort. I had always worked hard for my constituents, but to me this result meant only one thing. To survive as a Conservative MP in Scotland would be no easy matter. There was only one thing for it – to work harder and harder and harder!

CHAPTER 8

A Parliamentary Private Secretary, and Mrs Thatcher's Minister

To be re-elected as a Member of Parliament by your fellow countrymen and women is a great honour and a privilege. It also brings with it many responsibilities including unceasing work on behalf of all constituents who ask for advice or assistance.

At the House of Commons I had the help of a wonderfully able and conscientious secretary, Mrs Rosemary Creagh, wife of a colonel who had fought with General Wingate's Chindits behind Japanese lines in Burma during the Second World War. She would tell me anything, but not under any circumstances her age. Since she had worked valiantly for MI6 in the Second World War, putting together plans to help members of the Parachute Regiment escape to freedom from behind enemy lines after the Battle of Arnhem, I knew the approximate answer to the question I never dared ask. She was wise and farsighted and had a prodigious capacity for hard work.

Each day, without fail, dealing with constituency correspondence would take at least one hour and sometimes more, before attendance at Standing Committees or other meetings, including All Party Committees – such as the Scottish Penal Affairs Group which I chaired for some years.

Amid all the interest and bustle of Parliamentary life, Malcolm Rifkind, who was still at the Foreign Office, said he would like to put forward my name for consideration as his Parliamentary Private Secretary. This had to be cleared with the Chief Whip.

As soon as I was appointed I learnt the rules applying to such a job. MPs who serve as a PPS are sometimes described simply as "ministerial bag carriers" but I found that the job involved rather more than that. For example you had to be present at all Whipped votes and any PPS who voted against the Government would be sacked. The PPS was part of what is called the pay-roll vote – meaning all those who hold Government posts, however lowly – but sadly they are not actually paid for the job. The primary task was to assist the Minister and keep him or her in touch with the mood of the House of Commons.

For example, the PPS should notice what Early Day Motions were put down on the subject matter for which the Minister was responsible and note who had signed them and whether this was likely to lead to questions and debate on the Floor of the House of Commons. The PPS had to follow the work of All Party Committees and let the Minister know if important initiatives of one kind or another were likely to take place. I had to be aware of inward and outgoing delegations on sensitive subjects relating to Malcolm Rifkind's foreign affairs responsibilities.

A Minister's PPS would also help to look after constituents or fulfil a speaking engagement when other commitments might cause the Minister to be at Cabinet Committees, at other meetings or on missions abroad. Two such cases spring to mind. Malcolm Rifkind had to welcome the Russian leader, Mr Gorbachev, to Edinburgh shortly before he became President, so I had to address Malcolm's Edinburgh Pentlands Constituency Executive in his place.

On another occasion Malcolm had missed the flight from Brussels to London and at two and a half hours notice I was asked to speak in his place at the dinner of the Anglo-Polish Society. This was no easy matter, since he always spoke without notes, and when I asked the Head of the Department in the Foreign Office for background information he sent me a file marked "Restricted." This of course meant that under the Official Secrets Act I could not disclose a single word of it. As the minutes were ticking away I telephoned him to say that the file he had sent me was absolutely useless for my purpose. From his reaction it seemed that nobody had ever spoken to him like that before, and he said he would come and see me. He came but gave me information which was turgid and not of much help.

When I attended the dinner I reminded my audience that Britain had gone to war to save Poland from Nazi occupation in 1939 and that it was a source of great sorrow to us that at the end of the war the freedoms which the Polish people sought had not been restored. I also said that all the aid which we had given during the Warsaw Uprising had been in vain as Stalin's armed forces held back until the German army had crushed the uprising.

I told them that the Foreign Secretary, Sir Geoffrey Howe, was about to visit Eastern Europe and that I would personally make a note of all the points which they raised with me and would make sure that he was aware of their concerns before his forthcoming visit. I conveyed their views to Malcolm Rifkind and Geoffrey Howe and I was most interested to see reports in the press that the Foreign Secretary had taken up some of the points during his subsequent visit to Eastern Europe.

It goes without saying that a PPS has to keep out of trouble. They are not allowed to make speeches in the Chamber concerning their

Minister's responsibilities and have to be very careful about signing an Early Day Motion even if they agree with it. If the Opposition put down such a Motion for debate and the Government chose to oppose it, a PPS who had signed it might feel obliged to vote for it and of course would be sacked on the spot.

In addition when a colleague asks a Parliamentary Question it is useful to know what the supplementary is likely to be. It is essential in cases of constituents who have relatives in difficulties abroad that their cases are handled with all possible speed. In fact it is desirable to be well informed on everything.

One debate has stuck in my memory since it involved Malcolm Rifkind and Robin Cook with myself and George Foulkes present which was reminiscent of our days as Edinburgh Town Councillors. The subject was Europe, and Robin Cook, one of the Labour Opposition's foremost debaters, was expressing considerable reservations about the European Union. Out of the blue Malcolm Rifkind suddenly produced the card of the European Society at Edinburgh University in the mid 1960s which showed that Robin Cook, as its Secretary, had arranged a meeting on the subject of European Federation. This revelation gave rise to considerable merriment in the House.

Afterwards when George Foulkes came towards me I knew we would be in for some banter. He asked me who the "skunk" was who had leaked this document to the Government, so I sidestepped the question by saying, "all covered by the Official Secrets Act". I remember another Labour MP coming up to me on a different occasion and saying "You have to get up early in the morning if you want to take on Malcolm Rifkind".

Being a PPS however did not prevent me from going on a delegation to the United Nations Headquarters in New York in late November 1983, where we were welcomed by the Secretary General, Perez de Cuellar.

Among many subjects discussed was the future of the Falkland Islands. The Secretary General wished Britain to show flexibility in dealings with the next democratically elected government of Argentina and he wanted such a democratic government to be allowed to save face and to have a credible position with its own electorate.

He hoped that Britain would start a dialogue and make the first move "as the stronger side". The leader of our delegation, Sir Hugh Rossi, stressed that self-determination for the islanders was vital, and that any policy proposals would have to be acceptable to them. I made the point that there would also need to be a formal declaration of the cessation of hostilities.

I recorded at the time, in a report for Foreign Office Ministers, that the Secretary General "came across, with an engaging modesty, and a firmness of purpose, coupled with a sympathetic understanding of Britain's position".

The United Nations provides a place where countries which might otherwise become engaged in conflict, can explain their position and back off without suffering a loss of face. In addition, many of the world's developing nations see it as an institution in which they can advance the influence of their home country, and attract overseas aid. In this connection it has been referred to as a centre providing group therapy for Third World nations.

Just over a year later, as President of the Scottish Council of the United Nations Association, I welcomed the UN Secretary General to Edinburgh. His Chief of Protocol was a Frenchman and in his presence Perez de Cuellar asked me why the Scots held so many suppers in tribute to the immortal memory of Robert

Burns. I replied that the Scots liked his patriotism and humanity as well as his poetry and could feel associated either with his great strengths or his great weaknesses. I was asked what were his weaknesses and I gave the diplomatic answer that many Scots were descended from him. "Ah" said the Chief of Protocol, "But that is a strength!"

The visit to the United Nations was not the only delegation on which I would serve. On 27 November 1984 I led a group from the Commonwealth Parliamentary Association to Gibraltar. On the same day the Spanish Government opened the border between Gibraltar and Spain.

On our arrival the Gibraltarians confirmed that the present generation of residents had decided conclusively to maintain their relationship with Britain. The Rock of Gibraltar itself was full of secrets, being honeycombed with tunnels and caves, but it was the famous Gibraltar Apes who particularly took my fancy and I asked the First Minister, Sir Joshua Hassan, if he would very generously give one to Edinburgh Zoo. He said he would be delighted to oblige and I obtained a commitment from Lord King, Chairman of British Airways, that free transport would be provided to fly the Gibraltar Ape to Edinburgh, but the animal was never to reach the city. When I consulted the Director of the Royal Zoological Society of Scotland, Dr Roger Wheater, he told me that the Gibraltar Ape was too old to be transferred and therefore although he was grateful for my interest the Zoo could not accept the generous offer.

However, it was not foreign delegations that were uppermost in my mind, but the affairs of my constituents and how best to serve them. Being the holder of Scotland's smallest majority was enough to concentrate my mind wonderfully and infused me with the will to take my constituents' representations to the highest level if the need arose.

One such issue related to the Ferranti factory on the edge of Edinburgh West which had put in a bid to win the contract for the Inertial Navigation System for the Royal Air Force Harrier. A competitive bid had also been entered from a US aircraft company and the Treasury had become involved as the two bids were, I was told, relatively evenly matched. However a movement in the exchange rate made the Ferranti bid increasingly attractive as the months slipped by. I remember attending a meeting, along with the other PPSs, with Mrs Thatcher. When we were invited to volunteer any thoughts I took my courage in both hands and chirped up to say that, where all other things were equal, Ministry of Defence contracts should go to the home-based team and there was a particular contract which had been hanging in the balance for six months and was still undecided. This related to Ferranti of Edinburgh and I was asking that their case be sympathetically considered.

The Prime Minister gave me a steely look as though she was surprised that one of her MPs had dared to lecture her on patriotism. She said nothing. I hesitated, waiting for verbal fireworks. Had I stuck my neck out too far? Had I put the contract in jeopardy? I was tempted to say "After you, Prime Minister" and then get back below the parapet, but thankfully the moment passed and she went on to the next item on the agenda.

However I did not have to wait long for my answer. About three days later on 7 February 1985 the Minister for Defence Procurement, Adam Butler, announced by way of a brief but very welcome Parliamentary Answer that Ferranti had won the contract. I felt sure that a word from the Prime Minister's office had brought matters to a head. Later Mrs Thatcher would visit the Ferranti factory in the South Gyle and was very impressed by the expertise of the work force.

I had great admiration for Mrs Thatcher's leadership. My own approach to politics had been pragmatic rather than ideological, striving for calm and steady progress in assessing each issue on its own particular merits. But when she first came to power the economic situation was so dire that making the British economy competitive called for an exceptionally clear cut strategy which she would certainly deliver.

With the possible exception of Lord Hailsham, she was probably intellectually abler than anyone within her Cabinet and as well as dealing with individual policies could readily take an overall view. Of all the Prime Ministers I remember she was the most decisive and resolute. Then when the day's work was done she would return to 10 Downing Street at about 11pm. Her first thoughts would not be to rest but to deal with all the correspondence from the constituencies. If anyone had sent a bottle of whisky to be autographed by her for a Constituency Association raffle or had requested a message of support, she would just settle down and deal with such matters as well as a host of other letters. I knew this for certain from her PPS, Ian Gow. It was greatly to her credit that when she was meeting world leaders, she still found time to give detailed replies to MPs like myself with the most marginal of seats. As evidence of this in 1985 I received at least four substantial letters from her which were made public within my constituency.

My first approach to the Prime Minister arose out of the revaluation of properties in Scotland for local tax purposes in the mid 1980s. Revaluations were known to cause immense controversy, and in England had been repeatedly postponed. In Scotland, George Younger, the Secretary of State, had already asked Parliament to halt the revaluation due to go ahead in the election year of 1983 and decided not to do so again, so the exercise went ahead. Although it may not have been obvious at the time this decision to revalue acted as a catalyst and triggered a series of events. It led to George Younger urging the Prime Minister to reform local government taxation in Scotland as soon as possible. The discussions and meetings which ensued culminated in the introduction of the Community Charge.

The result of the revaluation was uproar. The Conservatives had promised to reform the rating system in the long term but had done nothing so far. Many electors were now faced with huge rises in rates and no very obvious action to bring in a fairer system. I wrote directly to the Prime Minister on 21 March 1985 telling her "I can say with complete certainty that on no occasion since October 1974 have I been so aware of a mood of growing and widespread alienation towards the Conservative Party over a single issue. Unless a Bill is introduced next Session, taking effect next year, I fear that a great many Conservative seats, both Regional and Parliamentary, will be lost in Scotland."

The Prime Minister's reply through me to my constituents was courteous and indicated the will to go ahead with reforming the system. She replied on the 2nd of April saying "I can understand only too well the deep anxiety felt throughout Scotland on this matter. But I found it especially helpful to receive your letter and enclosures, because it spells out in more personal terms the many examples in your constituency of the particular increases in rates which face both domestic ratepayers and businesses."

She went on to mention the allocation of £38.5 million to help reduce domestic rates and recognised the need to have a speedy appeals procedure relating to revaluations. She recognised that local government finance required a review and that once work was completed decisions would be announced. Mrs Thatcher ended her letter with these words "On a personal note, can I say again how helpful it was to receive your letter and learn at first hand the problems faced by your constituents. I want you to know that I have their interests very much at heart."

It was not only the Prime Minister who was gravely concerned. The Secretary of State for Scotland, George Younger, wrote to me on the 4th April saying "It has been an unusually difficult period for all sorts of reasons, and I know how great the pressures have been from many sides, but our Scottish backbenchers have been a great help in keeping our end up in the House."

At this time I was selected to go on a British-American Parliamentary Group visit to Bermuda for discussions with US Congressmen, and on 14 April I received an hour's briefing from the Head of the North American Department in the Foreign Office. I thanked him for his generosity in sparing me so much time and he said that he would not be busy unless the Americans attacked Libya, which he considered to be unlikely. What neither of us knew was that the US bombers had taken off that afternoon from their bases in Britain and were on their way to Libya. Clearly very few were in on this closely guarded secret.

The background to this action was that there had been a terrorist attack on a nightclub in Berlin on the 5th of April 1986 which had killed two American servicemen. President Ronald Reagan had claimed he had hard evidence that Libya had been responsible and on 15 of April, with the permission of the British

Prime Minister, the bombing had taken place by American aircraft using British bases. President Reagan asserted that the US was acting in accordance with its right to self-defence.

Our delegation was led by Labour's Merlyn Rees and Ken Clarke, then Paymaster General and Minister for Employment and we arrived a few hours after the attack had taken place. There was some anxiety at the time, as none of us wished the Soviet Union and the US to have an exchange of hostilities, and we knew that there had been a Russian destroyer visiting Libya not long before. Then we learnt that the Russians had been warned in advance and the destroyer had left.

We flew from Andrews Air Force Base in the Vice-Presidential aircraft to Bermuda for our private discussions. One of those in our delegation was Willie Hamilton, the Labour MP who was well known in the British Parliament for being strongly opposed to the Monarchy. When we were shown around Bermuda there was considerable merriment when we came to the area where the Queen had surveyed the beauty of the islands and ocean and which had been named the Queen's View. There were great calls of "Willie, come to the Queen's View" and to his credit he took this in good heart.

On returning to Britain I opened a further letter from the Prime Minister dated 16 April. This showed clearly the dilemma with which the Government was faced. Whatever system of local government finance was brought in the new arrangements would have advantages and disadvantages. She wrote:

"As you will no doubt be aware I share your concern about the continued effects of revaluation and overspending by local authorities which have led individual cases to high increases in rates. It was because of this concern that we have taken the unprecedented step of increasing Domestic Rate Relief by eight times."

She made it clear that it was the Government's policy to bring local government overspending under control and within guidelines. Authorities like Edinburgh would have to expect the Government to take action to compel them to keep their spending under control. She claimed there had been no good reason to postpone the revaluation a second time but admitted that some of the independent assessors valuations might appear "harsh" although she stressed they could be appealed.

Then she came to an important conclusion:

"However, as you will know, we have never been happy with the present system. It was a disappointment to us that in the last Parliament, despite considerable effort, we were not able to identify an alternative that was of itself acceptable or workable, and as a result of extensive consultation came reluctantly to the conclusion that it would be wrong to make a change without a replacement in which we and the country could have confidence.

"However, we have continued to work at finding a better alternative… There is further work to be done and it is not possible at this stage to predict the outcome. The purpose of the review is to see if a fairer, simpler and more stable system of local government finance can be found which would strengthen the accountability of local authorities while maintaining a reasonable balance between the interests of central and local government…

"You will appreciate that the Government is working to find a suitable and workable solution to this complex problem. It is our wish to do so as much as it is yours."

Clearly the issue of reforming the rating system was worrying the Prime Minister and I was surprised to receive a third letter from her. She wrote:

"You put down a question to me on 7 May about the rateable values of comparable properties in Scotland, England, Wales and Northern Ireland. I replied that comparable information is not available....

"On the domestic side it may be reasonable to look at the average rate bill for a domestic property, the Scottish figure including domestic water rate is £397 in the current year as against £430 in England when water charges are included....

"In the longer term there have to be further changes to secure continuing control of local government spending and improvements in accountability to the benefits of all ratepayers."

I made sure that those hundreds of constituents who had written to me all received copies of the Prime Minister's three letters and however angry they may have been, they knew that I had taken their representations as far as it was possible. The sequel is well known. Ministers came forward with proposals to introduce the Community Charge, which we were to learn would solve one set of damaging problems but would create another. It was introduced in Scotland a year earlier than in England and Wales, because the

Secretary of State considered that such reforms would help ease the huge resentment over the recent revaluation. Far from Scotland being used as a guinea pig as popular myth would have it, George Younger had been actively pressing for the new tax to be brought in with all speed north of the border.

The Community Charge was not the only subject on which I received a reply from the Prime Minister which I made public in my constituency. I was conscious that the teachers' pay dispute in Scotland was upsetting parents who feared that their children could lose out at a critical time in their education. I wanted a negotiated settlement and said as much in the House of Commons. Margaret Thatcher's letter of 4 November was typical of the thorough treatment she gave to her correspondence.

She wrote:

"I was very grateful to you for letting me have your own assessment of the teachers' pay dispute in Scotland. It really was most helpful. I can well understand the anxiety of parents when they see the effect that the teachers' industrial action is having on their children's education..."

But she was not in the mood to be browbeaten by the Teachers' Unions.

"I cannot accept the suggestion that the Government is being intransigent. What we are doing is defending the interests of children and parents. After all the damage which has been caused, and now with a threat to the 1986 examinations, surely it is not unreasonable to insist that any settlement should include a clarification of a teacher's duties

– a point which has been the subject of so much dispute in the past? Our objective is to prevent another dispute arising on this matter which would again inflict chaos in our schools and further damage to the education of children."

She ended with a firm commitment and her overall view of the situation.

"The Government attaches high priority to improving the quality of education for our children and to ensuring that pupils are equipped with the skills and training which they need for the jobs of the future. I know that very many teachers are dedicated to achieving these objectives. The responsibility is shared by the profession, central government and local education authorities; and we must all discharge our responsibilities fully."

Apart from matters relating to education and local government finance I managed to get four Bills through that Parliament. Instead of introducing Private Member's Bills I discovered that through the Ten Minute Rule Bill procedure, a Scottish Bill could go straight in to the Second Scottish Standing Committee without having to wait in a long queue for Private Member's Bills. I got through the Husband and Wife (Scotland) Bill, which abolished praepositura, the presumption that the husband pays his wife's bills. In the days of equality of treatment for the sexes this concept had become out of date.

Then there was the Parent and Child (Scotland) Bill, which gave children of unmarried parents an equal claim to inherit possessions as children of married parents, where the parents died without leaving a will, something that happens in the majority of cases in Scotland. It also removed the stigma of illegitimacy and repealed the Bastardy Act, an appallingly patronising document.

My uncle, Geordie Selkirk had taken the Animal (Scotland) Bill, which imposed strict liability on the owners of potentially dangerous animals, through the Lords and I was able to pilot it through the Commons. However, the most controversial legislation was the Bill to allow the building of the Western Relief Road in Edinburgh, which I sponsored on behalf of Lothian Regional Council, as I judged it would create employment, lead to environmental improvements and reduce traffic congestion and accidents in West Edinburgh.

This Bill was strongly opposed by the Labour Party and on the night of its Third Reading, I was determined to do everything possible to win the vote so I wrote a personal letter to every Conservative MP. The North West of England Conservative Members told me it was absolutely impossible for them to attend the vote, so I asked why and was told that Margaret Thatcher was going to address them that same evening. I immediately telephoned her PPS and said it would be enormously helpful if she might feel able to come and vote at 10 o'clock, especially as the Conservative Group, which was running the Lothian Regional Council with the help of the Liberal Democrats, was totally committed to this cause.

When the vote came I was one of the tellers and out of the corner of my eye I was delighted and not a little amused to see Margaret Thatcher entering the Aye lobby, followed obediently by about 30 North West Members.

Sadly, in the Regional Elections that followed, the Labour Party won a majority on the council and the project was dropped, but at least my West Edinburgh constituents knew that they had received support directly from the Prime Minister.

I was to get further backing from No 10 when Denis Thatcher later agreed to attend the West Edinburgh Conservative Ladies Lunch and to speak to the patrons of the local association. It turned out to be a night to remember!

I had been told that Denis would give a real old humdinger of a speech, but that no reporters were to be present and to this day what he said has never been revealed. However I do feel entitled to mention his opening line. He said "I have just seen Margaret on television arriving in Moscow looking very nice in a Russian fur hat. Heaven knows what it will cost me!" After his speech, when someone praised the role of Sir Ian MacGregor in ending the miners' strike, Denis was unimpressed and said emphatically "It was my woman who did it." Years later, after his death, Baroness Thatcher, as she had become, told me in writing that Denis had been the most loving and supportive husband.

By the end of the Parliament my local campaign team was much better prepared. We were ready to put everything we had into the fight for re-election and I was surprised to receive a compliment from a Labour MP, who later claimed that it was sarcasm rather than praise. John Maxton said on 2 July 1986 "It really is rather strange that Hon. Members are debating one housing association out of all the housing associations in Scotland. It is all down, as was the Western Relief Road, to the Hon. Member for Edinburgh West. I am sure that the Dunfermline College of Education will be saved as well. The Hon. Gentleman is a powerful Member of Parliament."

I did not feel a powerful Member of Parliament at all, but merely an MP clinging on to his constituency by his fingernails, but I was going to make best use of the compliment. My introductory leaflet in the Election was entitled "Lord Jim will fix it" and John Maxton's reference to "A Powerful Member of Parliament" was the first headline as a recommendation to electors. It was no use for him to tell me later that he had not really meant it. It was all in Hansard and, as I was encouraging Labour electors to stay with their party rather than switch to the Liberals, such an apparent endorsement from the Labour front bench was not to my disadvantage.

The Conservatives won the Election and at the count on Thursday 11 June 1987 I was delighted when my majority went up from 498 to 1,234, but the situation overall in Scotland was alarming with the party having lost eleven seats out of the 21 it had held. This left us with the smallest number of Scottish members since the Second World War.

By the Wednesday after the election Malcolm Rifkind had been re-appointed Scottish Secretary but the ministerial team was still unknown and my telephone had remained stubbornly silent. I was enjoying a cup of tea at home when Susie suggested that I was not going to become a minister. I asked why she thought that and she replied that the telephone would have rung a long time ago. But twenty minutes later a call did come through. I was in my study with my son Charles who was then nearly eight years old. He said "Who was that?" I told him "No 10 Downing Street" and he said "What do they want?" I explained to him that Mrs Margaret Thatcher was going to speak to me in five minutes time. Charles, his eyes looking like saucers, was suitably impressed and exclaimed "MRS THATCHER!"

Sure enough the call came and I was asked to become one of the Scottish Office Ministers. When I asked the PM what my responsibilities would be she said it would be for the Secretary of State Malcolm Rifkind to decide and added kindly that I would be a popular choice.

With a lot of help from my supporters, I had pulled myself back from the political precipice over which I had been hanging in West Edinburgh, had managed to find a more secure foothold and was now excited at the prospect of my first real ministerial job.

CHAPTER 9

The Scottish Office and the tragedy of Lockerbie

A new Minister is expected to switch into top gear overnight. The civil service provides enormous bundles of papers to be read immediately, and suggests a great succession of countless meetings and conferences for the new boy or girl to attend.

In addition to receiving a locked red box, stuffed with papers, all of which require a decision or opinion to be given, a new Minister is provided with a chauffeur driven car, an impressive office and the assistance of a Private Secretary with other staff. I had become Minister for Home Affairs and the Environment which included responsibility for the structure of local government, housing, roads and construction, prisons and historic buildings in Scotland. One of the first things I did when sitting in my new office was to examine the red button on the telephone. When I pressed it the door opened at once, a civil servant came in and said "Yes Minister?" Instinctively I looked round to see who he was talking to and then realised "My God, it's me!"

A Minister's Private Secretary, who is a career civil servant, is his or her closest helper. He or she is a vitally important link with every expert in the civil service who can provide the answers to

Parliamentary Questions, obtain the information for important statements and key debates.

One of the issues which had been left in the ministerial in-tray as being too controversial in the run up to the election related to giving approval to the creation of sites for travelling people. My decisions led to at least one resignation from a local Conservative Association and I learnt again it is not possible to please all of the people all of the time.

It was a turbulent time politically to become a Minister, when Margaret Thatcher's most radical policies were being enacted. The Conservative Government had only ten MPs in Scotland while Labour had 50 and after doing so well in Scotland it was a bitter pill for Labour to have to accept a Conservative Government in the United Kingdom.

Shortly after the election I was fighting my way through a mountain of civil service briefings, and arrived in London to make my way to the House of Commons. On the way there I met Donald Dewar in the street. It seemed that he knew what was on my mind. I needed time to master all my briefs, but time was the one commodity which was not readily available as the civil service packed every kind of engagement into my diary for months ahead.

Donald said to me "James, I have problems too." I took this to mean that as leader of 50 Scottish Labour MPs he was in difficulties, as he could not deliver at that time what they wanted, namely a Scottish Parliament.

After meeting him in Berlin when we were both students, Donald had been a guest at my 21st birthday party. He hardly treated me as an opponent but more as a friendly acquaintance who had strayed into another political camp. I remember that before the election he had said to me, in an aside, that he would not be sorry if I was one who came through.

The first weeks in the job are when a new minister is most vulnerable, for Opposition MPs like to trip up the new incumbent and I made my share of mistakes, although fortunately not on the floor of the House of Commons.

The first mistake was to write letters to thank civil servants who had in my view gone the extra mile to be helpful. However a week or so later it became clear that they had not in fact received my letters and I asked the Private Secretary what he had done with them. To my astonishment he said "I tore them up, minister. I tore them up. It is quite simply not done. If you write to one, you have to write to them all, and if you don't do that they will all resent it."

Nobody had ever torn up my letters in such a fashion and this diminutive figure shouting at me seemed unaware of the precariousness of his position. But as the link with the rest of the civil service I recognised he was my lifeline to survival and so I swallowed my irritation, and proceeded with the day's work.

The next misunderstanding has taken on somewhat legendary status in my political life. It concerns a woman driver and the opening of ministerial car doors by both her and me. She was a civil servant who had been assigned to chauffeur Michael Forsyth and I in London. Apparently it was part of her job to open the car door for me but this went rather against the grain and on more than one occasion I admit I may have got to her door handle first!

I hope she was not put out by this, but as it happened she nearly embarrassed me on one occasion. I had to attend a lunch at the Savoy Hotel, in the Strand, in honour of Ted Heath's many years of service and then I had to be in the House of Commons to answer MPs at Scottish Question Time at 2.35pm, I made careful plans for the woman driver to collect me at 2.15pm so I would be at the despatch box on time.

However when I emerged from the lunch I realised she had parked the car in the bus rank and an angry bus driver had hemmed in the vehicle making it impossible for her to move. She had said to him "Please yourself, I am paid for out of your taxes."

Knowing that when a Prime Minister or Secretary of State says to a Junior Minister "I will be most awfully grateful if you will do something" it is an order which must be obeyed, I tried the same technique with the bus driver but it did not work. He looked at me as if I was from another planet and refused to budge an inch.

Eventually I took a note of his bus company and his number, but there was still no sign of movement and as it is unheard of for ministers to be absent when they are due to answer questions, I realised I had no alternative but to set off running along the Embankment towards the Houses of Parliament. I arrived just in time to save my ministerial career!

But the affair wasn't quite finished. A letter was sent to the bus company from my office complaining about the intransigence of the driver. The answer from the manager was a half apology. Without condoning obstruction, he said that the bus driver had not had a clue as to who I was, and in any case the Government car should not have been sitting in a bus rank. I passed a message to my driver that as far as I was concerned honour had been satisfied.

This reminded me of a confusing contretemps I had previously had with the British Railways Board when I was still a backbencher. One which I am glad to say did not reach the ears of the political journalists at the time.

The business in the House of Commons had ended earlier than expected and I had gone to King's Cross Station to get a ticket for the night sleeper to Scotland. As it happened my car had broken down and was being repaired in a garage near Drem station in East Lothian. Apparently the train was not automatically scheduled to stop at Drem as I had hoped so I asked the ticket collector if it could stop there. I thought some trains might halt at this little station if enough passengers wanted that. In response the collector asked for my ticket which had "Lord Hamilton" written on it by the ticket office. He said somewhat enigmatically "It can be arranged" He then disappeared into a telephone booth where it was impossible for me to hear his conversation.

It was at this point – had I but known it – that events had begun to spiral out of my control. When the ticket collector emerged he told me that the train would indeed stop at Drem Station. Sure enough next morning it did so and to my surprise I was the only person who got off. A few days later I learnt why. A letter arrived from the British Railways Board claiming that I had stopped the London-Edinburgh sleeper by invoking the Scottish Landowners Bill of Rights. Their staff had been searching all their records but had been unable to find any such entitlement. Would I care to furnish them with an explanation?

Not only had I never mentioned such a Bill of Rights but I was strongly of the view that no such document existed and rightly or wrongly I came to the conclusion that the ticket collector was trying to have a good joke at my expense. I telephoned the British Railways Board and wrote to them explaining that I had made no such demand, that I was not a landlord but a Scots advocate by profession and had actually once represented the Board in court. To my great relief my explanation was accepted.

However the Scottish Press, I am sure, would have had a lot of fun writing stories with such headlines as "Tory MP stops sleeper train under false pretences for his own convenience!" Protestations to the contrary might have fallen on deaf ears. All publicity is not necessarily good publicity for a man with the third smallest majority in Scotland!

After I became a minister, another tricky incident took place, for which I was really not to blame. I had to address a conference of the Institute of Housing and when I saw the draft press-release of my speech I vetoed it as it suggested I had no confidence in the Government housing policy. As a result a new perfectly satisfactory release was prepared.

Imagine my horror on the day after the conference when it became clear that a press officer had issued the wrong release. The editorial in the *Scotsman* later claimed that it was refreshing to have a new minister who had no confidence in his own policy and to make things much worse all this had happened on the day that the Prime Minister, Margaret Thatcher, was visiting Scotland. I immediately had visions of disappearing in the next re-shuffle.

I had an urgent meeting with the Government press officers. They did not want me to say anything, as the journalists would enjoy the fun if we admitted the wrong press-release had been issued. So I decided to let the matter go and more importantly Mrs Thatcher appeared not to have noticed.

In the brief period before the House of Commons recess, a great deal of contentious legislation was going through. I found myself on a Standing Committee supporting the bill on competitive tendering for council services and successfully resisted a Labour amendment from John Maxton to remove Scotland from the bill's provisions.

It had been claimed that the introduction of competition to supply council services would put many thousands of local government employees out of work. This did not happen.

Competitive tendering meant that authorities had to compete with the private sector but the tender specification was often drafted by the councils' lawyers in such a way as to give their own direct labour departments an inbuilt advantage.

When the summer recess arrived it felt like emerging from a tunnel into the sunlight and now there really would be time to develop a close working knowledge of Scottish administration from top to bottom and fully master my portfolio of responsibilities.

However in the weeks ahead there was still much work to be done; roads to be opened by Loch Lomond and in Mid-Fife and the acceptance of the island of St Kilda as Scotland's first UNESCO World Heritage site. Preparations were going ahead for a major housing bill and a bill to privatise the Scottish Bus Group as well as an amnesty for those who were in illegal possession of firearms.

The amnesty did not mean that a person could not be prosecuted if he or she had committed a crime using such weapons, but did mean that for the duration of the amnesty possession of firearms would not be treated as an offence if they were handed in to the police. I announced progress with the amnesty in Strathclyde Police headquarters in Glasgow, with a huge assortment of every kind of vicious weapon in front of me. Clearly it was in the public interest to reduce the number of weapons which for one reason or another were floating around in the community.

On my way home that day I remembered that more than 25 years before I had won a shotgun at a shooting booth in France. I had been attending a course at the university in Tours before going to Oxford and one afternoon went by bus to watch the 24 hour car race at Le Mans. There they had a shooting booth, and one thing the Cameronians (Scottish Rifles) had taught me at my first TA camp was how to shoot with pin-point accuracy.

The first prize, which I wanted, was a transistor radio and the second was a shotgun. For the first prize I had to fire every shot through the bullseye twice and for the second prize only once. At first everything went according to plan. Every shot was through the heart of the bullseye on the target, and I noticed that the man in charge of the booth was beginning to look disgruntled. Each time I paid to take aim at the target I got every shot through the centre but he would haggle with me suggesting my shots had been a tiny fraction less than perfect.

I was sure that a court of law would have supported me but he was determined not to part with his transistor radio. In this case possession was nine tenths of the argument and I abandoned hope of justice being done. I was so annoyed that I laid claim to the shotgun which was parcelled up for me.

By this time it was nearly midnight and as the bus was not returning until the next afternoon I slept under a bush in the central area within the race track while the Ferraris continued to battle it out.

When I got back to Heathrow Airport I told the customs officer that I had something to declare. "What is it?" he asked, so I told him that in my golf bag among the clubs was a shotgun. "You are joking of course" he said, but I assured him that I was not. The officer became extremely stern and asked me to explain myself. So I told him the story of my prize-winning efforts in Le Mans. After listening he informed me that he would have to impound the gun and my golf clubs, which he did, and it was several months before I saw any of them again.

For more than 25 years after that, this gun, which was apparently a collectors' small bore shotgun of the kind used in Europe but not in Britain for shooting very small birds, had been locked up in a reinforced gun cupboard. I had absolutely no use for it and had never fired it so I handed it into the police during the amnesty and it was destroyed within a few hours.

Amnesties of this kind for weapons can produce some remarkable items. On this occasion I was told that an ancient monks' bible had been handed in, which, when opened, revealed a pair of pistols. It was sent away for them to be made safe before being handed over to a museum. In Edinburgh the Chief Constable William Sutherland showed me a sinister looking walking stick which was in fact a shotgun. I was glad to know it was going to be destroyed.

The work which took up most time related to housing and the major reforms which were in the wind. It was the intention of the Government to set up a body to be called Scottish Homes to help bring in private sector money to enable public spending on housing to go much further. This was to be done by combining the expertise of the Scottish Special Housing Association with that of the Housing Corporation, the latter being responsible for the funding of housing associations.

On a visit to Glasgow I saw Provan's Lordship, the oldest house in the city and while looking at the paintings on its walls, I felt that I could see much of Scotland's housing history unfolding before my eyes.

After the disastrous Irish potato famine in the mid nineteenth century, in the interests of survival, many thousands of Irish families made their way to Scotland. There they had been accommodated in housing, where many of the landlords charged rents which the new arrivals struggled to afford. This had left a legacy of bitterness and resentment against private landlords.

It was the Government's policy under Mrs Thatcher to encourage a revival of the private rented sector throughout Britain. However my own view was that this market would be relatively small in Scotland, especially in the West Central Belt, where the bulk of Scotland's population lived. This was because there were too many folklore memories of hardship suffered as a result of rents perceived to be too high in accommodation which was sometimes substandard.

The policy of home ownership was one I had always supported and I was given the opportunity to allow more public sector tenants to buy their own homes. An example of this was the thousands of council tenants who lived in houses which were subject to 999 year leases. Scots law had to be changed to enable them to acquire the right to buy for that length of time. As a result of the policy of expanding home ownership more public funds were freed up for spending on improving the housing stock.

In addition the housing association movement with its fair rent policy had turned out to be one of Scotland's success stories. This too would need maximum support, so that in cooperation with local authorities, the housing associations could build homes for rent, homes for the elderly, frail and disabled and homes for low-cost ownership, in accordance with the aspirations of the local community.

In order to ensure close working relations between the public and private sectors, I made it my job to visit every single local authority in Scotland, along with Government officials. In the autumn we went ahead with the housing bill and despite some attempts at scaremongering by the Opposition, gradually the purpose behind the setting up of Scottish Homes became clear and the new organisation flourished.

Some years later the policy of allowing tenants to convert rents into mortgages, or RTM as it was referred to, was implemented. The first RTM sale to former Scottish Special Housing Association tenants was in Uphall in West Lothian, and the Prime Minister agreed to attend the occasion, along with Michael Forsyth and myself. This proved to be a very interesting event and the married couple enjoyed welcoming Mrs Thatcher for a cup of tea, while an angry demonstration against the Community Charge was held at bay at the end of the street.

I had no idea what the politics of the husband and wife were, but suspected that they might not necessarily be Conservatives! Some months later a newspaper claimed that one supported the SNP and the other the Labour Party. The Prime Minister in these circumstances rather resembled an auntie who had dropped in for a cup of tea. A girl who was Editor of a school magazine wanted to interview Mrs Thatcher and asked her what her favourite sport was. She replied somewhat improbably – skiing – but then went on to say firmly that neither she nor any of her Ministers would actually be doing any skiing, as none of them could afford the time off if they broke a leg. I exchanged glances with Michael Forsyth as we had both just completed plans to take to the slopes in the recess starting in a few days. We smiled at each other but were very careful not to disclose our plans at that moment.

After the official ceremony in marking the transfer of ownership, I was invited to travel in the same car as the Prime Minister. As we neared the end of the street, where the police had kept the demonstrators, we came to the entrance through the cordon and one of the protesters hurled an egg straight at us. At that moment the driver accelerated, and the egg landed harmlessly in the road. I looked at the Prime Minister who was sitting with an impassive expression on her face as though nothing had happened. The whole incident made me realise she was not called the "Iron Lady" for nothing.

The first rent-to-mortgage sale represented a landmark in Scottish housing history, but the result was slightly different from what might have been expected. Not very many people bought their houses through RTM, but the publicity encouraged a great many more tenants to buy their homes through the statutory Right to Buy policy, as they rightly believed that this would be a better bargain. By the end of Margaret Thatcher's term of office, Scotland's housing profile had changed dramatically with home ownership having risen from only one third to almost two thirds.

The Prime Minister was not only concerned with major policy issues and great events. She had promised to respond to every MP who had asked for a meeting with her to discuss the closedown of a factory in his or her constituency. One day I received an order to report immediately to Mrs Thatcher, the reason being that Dennis Canavan, the Labour MP for Falkirk West had demanded a meeting with her because a small sheltered workshop in his constituency had been closed by the Scottish Transport Group. This had been the indirect result of legislation which I steered through Parliament to privatise the Scottish Bus Group.

The meeting took place in Margaret Thatcher's office in the House of Commons and during its progress she offered Dennis Canavan a cup of tea which she dispensed from a silver teapot. He put his case on behalf of his constituents and treated the PM with great respect. She responded with great courtesy but I have to report that there was no meeting of minds. I was left with two impressions, both favourable. Mrs Thatcher was prepared to take trouble over detailed issues which were important to individual members, at the same time as looking after national affairs. Dennis Canavan was prepared to take his local problems to the very highest authority and in years to come I was not surprised that when he was not in favour with his own party his constituents continued to support him strongly.

A few months later we were in the run-up to Christmas 1988 and none of us had an inkling of the tragedy and horrors which lay ahead. On the evening of 21 December, at about 7.20pm in the House of Commons, I bumped into Jim Sillars, the MP from the Scottish Labour Party. He told me he had just seen the latest news from Reuters which reported that a jumbo jet had come down at the town of Lockerbie.

I immediately made my way to the Office of the Secretary of State for Scotland in Dover House. There the officials told me the tragic news that Pan Am Flight 103, fully laden with passengers had crashed at Lockerbie. The Head of the Home and Health Department, William Reid, had contacted the Ministry of Defence, so that a jet aircraft would be on standby to take the Secretary of State to the site of the tragedy. I made it clear that I too would be available, and as I was the only Minister on hand, the officials requested that I should remain with them in the Secretary of State's outer office.

Soon the news got through to the relevant Ministers and I was told that Paul Channon, the Secretary of State for Transport would make a statement at 10pm. Malcolm Rifkind saw me shortly before the statement, and I said that I was ready to drop everything and fly up to Scotland. He told me in his usual decisive way to be ready five minutes after the end of Paul Channon's statement. I told him that the local MP, Sir Hector Monro, was ready to go and that Donald

Dewar, the Shadow Secretary of State for Scotland, wished to accompany us.

At the appointed time I left the House of Commons entrance with Donald Dewar, was driven to RAF Northolt, and with the Secretary of State and Sir Hector Monro, MP for Dumfries, boarded a small jet aircraft, which flew us to Glasgow Airport. On the tarmac we were met by Officers from an RAF Sea King Helicopter, and we flew down over the M74 dual carriageway towards Lockerbie, at not much over 1000 feet.

On landing in a field at Lockerbie we received a briefing from the Chief Constable, John Boyd. At first the Police thought that two small aircraft might have collided, as witnesses reported a flash in the sky. But with a great many bodies strewn in and around Lockerbie it became apparent that a major tragedy had occurred. A resident had found a dead body and had taken it to the local police station, where he was ordered to take it back to where it had been found. The Police wished to collect all the evidence with great care, and did not want any interference with what was a potential crime scene.

The nose of the jumbo jet had come down next to the Chapel at Tundergarth, and we were taken there to see the site. It looked as if the cockpit of the aircraft had been wrenched apart from the fuselage with indescribable violence. Around it lay bodies, covered with blankets, so our eyes were spared the worst of what had happened, and we felt to some extent anaesthetised by the darkness.

Back in Lockerbie the Chief Constable took Malcolm Rifkind around the areas most adversely affected by the massive impact of the aircraft's wings as they crashed into the houses below leaving in their place a giant smoking crater.

Together with Donald Dewar we were escorted towards the cordoned off area, past rows and rows of empty ambulances and many reporters and TV camera crews. On going through it into the crime scene, which had been taped off, we saw small groups of fire fighters, police officers and soldiers all in uniform. Before we had gone many steps we sank in mud up to our ankles, with debris all around us, and soon we became aware of smoking burnt-out buildings. It was as if I had been transported back in time and was seeing at first hand the effect of a wartime bombing raid.

We came to the smoking crater, where the aircraft engines had embedded themselves deep in the ground, and we were told that very attractive houses with people in them had stood there only a few hours before.

We were then taken to another site, where a traveller in the jumbo jet who had remained strapped in his seat had crashed into the roof of a house. That person too had been covered by a blanket, and as I looked at the roof I sensed that two feet away from me was another blanket, and under it were some shoes attached to feet. I realised that I was standing beside a person who had fallen some 30,000 feet on to a fence. The body had been respectfully covered.

As we walked back towards the empty ambulances it occurred to me that on the ground those most directly affected were either dead or had escaped harm, with relatively few wounded. In the days ahead I learnt that more people had died at Lockerbie in that one terrible event than had been killed on the British side during the pitched Battle for the Falkland Islands.

Donald Dewar said little to me while we took in the aftermath of what had happened, but on his way back to the hall where we met again with the Chief Constable, he remarked that he hoped he would never live to see another terrible tragedy like this. I shared his feelings about the horror of a night when bodies had rained from the sky, along with debris and fragments from Pan Am Flight 103.

Death and injury had struck Lockerbie before. During the First World War two troop trains had crashed into each other there with much loss of life to Scottish soldiers. That had been an accident, but this time we were left in no doubt that Ambassador Bruce of the USA, who had just arrived, believed that the destruction of the aircraft had been deliberately caused by a bomb placed on board. I shared his view, which would be confirmed a few days later.

We all joined a meeting, organised by the Chief Constable, where Malcolm Rifkind and the Ambassador each said a few words. Malcolm expressed his sadness at the grievous loss of life, expressed sympathy to the families of the victims, and confirmed that a further report would of course be made to Parliament. The Ambassador, who was accompanied by his wife, expressed similar thoughts and said that a large number of those who had perished on the flight had been young Americans. That was about all he would say and I felt for him in these appalling circumstances.

Donald Dewar parted from me after this and was driven to Glasgow. I was taken to my home in North Berwick where I arrived at 5.30 in the morning. On the way back I had identified what I saw as the immediate priorities. The Police must be given all the necessary resources and every possible assistance to investigate what had happened and why, and the local community must be given substantial support. At the first opportunity between Christmas and New Year I would go back to Lockerbie to make sure this was being done.

With me was William Reid, with whom I worked closely, and who had at one time been Private Secretary to Mrs Margaret Thatcher when she was Education Minister. I was glad to have his support on that day as well as that of Dr Gavin McCrone, another individual of great ability, who was the Chief Economist of the Scottish Office, and who would become Head of the Development Department. Our mission was to sort out the finances of Dumfries and Galloway Regional Council now that it had to deal with the after-effects of an international atrocity.

On arrival, wherever I went I was followed by television cameras and broadcasters asking questions, while at this point all I wanted to do was to listen and learn. The local school had been taken over for those working with the Emergency Services. The bodies and the personal belongings of the victims had to be found as well as every piece of the wreckage of the aircraft which would have to be taken away to be examined. It was indeed like a wartime episode, in which the whole of the Scottish community came together in assisting the smallest police force in Scotland. When I was interviewed I was able to pay tribute to the Emergency Services, and to the efforts of the countless volunteers from other police forces, fire services and social work departments, as well as other voluntary bodies like the WRVS.

The issue of finance was worrying, since under the current law a local authority had to foot the bill for its own emergencies, but in this case central government help from contingency funds would be necessary. In this connection the Prime Minister, Mrs Margaret Thatcher, was very supportive.

I again went to see the crater. The air was still permeated with the stench of heavy aviation fuel. It was evident that the contaminated earth would have to be removed. Meetings took place all day, and at nightfall we returned home. I switched on the television to learn that a British Government Minister had made his way to Lockerbie to pay his respects to the dead. I wondered who that could have been, and then I realised that in fact I was the person who was being spoken about.

It had happened like this. Late in the morning a police officer had told me that the relatives would like me to pay my respects to the dead and I had immediately gone to the Town Hall, which was filled with coffins. In the middle was a little silver coffin of a young child. I walked down the side of the hall, came to attention and bowed before it, in much the same way as we salute the fallen on Armistice Day. I then walked on and met those involved in identifying the victims. One of them said to me that his was the most awful job imaginable. I told him that he was carrying out an important duty of great service to the relatives, and that they were very grateful to him. He accepted this, but I did not forget what he had said to me. I could understand later why so many of those closely involved needed special counselling.

Apparently when I was in the Town Hall, without my knowledge, my actions had been caught by the TV cameras. What the British public wanted at that stage was not a statement about facts and figures, but a mark of respect. Without realising its full significance, this was something I had done automatically.

I returned to Lockerbie for a third time along with the Minister of State, Ian Lang, and we visited the cemetery when the last human remains were being buried. At the commemorative service respects were paid to the victims, to those whose bodies were never found, and to those who could not be identified. It was an extremely sad occasion which brought home to us all the huge loss of life which had been sustained, and the great and lasting distress experienced by all the relatives and the people of Lockerbie.

Looking back it was not difficult to imagine who might have had a motive for carrying out this outrage. The US had bombed

Tripoli not long before, and earlier, on 3 July 1988, the American naval warship the USS Vincennes had shot down a jumbo jet flying from Iran to one of the Gulf States, wrongly believing that their ship was under attack from a jet fighter.

In due course the Lord Advocate would prosecute two Libyan Intelligence Agents, and one of them would be convicted of the crime. I would not be involved with the preparation of the court case, although I would have to answer MPs' questions on behalf of the Law Officers as none of the latter had a seat in the House of Commons. I reckoned that it might be many years before every aspect of this monstrous crime would be uncovered.

On 20 August 2009 Kenny MacAskill, the Justice Minister in the SNP Administration at Holyrood, made the controversial decision to release Abdelbaset Ali Mohmed Al Megrahi, the man found guilty of the bombing, on compassionate grounds due to his terminal cancer, allowing him to return to Libya. Megrahi had dropped his appeal against conviction shortly beforehand and as a result it looks even more unlikely that the full facts of the tragedy will be revealed in the foreseeable future.

In fact Lockerbie was not to be the only tragedy with which I became involved. In December 1988 there was a substantial earthquake in Armenia, followed by an appeal from the Russian Government for assistance.

Lothian Regional Council asked whether the Scottish Office might donate 20,000 blankets from the Civil Defence Store at Cambusbarron, and on 16 December I went to Turnhouse, next to the airport, where sixth form pupils from West Edinburgh were helping to bundle up the blankets for onward transmission to Armenia.

171

In thanking all those who had participated I said that "the disaster in Armenia was of such a size that it is difficult for us here to fully take in the grief and the suffering of the Armenian people." In terms of humanity and respect for human dignity we wished to make a contribution, even if our best efforts might seem relatively small in comparison to the extent of the tragedy.

In accordance with the request of the Russian Government the 20,000 blankets were sent via the Red Cross to help improve the lot of the survivors and I hoped they were put to the best possible use.

The next big parliamentary issue with which I had to deal was the Law Reform Miscellaneous Provisions (Scotland) Bill. This proposed legislation put forward measures to reform the law on charities, to introduce competition into such legal services as executry and conveyancing work, as well as giving opportunities for solicitor/advocates to practise in the highest courts of the land. In addition there were licensing and penal reforms, including the provision of supervised attendance orders for minor offenders, and the changes made by the legislation resulted in the use of video links to protect children giving evidence in court.

Some of these measures were controversial, and there were just over six weeks to go before the summer recess. Sir Nicholas Fairbairn, the maverick Scottish Conservative MP and a former Solicitor General, made it apparent that he would oppose the Bill in its entirety, and some of his criticisms were echoed by two other backbenchers, Bill Walker and Allan Stewart, a former Scottish Office Minister. It was quite clear that at the end of the Session, there would be a great deal of hard work to be done in Committee, and not everyone looked forward to it.

The Secretary of State, Malcolm Rifkind, was determined to proceed, while Michael Forsyth, who was Chairman of the Scottish

Conservative Party and a Junior Minister, wished at least part of the Bill to be delayed until the autumn. I could see that there were good arguments to be mounted for both options but I felt the Secretary of State had the right to make the final decision. As the Minister responsible for the Bill's passage it would be my job to steer it through the House of Commons Committee.

Working out the figures, with Nicholas Fairbairn voting against virtually everything and receiving some support from one or two Conservative backbenchers, it seemed to me that it would be touch and go whether the Bill would get through intact. However I did have one advantage. There was one English backbencher on the Committee, no less a person than the young William Hague, and I was confident of his total support.

Piloting a highly technical bill through its parliamentary stages can prove very challenging both intellectually and physically and especially when it is subject to detailed line by line scrutiny by a committee of MPs. As the minister it is vital never to lose your concentration as dozens of possible amendments have to be debated and either accepted by the Government or more usually rejected.

I spent around 82 hours in total dealing with the bill during the Committee stage and at one point, when there was to be a crucial vote, Malcolm Rifkind produced an agreement which had been reached with the Law Society of Scotland on various key aspects of the legislation. Fortunately he was the kind of Cabinet Minister who could pull white rabbits out of hats, and as a result the division was won by one vote.

Thereafter Sir Nicholas Fairbairn's opposition began to lose its edge and one day we proceeded with the Bill well into the night. At 3.30am. Sir Nicholas flounced out. He had had enough, and between 3.30 and 5.30 in the morning, without his presence, rapid progress was made.

By the end of the Committee stage, both I and the civil servants advising me were beginning to be short on sleep and we welcomed the arrival of the recess. In the autumn the Bill went through and on 17 October Donald Dewar paid me a compliment on the floor of the House of Commons: "The Under Secretary of State gets tired of people paying tribute to him, but I must do so on this occasion... Never have I seen briefs put to such determined use when all around him there was chaos and confusion!" Similarly Menzies Campbell, the Liberal Democrat kindly congratulated me for "indefatigability and continuing courtesy to all sides".

I did not receive any such praise from Sir Nicholas Fairbairn, who stated: "All I wanted to say is that I hope that our Government and our Party will not break the rule that rules should not be multiplied and that legislation of any kind is a bad thing." I told him that the considerable number of amendments were an example of parliamentary democracy "operating at its best".

Brian Wilson the Scots MP who had been acting for the Labour Front Bench in Committee, was kind enough to write that I had "performed a very difficult task" and that he hoped and believed that a lot of good had come from our deliberations. This was followed by a letter from Prime Minister, Margaret Thatcher, dated 23 October 1990. "I am writing to congratulate you on carrying through the Law Reform Miscellaneous Provisions Bill (Scotland). I know it has involved you in a considerable amount of very hard work and indeed some difficulties as well. I really am grateful to you for all the effort which you put into it."

It was shortly afterwards that a reshuffle of ministers took place and I was confronted with the news that I was expected to accept responsibility for the Community Charge. I told my Private Secretary who looked at me with undisguised horror and asked if it was an order. I explained that the Secretary of State's Private Secretary had said to me that he would be "most awfully grateful" if we would take it on.

The first aspect of the flat-rate local tax which I thought needed immediate change related to those suffering from Alzheimer's and other forms of dementia. This was taken up with the Secretary of State for the Environment, David Hunt, who took the same view and the necessary exemptions were made.

I remember being asked to a lunch with the Prime Minister in 10 Downing Street, on the same day that Michael Mates, the English Tory MP, had an amendment down to the Bill introducing the Community Charge in England, this legislation being debated a year after the Scottish Bill had gone through. I went prepared to answer any questions on any subject relating to Scotland, but the sole topic of conversation was the English Bill and the working of the tax south of the Border. The Prime Minister was resolved to resist amendments in Parliament and I received the very clear impression that she had decided to reject any changes to what her opponents had dubbed the poll tax.

When the Bill relating to England became an Act and was implemented, the level of Community Charge levied by English authorities turned out on average to be much higher than anticipated. Also it was considerably higher than the average level of the charge in Scotland. I remembered the iron rule of politics that those who gain tend to say nothing, and those who lose cry blue murder. The situation was made worse because the losers had to pay far more than was expected.

I remember considering drafting a minute detailing the case for corrective measures to the Community Charge legislation. There were any number of ways this could be done. One method would have been to increase the Rate Support Grant to councils so that the level of Community Charge could be reduced. Another way of dealing with it might have been to introduce exemptions or concessions for interest groups such as students. As it was some of the student trade unions were threatening to target every marginal Conservative seat by encouraging voters to opt for the party most likely to defeat the Conservative candidate. It was becoming ominously clear that the Community Charge was acting as a focal point for discontent and that in its application it was not working exactly as intended.

When I mentioned the idea of further exemptions to a Special Adviser I was told to forget it. This was not the time for such a Minute. The Prime Minister had taken a hard line against changes, and the Cabinet had accepted her position. The actual words used were "The boss has decided to tough it out and the Cabinet has rolled over." I felt a sense of uneasiness, as I believed that we would have to revisit this subject in due course. The problems would not go away and the Government would continue to be pressured to take steps to address the growing discontent. I remember going into John Nelson's print shop in Edinburgh and feeling uneasy when he showed me a depiction of Wat Tyler, who led the so-called Peasants' Revolt against the imposition of a tax of three groats back in 1381. In the portrait Wat Tyler was slaying the poll tax collector!

The subject would indeed be revisited and came back onto the agenda in a surprising way, as a result of a resignation speech. On the afternoon of 13 November 1990 I was working in my office dealing with constituency requests sent to me by MPs from all over Scotland. My Private Secretary Owen Kelly had turned on the television and from his loud exclamations I realised that Sir

Geoffrey Howe, the Deputy Prime Minister, was making a very damaging attack. Standing a few rows behind the Prime Minister in the Commons and using a striking cricketing metaphor, he claimed that when it came to our European policy and in particular negotiations over the Single Currency, Britain's opening batsmen got to the crease only to find their bats had been broken before the game by the team captain.

I recalled Mrs Thatcher's recent statement on Europe, when I had been on the Front Bench to deal with some minor environmental matter. At that time she had to answer MPs' questions for an hour and a quarter and, towards the end, next to her on the front bench, only John Major, myself, and the Government Whip remained. I now understood why Sir Geoffrey had absented himself. He had disliked her forthright opposition to a single European currency, and had been uncomfortable with the tone of her response. I did not share his view on this as it seemed to me that if any individual had to answer critical questions for more than an hour it was not surprising if the exchanges were combative. In any case, while I had strongly supported Britain's entry into the Common Market, I was opposed to British freedoms, which had been built up over centuries, being overridden by European laws and sovereignty being whittled away.

Sir Geoffrey's resignation led to Michael Heseltine issuing his challenge for the leadership and to Margaret Thatcher winning the first round of the contest by four votes. I had voted for her and wanted to find out the reasons for her very narrow victory. Talking to my colleagues, it seemed to me that the main reason for what had happened was that many Conservative MPs with marginal seats had not supported her because of their constituents' dissatisfaction with Community Charge levels. Whatever the

Prime Minister and the Cabinet had previously decided, pressure from the back benches during the leadership election inevitably meant that the matter would come back onto the agenda.

During this time I felt like a stoker in the engine room of a ship, working to keep it moving while up above grenades were going off on the bridge. I had certainly expected the Prime Minister to win the first round of voting but not by such a slender margin. For a short time I kept my own counsel while rumours and intrigue swirled around Westminster. I decided that I would vote for Mrs Thatcher again if she stood in the next round, but I did not personally urge her to fight on as I was not convinced that she would win the next General Election, mainly because she had been so opposed to further changes to the Community Charge system.

On the Floor of the House of Commons John Maxton, the Labour MP with whom I had clashed previously, accused me of having voted for Michael Heseltine. I rejected his false claim by telling him that Margaret Thatcher was like Monty, a victory-winning general. Just after that by a remarkable coincidence she came in and sat down next to me on the Front Bench.

She must have shared the uncertainty felt by a considerable number of Conservative MPs because after consulting with her Cabinet colleagues she withdrew from the contest. Before the new leader was in place, she went on to make an extremely powerful and passionate speech in the Commons full of defiance and vitality, stressing the importance of a competitive economy and a property owning democracy. It was described as "Bravura Thatcher" in the press.

Looking back, her contribution to political life was enormous. It was sometimes said of her that she had won the Hot War with

General Galtieri, the Civil War with Arthur Scargill and the Cold War with Mr Gorbachev. On the economic front Thatcherite policies had made Britain much more competitive, had largely abolished restrictive practices and had hugely increased home and popular share ownership. At the outset she had made the correct strategic decisions to bring public spending and inflation under control and set Britain firmly on the road towards economic competitiveness and prosperity.

In the subsequent leadership election I voted for John Major who became Prime Minister while Ian Lang became Secretary of State for Scotland. I was asked to continue in the Scottish Office as Minister for Education and Housing and soon we were into the next Election campaign in 1992. I knew that my seat was once again the top target for the Liberals in Scotland and to my dismay the Accident and Emergency Service at the Western General Hospital in my constituency had been closed.

The Lothian Health Board had substantially overspent. The first year the Secretary of State had bailed them out but the second year they had been required to bring their spending under control. I had campaigned strongly for a Minor Injuries Service at the Western, which was agreed, but I knew that the loss of an A&E Unit at the hospital in the north-west of the City would cost me vital votes.

My campaign team learned that the Liberal leader Paddy Ashdown was coming to meet voters at the Corstorphine Shopping Centre so we flooded the place with Conservative supporters and I had a short face to face exchange with Mr Ashdown who I understand was not exactly enthralled by my appearance. Nevertheless he said "Pleased to see you" and I replied "I must come to visit your constituency sometime." The watching reporters were amused by our spoiling tactic and a photograph of our encounter appeared on the front page of the *Evening News*. Incidentally sixteen years later I would keep my word to Paddy Ashdown and would give a lecture on my father's first flight over Everest in his former constituency at Yeovil near the Westland factory which had built the experimental aircraft in 1933.

At the outset of the Election campaign Michael Forsyth had made arrangements for Margaret Thatcher to visit my constituency activists. Before her arrival a suspicious package had been found in the car park and had been blown up by the police. Understandably we were all rather tense as we awaited her arrival, although we later found out the package had only contained photographic equipment.

She spoke in her usual inimitable way, without any notes, and when a message was passed in saying that the press wished to interview her, she said what they really wanted to do was to get her to say something different from John Major. "We really do not need that." She then went on her way to her next appointment.

During the campaign I was visited by the journalist Edward Pearce who was writing a book called *Election Rides*. His work appeared a short time later and in it he wrote "James Douglas-Hamilton has his hands full, but he has run hard and has demonstrated that personal trouble-making, private popularity and hard work can combat a Scottish state of affairs reminiscent of the old Glasgow Empire. 'If they liked you they let you live.'"

On election night, to my relief, I did indeed stay alive and my majority only went down from 1,234 to 879. The loss of the A&E Unit had not cost me the seat as I had feared and the Conservatives led by John Major beat Neil Kinnock's Labour Party.

As a Minister I had been told that I would remain in post if re-elected until relieved of my present responsibilities, so I was

14) The author and his wife Susie celebrate victory in the 1983 election in which he managed to hold on to his West Edinburgh seat with the smallest majority in Scotland.

15) The Speaker of the House of Commons, George Thomas (standing, second left), meets the Conservative Opposition Whips before the 1979 General Election – the men who helped bring down the Callaghan Government.

16) The Scottish Office team in 1987. (From left to right: Michael Forsyth, Ian Lang, Malcolm Rifkind, Russell Sanderson and the author.)

17) As division bells ring in the Commons, the author reassures Margaret Thatcher that there will be time to vote as well as to have the photograph taken.

18) The Prime Minister and the author visit the home of Mr and Mrs Mowat – the first couple to buy their house in the government's rent-to-mortgage scheme.

19) The author persuades public sector tenants that the government scheme for regeneration and housing association activity would assist their community.

20) The author as Minister for Home Affairs announces an amnesty for the handing in of weapons in the summer of 1987.

21) The author deep in discussion with John Major.

22) An unexpected General Election meeting with Paddy Ashdown, Leader of the Liberal Party, 1992 in West Edinburgh.

23) The author, about to be introduced as a Life Peer to the House of Lords in 1997.

24) Walking down the Mound in Edinburgh from Parliament House to the opening of the Scottish Parliament with fellow MSPs (left to right: Margaret Ewing, Henry McLeish, Sam Galbraith, Annabel Goldie and Lord Hardie).

25) The author is sworn in during the first session of the Scottish Parliament in 1999.

26) The author and his sons (Jamie, Charles and Harry) in Iceland, at one of the largest waterfalls in Europe.

27) The author beside a statue of Thomas, fifth Earl of Selkirk, who helped settlers displaced by the Highland Clearances to emigrate to Canada in the early 19th century, outside the Manitoba Parliament.

pleasantly surprised to be told that I would in fact be remaining in the Scottish team.

This reminds me of a tussle of wills which I had with the civil service. During my previous term as a Minister, they had sought to redecorate my office in St Andrews House at great cost renewing all the furniture, carpets and repainting the walls. When it was clear that they were not going to do this for all the other offices, I had refused permission. However when I returned to my previous domain after the election I realised that the Civil Service had won. During the Election period the whole office had been redecorated with state-of-the-art new furniture, not to mention bright new carpets and beautifully painted walls. The decision had had absolutely nothing to do with me, but I suspected the Civil Service had been anticipating the arrival of a different government and a different Minister!

CHAPTER 10

The Earldom of Selkirk – Earl for four days

It was just two years after the unexpected victory of John Major in the 1992 election that I was suddenly barred from voting, speaking or even entering the House of Commons Chamber. The reason for my exclusion was the death of my uncle to whose hereditary peerage I was the heir. It became a collision between political duty and family history.

Since the Conservatives had a very small majority the disappearance of the Member for Edinburgh West could have threatened the Government's continued existence, especially as a confidence vote against the Prime Minister on Europe was imminent.

If I was to support my constituents and the Government, I felt I would have to disclaim the Earldom of Selkirk, but what I did not know was that ahead would be a legal challenge from a relative as to whether the Earldom was mine to disclaim in the first place.

My uncle Geordie Selkirk, a tall forceful man, had always been a very important figure in my life. During his career he held high office as Paymaster General, Chancellor of the Duchy of Lancaster in the Cabinet, First Lord of the Admiralty and Commissioner General for South East Asia. While in Singapore he worked with

Lee Kuan Yew, the eminent Prime Minister, who wrote to me after my uncle's death that "from a Singapore point of view, he was supportive, effective and friendly... He had this deep voice and an unconsciously haughty way of talking. This tended to put Singaporeans off, until they got to know him. But then he had a knack of putting people at ease, probably part of his training or culture as a nobleman. He was convivial and a practical man."

While in Singapore, my uncle resisted calls to involve British Forces in Laos and Cambodia, advice which was accepted by the Government of Harold Macmillan. Afterwards he visited Canada to become an Honorary Chief of the First Nation Saulteaux and was presented with a war bonnet. His ancestor, the Fifth Earl, had committed his fortune, taking Highlanders to Red River Settlement which would be the beginnings of Winnipeg.

Uncle Geordie took an interest in me from an early stage and receiving a letter from him was a significant event. He had the old Scottish quality of believing that young persons should not get above themselves but at the same time should be encouraged. On 17 October 1960 on learning about my interest in debating he wrote to me from Singapore to say "There is no greater accomplishment than to be able to speak concisely, clearly and humorously, but it is an accomplishment rather than an achievement."

On 26 October 1962 he again wrote to me, this time on the subject of an Oxford Union debate, saying that the problems of the world cannot be faced passively, and as Pericles stated "The secret of happiness is liberty, and the secret of liberty is courage." My uncle went on to say that the balance of terror had prevented the outbreak of anything but a minor war, but the balance would not continue if Russia passed on nuclear weapons to other countries.

The choice was not between co-existence and peace, but between an unstable co-existence on the one hand and chaos and starvation on the other.

On 2 February 1963 he warned me after another Oxford Union debate that popular applause is "always a very transient element" from which it can be dangerous to derive too much satisfaction. He was glad that I had given up boxing which he believed required "a rather more well-knit and stocky body than your own" but he was delighted to learn about my promotion in the Territorial Army to Lieutenant in the Cameronians Scottish Rifles.

He gave me some timely advice in his letter of 22 August defining the object of the House of Commons as being the attempt to bring together the politicians who seek power and the rest of the population who are interested in good, efficient, uncorrupted government. There was, he believed, therefore a consistent conflict between liberty and authority. The real danger of democratic governments was that they proved to be too weak, not too strong. Interestingly enough he concluded by urging me to remember that half the world consisted of women, so they were well worth trying to understand!

After I became an MP, he wrote to me on 28 December 1974 saying that it was interesting to find how many MPs of his generation had noticed my maiden speech opposing the general reintroduction of the death penalty, which he described as a first class start, although I rather fancied that he might have taken a different view on the subject.

On 16 November 1979 he set down his recollections of what he and his three brothers did in the Second World War and some time later he asked me to discover what the Luftwaffe records had to say about the five German Junker 88s who had attacked him when he was piloting a Wellington bomber over the Bay of Biscay on 9 September 1943. The information came back to me that, on that day, four of their JU 88s, each carrying four men, had failed to return to their base at Montpelier in the south of France.

After giving the matter some thought my uncle believed that his sergeant gunner had accounted for one plane and that the others had run out of fuel on their way home. When attacked, instead of turning away which would have made him a sitting duck, he had turned towards them and dived down towards the water. At that moment his windscreen was shot away, with a canon shell going through his sleeve. He then zig-zagged, at low level, over the sea out towards the US into cloud giving his assailants the slip. Geordie told me he was extremely irritated that whenever the crew brought him a cup of coffee in the cockpit, without a windscreen, the coffee blew away.

In 1992 he became involved with raising the funds for a monument in Teba in Southern Spain, to Lord James Douglas, known as "the Black Douglas", the great Scottish warrior in the Wars of Independence in the early fourteenth century. He was killed by the Moors at Teba, near the Castle of the Stars, while fighting alongside the King of Spain. When he met his death Lord James had been on his way to the Holy Land with the heart of his great friend King Robert the Bruce in a special casket around his neck. In 2007 with the help of Ronnie Browne of "the Corries" skills as an artist, a commemorative representation of the Black Douglas was unveiled at Lennoxlove.

In 1983 Geordie had warned me that I might be the heir to his title. An Opinion to that effect had been expressed by Sir Crispin Agnew of Lochnaw at that time and my cousin Alasdair had been informed. Geordie had written to me on 11 June drawing my attention to the fact that, from the date of his death, I would have thirty days in which to disclaim the Earldom. If the official decision was in my favour I would automatically lose my seat in the Commons.

In fact the position was more complex than that, since the outcome of a case before the Court of Lord Lyon would take many months and a disclaimer of the heir to the title has to take effect within 28 days from the death of the hereditary peer.

On 29 January 1991 Geordie had written to me again giving his view as to the future of his title after his death. Since he had no male heir, the Earldom would go to the immediate younger brother of the Duke of Hamilton, which was myself. "If I die before Angus (your older brother), the title descends to you; if on the other hand, Angus dies before me, his eldest son becomes Duke, and his younger brother becomes the Earl of Selkirk. The latter is, of course, less likely than the former" he explained.

On 16 September 1991 he sent me a copy of the letter he had written to the Editor of Dods (which includes lists of all MPs and Peers) making the same point and making clear that as an MP I could disclaim the title if I so desired. In his letter to me he wrote "you do realise that you may have to make a final decision at fairly short notice".

On 24 November 1994 I wrote to the Conservative Chief Whip, Richard Ryder, to inform him that my uncle had died that morning. I told him:

"The reason I am writing to you is because he was a hereditary peer and in terms of the three Opinions, which are enclosed, the heir to the hereditary title is myself. I have been aware of this for some time although I did not talk about it. This may be the first time this situation has arisen with a sitting MP and there are 28 days within which the person concerned has to make it clear whether he is going to renounce. I propose to say nothing about this until after the funeral at which time I will make an appropriate statement....

"My inclination is to stay on in the House of Commons. When this happened to Tony Benn the law had not been changed and he was excluded from Parliament. After the change in the law Lord Home and Lord Hailsham made use of the legislation to renounce and re-enter the House of Commons. What slightly complicates the issue in this case is that it might be some time before the Lyon Court could deal with this officially."

During the Civil War between King and Parliament, the first Duke of Hamilton had led an army of 12,000 Scots into England on behalf of King Charles I, but had been outmanoeuvred at the Battle of Preston by Oliver Cromwell and had subsequently been beheaded. His brother, the 2nd Duke, led a smaller Scottish force of horsemen at the Battle of Worcester against Cromwell and he too was defeated and died from his wounds. The Earl of Selkirk married Anne, the daughter of the 1st Duke and was allowed to call himself Duke for life after the Restoration of the Monarchy under Charles II. In 1688, shortly before the Glorious Revolution, King James II and VII issued a document outlining the descent of the Earldom, the King being mindful of the sacrifices of the Hamilton family for the Royal Cause. This Novodamus as it was known was in Latin and made the next younger brother of the 4th Duke of Hamilton the Earl of Selkirk.

I could not resist the temptation of putting a PS into my letter:

"It occurs to me that Oliver Cromwell would be turning in his grave if he thought whether or not a person became a

Peer in the 1990s depended on who had been a close friend of King Charles I".

On the same day I received a letter from the Secretary of State for Scotland, Ian Lang, which put me under some pressure.

He wrote:

"I was so sorry to learn the sad news of your uncle Geordie's death. My condolences. You and I discussed the question of your renunciation of the Earldom. I can understand your anxiety not to show undue haste over this lest it be misconstrued as discourtesy to his memory.

"However, we are unfortunately in a very serious political situation at present, with the real possibility that the Government could fall as a result of a defeat in the lobbies next Monday.

"As a result, your vote then is very important and could be critical to our survival. In these circumstances I am sure everyone would understand why it is so important that your renunciation should be taken at the very earliest opportunity, and before Monday."

That evening I was due to answer a debate on the withdrawal of some maternity services at the Western General Hospital in my constituency. My friend and colleague Allan Stewart accepted the task of answering on my behalf as I informed him that if I even entered the Commons Chamber it might cause a by-election.

On the Monday following I acted on the advice of the Clerk of the House of Commons who said that it would be altogether appropriate for me to disclaim even before the Lyon Court formed a view as to whether I was in fact the Earl. All I would be doing would be disclaiming an interest in a title on my own behalf in so far as I had the right to do so. I then went to the House of Lords with the Lord Advocate, Alan Rodger, who told me that I had a job now as a Government Minister but that there would be no job waiting for me in the House of Lords. I went in to see the Clerk in the Lord Chancellor's Office who in contrast to the Clerk in the House of Commons said to me "Is this something you really want to do?" I had been Earl for four days, but my mind was made up and had been for a long time.

I signed the document of disclaimer which applied for life but I knew that my eldest son would succeed me on my death, if the Court of Lord Lyon in Edinburgh confirmed that I had been Geordie's heir. I then went to the House of Commons to receive a copy of the receipt of an Instrument of Disclaimer sent from Sir Thomas Legg, KCB in the Lords to the Clerk of the House of Commons. Shortly afterwards Andrew Mackinlay, the Labour MP raised a point of order in the Chamber for a Statement on my position. He was reassured by the Speaker that the necessary evidence of disclaimer had reached his office.

That night as it turned out the Government won quite easily and although my presence had not mattered on this occasion, it would later. During the debate on the Arms for Iraq Inquiry the Government won by only one vote. If I had not been present to lend my support then, a tied vote could have been a serious embarrassment for the Government and would have piled on the pressure for an earlier General Election.

After disclaiming the hereditary peerage, John Major asked to see me in his office to thank me for my support. I also met Tony Benn in the Commons Lobby and thought to myself how ironic it was that I was following in the footsteps of somebody whose political views totally diverged from mine. I got the impression from speaking to him that he had not anticipated that the Act for which he had fought would benefit the likes of myself. Because he had been determined to disclaim the title he inherited, he had campaigned successfully for a change in the law. While Parliament had deliberated at length, he had been excluded from the House for three years. After all, in my case far from waiting for three years I had dealt with the whole business in just over three days! He had been the first MP to disclaim, but, as it turned out, I would be the last. At the time of my disclaimer the journalist Magnus Linklater wrote that I had been given a walk-on part in the harsh world of politics. In 1999, the House of Lords Act allowed hereditary peers to stand for election to the House of Commons, thus eliminating the need to disclaim. Under the new arrangements Viscount Thurso was elected MP for Caithness and Sutherland in 2001.

However, the issue as to who would succeed to the Earldom of Selkirk was not over. My cousin Alasdair expressed the view that the title was not mine to disclaim and in due course raised an action before the Court of the Lord Lyon.

My first reaction to the information that my cousin thought he was the heir was that this matter should have been sorted out in my uncle's lifetime. While my father was Duke of Hamilton my cousin Alasdair would have been in line to succeed, however, on my father's death, when my brother Angus became Duke, I was in line to succeed. More confusingly, had my brother Angus died before Geordie, it would have been his (Angus') second son who would have succeeded. The date of Geordie's death would decide who inherited the title.

It seemed to me that the succession had elements of a lottery about it, as everything depended upon who died when. My own view was that any argument my cousin had on this subject was not with me but with King James II and VII for having authorised the Novodamus laying out such a procedure. If anybody had told me that one day I would be involved in a legal action concerning a document in Latin written in 1688 I would have found it hard to believe, but that was the situation in which I found myself. The case came to an end in March 1996. My Counsel were Bill Nimmo-Smith, QC, who became a distinguished judge and Sir Crispin Agnew, who was a Scottish Herald. The Judgement interpreting the meaning of the Novodamus was in my favour.

All this had not gone unnoticed by my colleagues and I received a generous letter from Michael Forsyth, who was by then Secretary of State for Scotland.

He wrote:

"I was pleased to hear of your victory in Lyon Court – many congratulations.

"We were all very grateful for your swift disclaimer of the earldom when the situation first arose. It was typical of your sense of public duty and our unswerving loyalty to the Prime Minister and the Government.

"It is good to know, however, that this ancient title will now pass on, to be enjoyed by your son and his descendants, while leaving you free to pursue your Ministerial career and to continue to give me the strong support which I value highly."

This seemed to be the end of the saga but there turned out to be one more hurdle to jump. I wished the position of my eldest son

Andrew as heir to the Earldom of Selkirk to be accepted by the Lord Chancellor's Office. So I told them the decision of the Court of Lord Lyon. To my surprise they would not accept it without confirmation that I was the immediate younger brother of the Duke of Hamilton. I said that my mother could confirm that fact only to be told that in case my mother had had a secret love child somebody else would have to attest to my status as a second son!

Quite apart from the fact that my mother would not have been amused by this suggestion and that pregnancies cannot easily be concealed, it occurred to me that this was a throw-back to former centuries when it had been claimed that babies had been smuggled into beds in warming-pans, or even lowered by rope from castle walls in a basket. Surely to goodness such processes are laughably old fashioned.

But the Lord Chancellor's Office was adamant, so Lord Renton of Huntingdon who had known my mother for thirty years obliged with an affidavit. To my dismay this too was considered to be no good, since he had not known my mother at the time of the birth of her first child and immediately afterwards. I then went to my aunt by marriage, Mrs Prunella Power, who had known my mother before she married my father and her evidence was considered to be sufficient.

All of this was not allowed to distract from work at the Scottish Office where a large number of issues had come across my desk. While looking after the environment brief, I had helped introduce a Bill to establish Scottish Natural Heritage, a more powerful environmental agency to protect the countryside and wildlife. The most contentious issue which arose was whether wolves should be reintroduced into the Scottish Highlands and Islands, but the prospect of young mothers pushing their babies in prams with wolves on the loose served as a deterrent to this interesting suggestion.

Later I took over the education portfolio and began by having consultations on the most acceptable form of testing for schools. The *Times Educational Supplement* on 6 November 1992 asserted that a skilful hand was being played on testing and that enough had been done to obtain the agreement of local authorities, parents and teachers. The purpose of the policy was to have an educational system second to none with education serving young people as the passport to jobs and fulfilment.

It had been my good fortune to serve, under three Secretaries of State, all of whom were extremely bright. Malcolm Rifkind who had been my closest friend as a student at Edinburgh University had enormous capability and an extremely quick mind. He would serve as Secretary of State in four great departments, including those of the Scottish Office, Transport, Defence and Foreign Affairs.

His successor, Ian Lang, was in an impregnable position as he was an extremely close friend of the Prime Minister, John Major, and had previously acted as his Campaign Manager in the contest to succeed Mrs Thatcher. As a result the Prime Minister would support him in virtually all circumstances. Ian Lang was generous in allowing me to retain responsibility for Historic Scotland whose jewels in the crown included Edinburgh Castle and Stirling Castle. These Heritage Centres attracted a great deal of tourism for Scotland and had been steadily improved. My four sons took part in their first public engagement at Edinburgh Castle when they had to detonate a small charge to begin the creation of a special tunnel which would allow essential services to be carried out without impeding tourists.

I was able to advance efforts to secure more tourism for Scotland during an official visit to the US. I told the American travel agents in Washington and New York that my wife's grandfather, the author John Buchan, had invited President Franklin Delano Roosevelt to Canada when he had been Governor General there. This had been the first such visit by an American President to Canada since the War of Independence and I mentioned to them that as a gesture of friendship President Roosevelt had given John Buchan the American flag from the front of his Presidential car, which was now proudly on display in our home in Scotland. This paved the way for a friendly question and answer session.

One of the most moving experiences I shared with my wife, Susie, on that trip was the visit to Ellis Island, where some 25 million poverty stricken Europeans had arrived in the US, in their search for a better future. The first generation had a really tough time. The second generation had done reasonably well, but the third generation had made it in a very big way. However, two per cent of those arriving had been sent back either because they were criminals or because they had infectious diseases – or because they were anarchists! Thus Ellis Island would always be known as the "Island of Hope and Tears".

Back in Scotland Ian Lang's successor as Secretary of State for Scotland was Michael Forsyth, who was a passionate supporter of Margaret Thatcher and a person of great ability, with considerable gifts in communication. It was very enjoyable working for him since he might have six new ideas before breakfast each day, some of them extremely good and others just good. One of his most original ideas was to return to Scotland the Stone of Destiny, which, in the eyes of most Scots, had been pilfered and taken to London by King Edward I.

Years earlier it had been removed from Westminster Abbey without authority by the Scots Advocate Ian Hamilton, QC, then a student at Glasgow University, an adventure described by him in his book, *The Taking of The Stone of Destiny*. The Stone was returned to Scotland by the long arm of the law at the time, although very wisely the Law Officers decided not to prosecute. There was an apocryphal story that a Scotsman in a remote area had let the police know that he knew the identity of the person who had stolen the Stone. The Police arrived with their notebooks to be told the name of the culprit – King Edward I.

I later had to answer a debate on this subject in the House of Commons on 16 July 1996 raised by Bill Walker, a Conservative MP for North Tayside, who wished the Stone to go to Scone which had been the site for crowning of Scottish Kings. I told the MPs that "the Prime Minister's historic announcement to the House on 3 July 1996 could be regarded as a belated carrying out of the wishes of Edward III and of English obligations under the treaty of Northampton. In contemporary terms, it should be seen as a gesture of good will to the Scottish people and a confident assertion of their full and equal partnership in the Union."

I paid tribute to Michael Forsyth and John Major for having "the foresight and vision to see that the matter was of tremendous importance to the Scots. It will never be forgotten by the Scots that this gesture has been made when there has been a refusal to return it for 700 years."

After securing the support of the Prime Minister, Michael Forsyth and I visited Edinburgh Castle and announced to the press that the resting place of the Stone of Destiny would be alongside the Crown Jewels known as the Honours of Scotland. It was also agreed that it would be returned to Westminster Abbey in a vehicle, known as a Stone Mobile, for Coronation ceremonies, the Coronation Chair symbolising the Union of Scotland and England under the Crown of the United Kingdom.

Notwithstanding some such good news stories, the political climate was bringing stormy weather for the Tories. After nearly 18 years there were clear signs of the voters becoming restive and to add to our problems the issue of sleaze came to the fore. The Prime Minister's "Back to Basics" campaign was interpreted by some commentators as a return to Victorian values. However some MPs managed to walk backwards into the limelight, whether because of sexual peccadilloes or allegations of financial impropriety relating to a few MPs being paid for asking questions in the House. I remember on one occasion trying to lighten the atmosphere at an Election meeting when I was asked for my views on the issue of cash for questions. I replied that actually as a Minister, I was one of those who had to answer parliamentary questions not ask them.

"Black Wednesday" on 16 September 1992 came a few months after the Election and was a disastrous setback to the Conservative Government. Britain was forced to withdraw from the European Exchange Rate Mechanism and the devaluation of the pound which followed threw the Government's economic policy off course. It dealt the Conservatives' reputation for economic competence a devastating and lasting blow, and the Tories' rating in the opinion polls slumped and never recovered.

I watched that debate from the Gallery directly behind and above the Opposition Benches and remember John Smith saying that the President of the Board of Trade, Michael Heseltine, had advised Tory backbenchers to support the Prime Minister today. "He did not say tomorrow, next week or next month, merely today." This caused enormous merriment in the House of Commons as a humorous intervention devastatingly timed.

Later, before the vote I passed John Major sitting on the frontbench and caught his eye. He gave me a look as though everything was going wrong for him that day, and indeed it was. A tidal wave was coming in the direction of the Conservative Party, however much we might seek to do business as normal.

On 19 October 1994, I received a typically supportive letter from the Prime Minister concerning the anniversary dinner of the Edinburgh West Conservative Association to mark twenty years of service to my constituents. He wrote:

"I understand that on Friday you are celebrating your twentieth anniversary as Member of Parliament for Edinburgh West and I wanted to take this opportunity to send you my congratulations.

"You justly have a reputation for being a hard working and conscientious Member of Parliament who fights vigorously on behalf of his constituents. I know they would like to join me in sending you my very best wishes on this special occasion."

The evening was a light hearted one. In my speech I said:

"This constituency has the honour to be in the Front Line. And I pay tribute to those others whom I have not mentioned tonight, to the unknown heroes of Edinburgh West. I refer of course to those people in Edinburgh West who live in Liberal, Socialist or Nationalist households, but who secretly place a cross in the right place. They too will always have their part to play.

"In one respect the House of Commons never changes and that is when Members of Parliament drop off their perch. Somebody will come up to you and say 'Have you heard? Poor old Tomkins has gone.' 'Very sad! Very sad! Now do tell me, what was his majority?'

"Tonight I am grateful not only for the many friendships which as an MP I have been able to make, but also for the sure and steadfast support of the very many members of the Edinburgh West Conservative Association."

It was not long after this that the Leader of the Opposition, John Smith, died suddenly. He had rendered a great service to the Labour Party in making it more electable and I remembered all the discussions I had with him on our delegation to India and as an advocate during cases in the High Court. He was very entertaining company with a pawky sense of humour and full of joie de vivre when off duty.

I attended the funeral service near his home in South Edinburgh before his burial on the Isle of Iona where St Colomba had brought Christianity to Scotland. At the last moment before the service I was asked to squeeze up for a late comer. It was Dick Spring, the famous Irish Rugby International who was Deputy Prime Minister of Ireland. I remember in the service one of the hymns chosen started with the words "Courage brother do not stumble". Donald Dewar made an impassioned address which compared the loss of John Smith to that of Hugh Gaitskell, both Labour Leaders who had very sadly died before their time.

John Smith had been a friend of mine and friendship between members of different parties has to be on a strictly correct basis. On one occasion I had to start a debate on reform of legal aid provisions throughout Britain and he told me beforehand that it would be my first real test as a Minister. As it turned out it was a friendly debate with a routine knockabout for which I had the necessary answers. But his warning had been the action of a friend who had wished to let me know that I would have to be thoroughly prepared.

Some time later, at the reshuffle when Michael Forsyth assumed the office of Secretary of State, I was summoned to 10 Downing Street to see the Prime Minister. I had to inform his Private Secretary that I wished to be taken out of sequence as I had to answer a "Prayer" raising special objections to some Order in a House of Commons Committee. The Prime Minister said that he hoped he would have good news for me at the end of the day. After my Committee I telephoned 10 Downing Street to be told that I was now a Minister of State and would be responsible for Health and Home Affairs at the Scottish Office.

One of the first initiatives introduced was the launch of a "Diet Action Plan" which involved leaflets being sent to every home, giving householders advice on the decisions which, even on a low budget, would improve health and quality of life and in many cases help them live longer. It seemed to me unacceptable that on average the English lived two years longer than the Scots, and the suggested explanation was that diet was a main contributory element. Of course with improved diet and improved medical care people were in general living much longer throughout Britain, but it was clear that, with a high incidence of heart disease, stroke and cancer in certain parts of Scotland, a genuine attempt at increasing the prevention of ill health must be attempted.

Health issues attracted headline publicity, as did matters relating to young people, and I was proud to have helped put the

Children Act of 1995 on the Statute Books. The lead Minister at the time of its passage was Lord Fraser of Carmyllie, but as he was in the House of Lords I had to take the Bill through the House of Commons. The key principle established was that the interests of the child must be paramount and it represented an important legislative milestone for children in Scotland.

When I spoke on the subject I reminded the audience of the fate of two of the young Douglas heirs who were invited to Edinburgh Castle for dinner hundreds of years ago, but, just as a boar's head was brought in on a platter, they were taken out to the courtyard and stabbed to death. I said that ever since hearing that story I had been very much in favour of increased rights and protection for children.

However, violence against children is not restricted to any one century. I was on my feet in the House of Commons at the Despatch Box when the news came through, of the atrocity committed in Dunblane by Thomas Hamilton, who in an act of calculated wickedness had murdered many schoolchildren, before turning his gun on himself.

On 28 October 1996 I had to speak in place of the Secretary of State during The Queen's Speech and I made it clear that Lord Cullen's recommendations following the Inquiry into the Dunblane shootings would be implemented. These related to improving school security, the need to have vetting and supervision of adults working with children and young people and in particular accepting that a partial ban on handguns would lead to the destruction of 160,000 weapons. George Robertson, the Shadow Secretary of State for Scotland, asked me why the Government was against a free vote on handguns and I replied that a firm and decisive response was strongly expected by the public. Somehow by the time I sat down I felt that I had caught the sombre mood of the House of Commons on this most distressing subject.

Earlier that year, on 23 July, I had been made a Privy Councillor by the Queen. In the line-up I stood between Gordon Brown and Robin Cook, and since they had no Government car I gave them a lift from Buckingham Palace back to the House of Commons. I sensed that even then the Opposition was anticipating victory in the forthcoming Election. George Robertson had been heard to remark on another occasion that I had a very nice office but that I would not have it for long!

One of the Ministerial duties to be carried out was attendance at the official openings of new roads and bridges. The Queen Mother opened the Dornoch Bridge and by some extraordinary chance the overcast sky melted away into bright sunlight as she came forward to perform the opening. She was presented with a large gift by Morrisons, who had built the bridge, and the local schoolchildren asked me to give her the cassette of tunes which their pipers had recorded. The Queen Mother was just as delighted with that small present as she was with the larger one.

But it was the new Skye Bridge which caused most controversy. The people of Skye were quite happy to have a bridge but did not wish to pay for it. I had provided approaching £8 million from the Scottish Office block for the approach roads. This had incurred the grave displeasure of the Treasury who wanted these roads to be paid for from the bridge toll. I believed that on balance most people would prefer a bridge with tolls to no bridge and the Government went ahead with the proposal after a majority of the Highland Regional Council voted for it.

One of the struts of the controversial bridge was sited on the small island of Eilean Ban and one of my last acts as a minister had an important impact on its future. I received a letter from Will Travers of the Born Free Foundation telling me the island was about to be sold on the open market by the Scottish Office's Roads Department. Will Travers, who is the son of actors Virginia McKenna and Bill Travers, urged me to ensure that Eilean Ban could be preserved as a haven for wildlife. I was reminded that Gavin Maxwell, the conservationist and author had lived on the island in the late 1960s and planned a number of wildlife enterprises there before his death in 1969. Around the same time Virginia McKenna and Bill Travers had starred in the film version of Maxwell's book *Ring of Bright Water* about his life with Mij the otter.

As soon as I learnt that the Secretary of State had not made any decision about the island's future, with his approval, I stopped the sale with a few hours to go. I am delighted to say that the island went on to be run in cooperation with the Bright Water Visitors' Centre by the Eilean Ban Trust as a conservation site, and Virginia McKenna was heavily involved in creating the Gavin Maxwell Museum there.

When the Election finally came in 1997 the polls foretold that there would be a grim result for the Conservatives. Watching the votes being counted at Meadowbank Stadium in Edinburgh, I realised the extent of it when I was told that Michael Portillo had lost his seat and that no Tory was likely to be elected North of the Border. Having had the most marginal seat in Scotland for at least 14 years, I knew that there would be no way I could survive a landslide. Even so, after the result was announced and Donald Gorrie of the Liberal Democrats, whom I had twice beaten before, was declared the new MP, I saw a host of journalists coming towards me to see how I would react to the result. One of my friends suggested an appropriate movie soundbite from *The Terminator* so I went to speak to them and said, "In the determined words of Arnold Schwarzenegger 'I'll be back.'" This amused the press, who thereafter left me alone.

On returning home that night to North Berwick I told myself that the country had tired of the Tories and I had been powerless to buck the trend, in much the same way that King Canute could not prevent the ebb and flow of the tides. When I went for some sleep I remembered the words of Scarlett O'Hara in *Gone with the Wind* after Rhett Butler left her. Tomorrow would indeed be another day, my first as an ex-MP, outside the House of Commons after twenty-two and a half years, but I was determined to get back into politics in some capacity, when the opportunity arose.

CHAPTER 11

Out of office and out of power

Work as a Member of Parliament for almost 23 years and as a Minister at the Scottish Office for ten years had meant hard labour, long hours, and a great deal of commitment. Losing all that overnight is not easy for every ex-Minister to accept with immediate and absolute equanimity, even if it is a very well-recognised risk, which all democratically elected politicians face on a regular basis. A losing candidate is expected to take his or her defeat in good spirit and must be seen congratulating the victorious opponent in front of all the cameras.

In the case of ex-Ministers it comes as a bit of a shock to them when they jump into a car and find that it no longer moves off immediately. No more for them the well-organised official Diary, nor the protective umbrella, which appears miraculously from nowhere at a rain-soaked destination. The loss of their job and livelihood certainly provides the time for some sober reflection but in my case not too much! I was determined to get back to some form of elected activity as soon as possible.

Joining the ranks of the unemployed is a test of character, and some confront the challenge better than others. Sir Winston Churchill, who knew all too well what life was like in the political wilderness, put the dilemma quite well when he wrote that

204

politicians are "ready to take the rough with the smooth along the path of life they have chosen for themselves. Yet even politicians suffer some pangs."

For me an obvious solution might have been to return to the law. Technically I was a QC, but having not practised since the mid 1970s it seemed to me that I would need to undertake a refresher course for a year or two to get totally up to speed with all the new laws relating to Scotland, Britain, Europe and Human Rights, the practice of the law having become more specialised.

Two years seemed to me too long to wait, so I thought momentarily about applying for an English constituency, an option to which the Scottish press had been known to refer contemptuously, and in my view somewhat unfairly, as the "Chicken Run". However, I rejected this possibility almost immediately. There would be great competition, and in any case I was a Scot with deep roots in Scotland. Others who lost their seats reached different conclusions but I wanted to serve North of the Border. To have departed in search of an English seat would have been the wrong road for me to take.

What then was there to be done? Apart from forays into occasional journalism the question was in part answered for me by a telephone call from John Major at 9.45am on 7 June 1997. He said, and I took down his words, "I recall that you stood aside in the Government's interests and disclaimed an hereditary peerage." Then he told me that he was minded to put my name forward for the Resignation Honours List and wished to know whether I would accept a Life Peerage. I said if it was offered I would accept. He then explained that not all ex-Cabinet Ministers could be offered one but there were special considerations in my case.

While he could not offer me an absolute guarantee of a move to the House of Lords he said it was very likely to happen. He also told me how frustrated he was that Tony Blair was now adopting all his policies and that he was not getting credit for it. This conversation was followed up by a formal letter from him on 24 July. It said:

> "I should be grateful to know if you are agreeable for your name to be submitted to The Queen with a recommendation that Her Majesty may be graciously pleased to approve that the dignity of a Barony of the United Kingdom for Life be conferred upon you in my Resignation Honours List.
>
> "If the proposal is acceptable to you, I should be glad if you would reply by return of post to the Principal Private Secretary at No. 10 Downing Street."

Almost immediately afterwards on 28 July he wrote me a much longer letter, which indicated his thinking on the landslide Election result which had caused about half of the Conservative MPs to lose their seats, including all of the Conservative Members in Scotland – a similar fate befell the Liberal MPs in Scotland in 1923 after the partition of Ireland.

There could be no doubt that the 1997 Election had been a disastrous setback for the Conservatives. This became evident to me when I joined 160 defeated former MPs at Conservative Central Office to hear speeches from Ken Clarke and William Hague who were battling it out for the Conservative leadership. I remember William Hague saying he was tempted to insist on a duel with pistols at dawn, since Ken presented a larger target!

Despite all the good humour, I looked round the room and realised that most of those present would never make it back to Parliament.

In his generous letter to me John Major recognised the difficulties for former MPs forced to make a career change:

"I was so sad about the result in your constituency and the fact that you are no longer with us in the House of Commons. Politics is sometimes a cruel trade, and it is a very poor reward for all that you did that you were not safely and securely returned to the House. You deserved to be, and the House is poorer for your absence...

"It must be extremely difficult – as well as dispiriting – to return to private life and to have to establish a new routine. I hope things are settling down and that the future is beginning to take shape for you. You can be very proud of what was achieved during your period in Parliament, and your part in achieving it. It may not be fashionable to acknowledge those achievements at the moment but in time, it will be."

At the end of his letter he added "I'm so glad you will be resuming your Parliamentary career upstairs."

In August 1997 my Life Peerage was announced and I received letters of congratulations and best wishes from William Hague and Ted Heath, and on 28 October was formally introduced to the House by my sponsors Lord Renton of Huntingdon and Lord Crathorne. David Renton had been a close friend of Margaret Thatcher and John Major. He had introduced her to Lincoln's Inn and John Major succeeded him as MP for Huntingdon, which had once been the constituency of Oliver Cromwell. He had also been the closest friend of my late uncle Geordie Selkirk. Lord Crathorne was a very active Parliamentarian who had served for many years as Secretary of the All Party Heritage Group on behalf of the members of both Houses of Parliament.

Two other Scots were introduced as Life Peers at the same time, namely the former Secretary of State for Scotland, Ian Lang, who would sit as Lord Lang of Monkton, and Jimmy Gordon, the former managing director of Radio Clyde, who would sit as Lord Gordon of Strathblane. The ceremony involved putting on the red gown of a Baron covered with ermine, doffing of caps (which the Labour Government would soon abolish as being outmoded) and the swearing of the Oath of Allegiance at the Despatch Box. After being sworn in, flanked by their sponsors, the new Life Peer leaves the Chamber, in my case duly impressed by the solemn splendour of the occasion.

Before any possible move to the Lords I had already been thinking about the possibility of standing for the Scottish Parliament, since I believed that it would soon come into existence. I increasingly became convinced that the Conservative party in spite of its drubbing at the General Election, and its previous opposition to devolution, must play a part in the future of Scotland's public life. Therefore when I wrote to John Major hinting that I was interested in being elected to the Scottish Parliament my letter went as follows:

"The White Paper on Scottish Devolution came out yesterday and I was reassured to see Peers would be allowed to participate in a Scottish Parliament if elected. In view of the General Election result it looks likely a Scottish Parliament will be a reality. It is a process which Labour will start but I do believe they will not be in a position to finish it.

"I am very grateful to you for putting my name forward and I look forward to keeping in touch in the years to come."

It was not many months later that the Referendum on whether or not a Scottish Parliament should be created was held. An overwhelming majority voted in favour of a devolved Parliament, which was accepted as the settled will of the Scottish people. The Tories had officially campaigned against Labour's devolution plans but it was clear even then that enough Scots would vote Conservative at the first Holyrood election to produce a sizeable group of MSPs in the Scottish Parliament, under the additional member system of proportional representation. It would therefore have been very foolish for the Conservatives not to have participated in the future Parliament in order to make a difference. I was sure that I wanted to be one of them.

As soon as the opportunity arose, I applied to fight Edinburgh West, my former constituency, with whose activists I had kept in close touch. I soon discovered that there was going to be intense competition to get into the new Parliament, perhaps even greater than that for getting into the House of Commons.

Before long I was one of a shortlist of two, to be considered for Edinburgh West, along with Jacqui Low, who had been a Special Adviser to Michael Forsyth. She spoke well, but over the years I had built up a bedrock of support in the area which was responsible for my selection that night.

It would be very hard to win back Edinburgh West from the Liberal Democrats and it was certainly not a foregone conclusion that I would get into the Parliament on the top up list. The Leader of the Conservative candidates, David McLetchie, would be first on the List in the Regional Constituency of Lothians and would not need to go through the selection. To be certain of making it to the Parliament I had to be in second place. There was a school of thought that after a landslide Election the Party should concentrate exclusively on new talent and say goodbye to the old guard. Only the constituency Chairmen, the President of the Party and the Chairman of the Party could vote. The person who had fewest votes would win. In other words if a Chairman wished to have a candidate he would put 1 opposite his or her name and rank the other candidates 1 to 5. This was a system under which an enemy could be more powerful than a friend and tactical voting would not be unknown.

I spoke as strongly as I could and was told that after I had left the room to await my fate, hoping that my appeal to them that "we have within our ranks a combination of youth and enthusiasm, wisdom and experience and there is a place for them all," had not fallen on deaf ears.

The Director of the Party, Raymond Robertson, an old friend and former Scottish Office Minister in the House of Commons, telephoned me to say that I had won as top of the List after David McLetchie by the closest of margins possible. But as Sir Winston Churchill always used to say "one vote is enough". After all, some of us were used to small majorities! In the next Election, four years down the road, I would press for all members of the Party in the Region to have a vote, in deciding the position of candidates on the List.

In the run up to the Elections the Conservative Party sought to connect with the people, which was no easy matter after a landslide Election with an adverse result. It was quite clear that one of the main causes of the landslide had been the fact that the

Conservative Government's economic policies had been blown off course some years before on "Black Wednesday". To reconnect with the electors a series of consultation meetings were arranged at which the candidates would listen to and learn from local people.

During the election campaign a curious episode remains seared into my memory. In Edinburgh's Davidsons Mains a man came up to me and said "You saved my life!" I was taken aback and asked how that could be. He replied that he had had a heart attack in a church and his heart had stopped. However the men and women of the Scottish Ambulance Service appeared with one of the brand new defibrillators which had been authorised by myself as the then Minister of Health out of the end of year savings. As a result his heart was started again and he lived. I got the distinct impression that he believed that as the Minister I had shared in the responsibility for his recovery and that what I had done might even be worth a vote!

Actually it was the ambulance men and women who saved his life and while it was correct that I had allocated more funds for defibrillators, I was only a small part of a big team and a healthy sense of humility was always desirable. Even so it was refreshing to know that the system was working, and I was glad to give him my very best wishes.

As I had anticipated, I failed to recapture the Edinburgh West constituency on a first past the post basis. There was to be nail biting drama for some over the counting of the List votes. With Council elections, constituency elections and elections for the List, the complexities that arose were great and at about 4am. those doing the counting at Meadowbank Stadium made it clear that they had had enough. Accordingly those trying to be elected as List Members for the Lothians were asked to return the next afternoon, which we did.

I found myself in the company of Lord Steel of Aikwood, the former Leader of the Liberal Party, and Robin Harper, the Green candidate, a most friendly and charming man with whom I had shared platforms in the Election campaign. It became clear that we were likely to be the last three to be elected on the top-up lists in Scotland. I came in third last, David Steel second last and then Robin Harper, who became the first member of the Green Party to become a Parliamentarian in Britain. What a relief for us all!

Then a row followed months later. It was discovered that by some mysterious mix-up, 2000 votes in Edinburgh West had not been counted, and the Secretary of State for Scotland was not minded to have them included, unless one of us raised a legal action at enormous cost. However, the Chief Returning Officer confirmed that whichever way the votes were counted we were all in the Parliament, although if they had been counted it was possible that Robin Harper might have been elected before David Steel. None of us were prepared to contemplate incurring the legal costs involved in seeking a count – so long as we were all well and truly in the Parliament that was all that mattered.

For me, becoming an elected Member of the first Scottish Parliament for 300 years was very exciting. It also felt a little like returning home. While the commercial and business sector of Edinburgh had congregated around George Street much of Edinburgh life revolved around the Royal Mile, where I had lived as an Advocate in Lady Stairs Close, next to the Museum dedicated to Scotland's Great Writers Robert Burns, Sir Walter Scott and Robert Louis Stevenson.

The new Scottish Parliament was to meet initially in the Church of Scotland's Assembly Hall at the top of the Royal Mile until the new permanent building was completed on the site opposite Holyrood Palace. As the Opening of the Parliament approached it brought back many memories of work as an advocate and as an interim Procurator Fiscal in the Scottish Courts across the road, and of acting as the Cameronian Officer in charge of the Edinburgh Castle Guard. I particularly remembered the excitement of calling out the Guard in the middle of the night when a window was left suspiciously open. I discovered that calling out the Guard meant that everybody came running, not just the soldiers but the police as well, and Special Branch Officers and Her Majesty's Civil Service. Everyone told me that I had done entirely the right thing, but I had the impression that it would be best not to call out the Castle Guard too often. I was also reminded of acting as an Army ADC to the Lord High Commissioner Lord Clydesmuir and escorting his guests from Holyrood Palace to the General Assembly of the Church of Scotland.

As all these old memories came flooding back, I was determined to play a part in the new Parliament, in the best interests of those whom we were elected to serve. Also I would be less than human if I did not admit that after two years in the political wilderness it was wonderful to have a Parliamentary salary again. Even so I was under no illusions that a great deal of hard work lay ahead, as I had been appointed the Business Manager and Chief Whip of the Scottish Conservative Group of 18 MSPs.

The Opening of the Parliament was a spectacular affair. Events got underway at 8.30am on Thursday 1 July at Edinburgh Castle where the Crown of Scotland was placed in the safe keeping of my brother Angus, the present Duke of Hamilton, who was to carry it ahead of the Queen into the new Parliament. The handing over was witnessed by the Lord Lyon, the Chief Executive of Historic Scotland and the Governor of the Castle.

This was the first time that the more than 500-year-old Scottish Crown had been feted in this way as part of a grand ceremony, since the procession of the Honours of Scotland – the Scottish Crown Jewels – during the year of the Queen's coronation in 1953.

In due course my brother would lay the Crown on the table in front of the Parliament's Presiding Officer where it remained throughout the opening ceremony. It rested beside the new silver mace which was presented by the Queen as her personal gift to the Parliament. The mace had inscribed on it the simple but powerful words to guide our deliberations "Justice, Integrity, Wisdom, Compassion."

Earlier the MSPs had gathered in the Advocates Great Hall, where as a young lawyer I used to wait to be instructed by solicitors to represent their clients in court, and at the appointed time we took part in a procession to the Assembly Hall for the official opening. I found myself walking between the Lord Advocate Andrew Hardie and Margaret Ewing, and thinking that as her husband Fergus and her mother-in-law Winnie were also elected SNP Members this must be a record for one family. Once we were all seated in the Hall, I looked up at the gallery where I could see my wife Susie sitting in front of Scotland's famous film star, Sean Connery. He was wearing a kilt and it almost looked as though she was sitting between his knees.

The Presiding Officer, Sir David Steel, warmly welcomed the Queen and as he did so it occurred to me that this was probably the first time that a British monarch had set foot on the floor of a parliament within Britain since King Charles I entered the House of Commons with soldiers to arrest five members. The Speaker, William Lenthall, had bravely told him then that he had no eyes to see nor tongue to speak except as the House directed him.

I particularly recall the Queen's description of Scotland as having a society "in which the qualities of cooperation, learning, entrepreneurial skill and national pride run deep." She went on "I have trust in the good judgement of the Scottish people. I have faith in your commitment to their service and I am confident in the future of Scotland."

Then the First Minister, Donald Dewar, after thanking the Queen for the gift of the Mace, made what I thought was the best speech of his life. He caught the significance of the historic occasion and the sense of Scottishness which pervaded it, telling us all: "This is about more than our politics and our laws. This is about who we are, how we carry ourselves. There is a new voice in the land, the voice of a democratic Parliament. A voice to shape Scotland as surely as, the echoes from our past"

He spoke of the different strands in Scotland's Story, linking the sounds of the Clydeside shipbuilders with those of the country people engaging in "the speak of the Mearns", throwing into the mix the influential philosophical discussions of the Scottish Enlightenment and finally the far-off battle cries from the days of Bruce and Wallace. All this along with the skirl of the Pipes evoked a great pride in the nation's history.

At about midday the Queen, the First Minister and the Presiding Officer went to a platform on the Mound while we, the MSPs, and the guests stood nearby. Then all eyes turned up to the sky. Concorde and the Red Arrows flew past in perfect formation leaving the familiar coloured vapour trails high above the city.

What I didn't know that day was that this famous aircraft's days were numbered and that within four years I would start a campaign to bring a Concorde to Scotland as an outstanding visitor attraction.

CHAPTER 12

On the trail of two heroes – Mussert's flag and Roosevelt's home

Members of Parliament who suddenly tell the media that they want to "spend more time with my family" often do so in advance of being sacked from their Government jobs or before some colourful misdemeanour hits the headlines in the Sunday papers. However such political euphemisms notwithstanding, many elected representatives do genuinely feel guilty about being away from home so much and often working unsocial hours.

My response over the years has been to try to seize what opportunities have been available to go on exciting and hopefully educational holidays with Susie and our four sons. I hope they enjoyed them as much as I did. They certainly offered me the chance to think about some wider issues away from the Westminster "bubble" and the complex and detailed work of taking a bill through Parliament. A few examples leap to mind.

On our first family holiday in the United States, while staying with friends north of New York, I remember how enthralled we all were to see our host David Rockefeller's helicopter landing on the lawn at 7am to pick him up and take him in to work in Manhattan, thinking as we watched that this was all rather different from boarding a crowded tube train in London or battling through the rush hour traffic in Edinburgh.

On a second visit to Washington we saw the great portrait by Peter Paul Rubens of "Daniel in the Lion's Den" in the National Gallery there – a picture which had once hung in our family's former home of Hamilton Palace in Lanarkshire before the building was demolished.

Staying in Montana a few days later we went riding on the slopes leading up to the mountains and one evening at our friend Lee Freeman's house, we were excited to meet the actor Peter Fonda, son of Henry and brother of Jane. He spoke at length about the cult film he made in the 1960s, *Easy Rider*, and I asked him why the line "We blew it" had been in the script without any obvious explanation. He replied that he intended that very question be asked, so that people would want to see the film again. This was exactly what I had done!

On a later occasion Susie and I chose Iceland as a potentially exciting destination for a family trip. The land of hot springs, volcanoes, glaciers, waterfalls, geysers and earthquakes, and one of the oldest democracies in the world was also the place in which the American astronauts had practised before their first landing on the moon.

We took off from Glasgow Airport on 3 August 2000 and on arriving in Iceland we made our way to Guesthouse Anna in the capital, Reykjavik, next to an aerodrome constructed by British Servicemen in the Second World War to help prevent the country being invaded by the Nazis. Early the next morning, my three sons, Charles, Jamie and Harry, who had travelled with us, went on a sea whale watch, Iceland having stopped all hunting of whales eleven years before

I still have vivid memories of Myvatn, an extremely attractive area in the north of Iceland, with a beautiful undulating plain of hay fields, stretching out into the distance around the local river Laxa. We went fishing with Oli Olafur, the chief cook of Hotel Selid, and under his guidance we returned home with two handsome trout caught by Harry which made for an excellent fish supper.

On another occasion we spent the night not far from the largest glacier in Europe at Vatnojokull. As the sun sunk in the horizon it seemed as if the glacier was on fire, set alight by the rays of the sun, the flames so bright that the human eye could only glance at them for the briefest of moments.

Later we found ourselves on top of Vatnojokull, as passengers in a super jeep close to many crevasses and a huge drop of at least a kilometre on the other side of the mountain next to the glacier.

I couldn't help thinking that, if one of us had fallen down one of the crevasses, a perfectly formed body might have emerged at the foot of the glacier in some thousands of years' time. The super jeep with its huge tyres drove across this hazardous ice and snow in convoy with two other vehicles and it was a comfort to know that if any of us had got into difficulties the others would have been on hand to help. Once away from the crevasses we were allowed to try out the snowmobiles, which could get up to a considerable speed.

We came down from the glacier and before long saw icebergs floating in the Jokulsa Lagoon which we decided to visit the next day. Early that morning we could see that the icebergs consisted of huge chunks of floating ice which had broken away from the glacier. We were offered a trip around the lagoon on board a large wheeled boat. These were used by the United States Army in the

Vietnam War for various purposes, including bridging rivers by lining the boats up side by side.

As the engine was noisily charged up, we were told that in the extreme cold of the glacial waters, we would only survive for three to four minutes if we fell in. When the vehicles entered the water the driver piloting the boat told us that nine tenths of the icebergs were under the water and I noticed he gave them a very wide berth. Some of them looked beautiful with their blue colouring and we were told that the ice was probably 1,000 years old. It was the only time in Iceland that we felt really cold and having such a close encounter with these icy monsters gave me some idea of the fear that must have gripped the passengers and crew of the liner *Titanic* before their tragic collision.

The following day we were ready to travel east and on the way visited a small church where what appeared to have been an extraordinarily effective sermon had been delivered more than 200 years before. A massive eruption of molten lava had taken place at Sida in 1783 and the fiery torrent had swept on towards the river Skafta. As the eruption reached its peak and the lava thundered on, the priest in the nearby town of Kirkjubaejarklaustur had prayed urgently for divine deliverance, promising the local population would repent their sinful ways. Lo and behold, the lava stopped just short of the town. "The Sermon of Fire" it seemed, had been answered.

A sign warned us against driving towards Mount Hekla and the sense of natural dangers all around, which I had experienced since we arrived in Iceland, was sharpened by the knowledge that not very far away was a volcano which had erupted many times over the centuries. The possibility that it would explode into life again served as a lure to some people but all were strongly advised by the authorities not to get too close. I certainly did not feel inclined to put my family's safety at risk. The very name Hekla seemed to have a menacing ring to it.

Later at Pingvellir National Park, at the gorge which was the site of the old Icelandic Parliament, established as long ago as AD 930, we saw a remarkable sight. It was a procession of about 300 young people, all carrying national flags including the flag of Iceland and the Union Jack. They were marching from the gorge towards the lake at the end of a dignified and solemn ceremony. I went down and discovered that what we had stumbled on was an international meeting of Boy Scouts who had staged this occasion at the site of one of Europe's oldest parliaments.

Another trip at holiday time with Susie and three of our sons took us to the Czech Republic, our son Charles by this time being hard at work as a geologist in the Central African Republic. We found the capital city Prague was full of interest, with splendid museums, galleries and excellent concerts. We also had another reason for wishing to go.

I wanted my sons to know more about the evils of Nazism and the Holocaust. They already knew the story of Anne Frank, one of the six million victims of the Nazis, and had visited her home in Amsterdam. I also wanted them to learn what happened when two Czech warrant officers fought back on behalf of their country and were eventually recognised publicly as national heroes. There was their link with the Scottish Highlands to add unexpected local connections to the story.

With the support of the free Czech Government and the British Special Operations Executive, they were parachuted by the RAF into Czechoslovakia on a mission to eliminate SS Obergruppenfuhrer Reinhard Heydrich, Himmler's Deputy in command of the SS, Head of the SD, the SS Security Service and Reich Protector of Bohemia and Moravia – the man regarded as the architect of the Holocaust.

I explained to Andrew, Jamie and Harry that the people who planned the mission knew that the SS were likely to exact some revenge against innocent civilians if Heydrich was killed but what happened was far worse than they expected and thousands died in an orgy of retaliation. The villages of Lidice and Lezaky were destroyed and most of those who lived there were murdered. In these circumstances neither the Free Czech Government nor the British claimed responsibility for the death of Heydrich.

We visited the National Memorial at what had been the village of Lidice, where the few women who had survived were sent to concentration camps and some of their traumatised children were taken by the German soldiers to be adopted by SS families. Our sons were shocked and taken aback at the enormity of the crime.

We also went on to see the famous ancient synagogues of Prague with more rooms whose walls were covered by a seemingly endless list of the names of victims of the Holocaust. We were told that Hitler had wanted to preserve the synagogues as museums of an extinct race.

The next day at the National Memorial in the Orthodox Cathedral, before our eyes there unfolded the story of one of history's often forgotten monsters and the courage of the two young men Josef Gabcik and Jan Kubis, who finally proved to be his downfall.

So how had Heydrich met his end? What actually took place was straightforward. Josef Gabcik and Jan Kubis were chosen for their mission to take out Heydrich, because they were warrant officers of exceptional courage, ability and commitment. They were parachuted into Czechoslovakia by Flight Lieutenant Ron Hockey and along with other members of the Czech Resistance hatched their plan.

They knew that Heydrich's overconfidence was such that he did not believe it was necessary to travel with armed guards when driving in a convoy. So they waited for him at a sharp bend in the road where his driver would have to slow down. The bend is still there and was examined closely by my sons.

On 27 May 1942 at 10.30am when Heydrich's car reduced its speed, Josef Gabcik tried to shoot him with his British Sten Gun but it jammed. Heydrich told his driver to halt the car and stood up drawing the gun from his holster to open fire at Gabcik. It was then that Jan Kubis threw the British-made bomb which exploded.

Heydrich fell over, then fired and missed. Gabcik and Kubis made off in different directions. They thought that they had failed in their mission, but they had done better than they knew. The horsehair from the seat of his car had been blown into his spleen and Heydrich died from blood poisoning.

Notwithstanding the countless murders committed in revenge, and a massacre of the innocents, the dreaded Gestapo could not discover the whereabouts of Gabcik and Kubis. It would be some time before any important clues would be forthcoming. Assistance would be given to them by a Czech Sergeant, Karel Curda. He had been a parachutist and chose to assume the mantle of a traitor, for which he would be executed after the War. He did not know where Gabcik and Kubis were, but he did know that parachutists had sheltered at the home of the Moravec family. He told the Gestapo and when the Gestapo arrived Mrs Moravec went to the washroom, where she took cyanide so that she would not have to answer any questions.

The Gestapo seized her son Ata, gave him alcohol and when he had been pressed to the limits of human endurance, he was shown his mother's head in the water of a tank for fish. He did not know where the parachutists were but horrified and unnerved at the treatment given to his mother's body, he gave the Gestapo the absolutely vital clue. His mother had told him that if he was ever in trouble he was to go to a certain priest of a certain church. Although he did not know it, sheltering inside the building were Josef Gabcik and Jan Kubis and their friends, some six other armed parachutists.

Early in the morning of 18 June 1942 around 800 soldiers of the Third Reich including a Battalion of SS Guards and many from the Waffen SS surrounded the Orthodox Cathedral in Prague. Within minutes a terrific firefight ensued with the parachutists outnumbered by 100 to one. Torrents of fire were poured into the cathedral and when some of the parachutists took refuge in the underground crypt the Germans were unable to storm it. When asked to surrender they shouted "Never." The SS then resorted to flooding the area with water, and after strong resistance, rather than drown, the remaining parachutists used their last bullets on themselves.

Only one terribly wounded man remained alive, namely Jan Kubis. By a great mercy he was dead by the time he reached hospital, sparing him the dreadful tortures and attentions which the SS would have given him if he had lived a few hours longer.

In the meantime the Bishop, the priests and other church members were taken away to be shot, along with thousands of others and the Orthodox Church was closed down. The Czech people suffered most severely in the wake of what came to be known as the Heydrich Terror.

Sir Winston Churchill's history *The Second World War* makes no mention of Heydrich or his demise. I have always believed this was because the British and Free Czech Governments did not wish to talk frankly about the operation which might not have gone ahead at all if the planners had known how many hundreds of innocent people would perish as a result.

Hitler was under no illusions about the impact of Heydrich's death. In spite of all the grief and misery inflicted and the innocent blood spilt on his orders, he apparently regarded the taking out of such a top Nazi as being comparable to a military defeat.

In some ways it was more than a defeat. Not only had a possible successor to Hitler been eliminated from the "Thousand Year Reich" but Heydrich's death was a signal that the people of Czechoslovakia had rejected Nazi domination and would throw off that yoke of bondage whenever it might lie within their power.

I asked my sons what they thought of Heydrich and they told me he had been a man of enormous ability who had turned his skills to thoroughly evil purposes which made him one of the most dangerous men who ever lived. And what was their view of Josef Gabcik and Jan Kubis? This was easy for my son Jamie to answer. In his opinion the two were "heroes and patriots", and his brothers shared that view.

On a more philosophical level the whole episode raises the question of whether it was all worth it. Could the slaying of Heydrich be justified in view of the risk it posed to so many innocent lives? It was a question which was not answered at all by the Allies at the time.

The nearest justification I could find was at the Cathedral, where I bought a booklet giving information about "A National Memorial to the Heroes of the Heydrich Terror, A Place of

Reconciliation." In 1992, in this document were recorded the words of Czech President Vaclav Havel to the effect that freedom was something "which has to be paid for". In his judgement the elimination of Heydrich "was one of the most significant acts of resistance on a pan-European scale" and substantially helped to make the Czech people feel that at the end of the war they had emerged victorious. If they were now "truly and fully free," they owed their freedom to those two men and to the victims whose lives were sacrificed.

For me the last words on the subject were inscribed in the book of tributes in the crypt of the Cathedral. Opposite the Star of David, the religious symbol of the people whom Heydrich had sought to murder and destroy, I read the words written in ink "This is hallowed ground where men died in the cause of freedom justice and humanity."

The SOE participated in many campaigns and the killing of Heydrich was their second most important individual mission. The most significant of all had been the support given to brave Norwegians who performed brilliant acts of sabotage in order to destroy heavy water in Norway so making it impossible for Hitler and his scientists to obtain the atomic bomb.

When I go to stay with my cousins at Traigh House in the Western Highlands near Arisaig House, both of which were used by the SOE in the Second World War, I think of Gabcik and Kubis training nearby, not far from the sands of Morar and its Northern Lights immortalised in the film *Local Hero*. I like to believe that in the incomparable beauty of the Highlands, during their training they did have some moments of peacefulness, before they set off on that final mission from which they must have known they had little chance of returning.

I wanted my sons to understand this traumatic story against a wider backdrop and that they should also be aware of how their maternal grandfather had a series of encounters with the SS, in none of which he came off second best.

Their great grandfather, the author John Buchan, the first Lord Tweedsmuir, who had only a few months to live, had signed Canada's declaration of war in his capacity as Governor General of Canada on behalf of King George VI. It was therefore natural for his son John to join the Canadian army. During the invasion of Sicily when his commanding officer was killed John, by now the second Lord Tweedsmuir, became Canada's youngest Lieutenant Colonel, in command of the Prince Edward and Hastings Battalion, nicknamed the Hasty Ps! He was immediately given orders to attack the Hermann Goering Division of SS, the Fifteenth Panzer Grenadiers as well as other units down the road. Knowing that they had their artillery trained on the approach route, he saw that a new strategy was required. He reckoned that if he carried out his orders as given there would be at least 90 per cent casualties, so he turned over in his mind whether there could be a better way to win. Then inspiration came to him. He remembered the advice given to him as a small boy by his uncle Walter who had held up his walking stick at a 45 degree angle and told him he could climb any mountain at that angle. As he raised his rifle in the Sicilian sun, John could see the side of the mountain above Assoro was no steeper than that.

The question occurred to him "Why not climb the mountain, take the enemy completely by surprise and from the commanding heights fire down upon them?"

A good account of the ensuing battle is given by a young officer, Farley Mowat, who would become a famous Canadian author and conservationist after the war. In his book *And No Birds Sang*, there is a vivid description of Lord Tweedsmuir as a young man in search of adventure. "Barely thirty years of age, soft-spoken, kindly, with a slight tendency to stutter, he was a tall, fair-haired romantic out of another age…" The afternoon before the attack Tweedsmuir went on a reconnaissance mission, and "looked up at the towering colossus of Assoro with the visionary eye of a Lawrence of Arabia, and saw that the only way to accomplish the impossible was to attempt the impossible."

That night the whole battalion climbed the mountain, under cover of darkness, and at first light took the enemy soldiers by surprise and dislodged them from their position. The enemy troops responded by firing light anti-aircraft guns straight at them, but it was too late. The top of the mountain had come alive with Canadian soldiers who were in no mood to shoot second. Within 20 minutes, John and his 500 strong Battalion, had radioed back the exact sites of the German artillery, which were destroyed one by one by Allied fire. Later on the enemy counter-attacked and came into contact with Dog Company of the Prince Edward and Hastings Regiment who were nearing the end of their ammunition. Fortunately they had just enough to repulse the attack. By the end of the battle Assoro was no longer under soldiers supporting the swastika but the young men from the farms and towns of Ontario, whose national emblem was the maple leaf. The Canadians had prevailed.

Farley Mowat, in *And No Birds Sang* and *The Regiment*, comes to the conclusion that John Tweedsmuir's plan to climb the steep mountain was "so daring that failure would have meant not only the end of his career, but probably the end of the Regiment." Oddly neither he nor his battalion received much in the way of recognition for success in this battle. He was, however, awarded the Order of Orange-Nassau with swords for actions at the end of the war.

John and the Canadians in Holland not only had to feed the Dutch population but John received orders to find, arrest and intern the whole of the Dutch SS and its Head Anton Mussert, who was also leader of the Dutch Nazi Party. John went to Mussert's home which was locked up and to gain entry the soldiers blew in the door with a mortar. Mussert was arrested by Canadian soldiers elsewhere, but as John searched the house he found Mussert's flag. Knowing that the Romans took the standards of their defeated enemies, he followed suit and confiscated the flag. It was eventually given to my wife Susie. My sons were interested in this artefact of war, because it had been seized by their grandfather and symbolised to them the end of an evil regime. However, because of what it represented, none of us were keen on it being kept in our home. It is now with the National Museum of Scotland as evidence of the defeat of the Dutch SS.

My father-in-law hardly ever talked about the considerable task which he had been given so I wrote to him asking if he would give me a personal account in writing and his reply was one of the most remarkable responses I have ever received.

He wrote to me on 7 September 1985:

"You asked me if I would write a note as to how the personal banner of that unholy scoundrel the Commander of the Dutch SS came to be in my possession. When the Germans surrendered in Holland in 1945, I was in charge of a great many of the activities of bringing the country back to normal, which included rounding up all kinds of traitors. I collected the Dutch SS and put them behind barbed wire at Harskamp. Their atrocities had been so frightful that every loyal Dutch hand was against them. And it must be one of the few cases in history where prisoners begged their captors to strengthen the defence of the place where they were enclosed, to prevent their fellow countrymen from breaking in and killing them.

Of all the traitor movements in the war, I think the Dutch SS was one of the worst, and the contrast was so vivid with the gallantry and patriotism of the loyal Dutch.

One thing that made our work very much easier was that each of the SS had his blood group tattooed under his arm pit. Many of them had removed the tattooing, leaving a scar, which was equally valid proof of their membership."

It was of further interest to my sons that Mussert's name was mentioned in the diaries of Anne Frank where the three words she used to describe him were "that fat pig". When she was arrested there is every reason to suppose that the SS driver was one of Mussert's men and the nature of some of their atrocious activities during the Holocaust were laid bare in her diaries. Mussert would not survive Anne Frank for very long. He was put on trial for treason and sentenced to death. His appeal to Queen Wilhelmina of Holland for clemency was refused and he was executed on 7 May 1946. Mussert's name will merely be a footnote in modern Dutch history as a murderous bigot, bully and braggart. However Anne Frank, in stark contrast, will be remembered down the years not just as a victim but, because of her idealism, her moral courage and her vision of the better world which would certainly come. Through her literary gifts her poignant story imparts to all humanity a very personal picture of what happened to six million others in the Holocaust.

Certainly our holidays were intended to be educational and memorable, but not all of our trips dealt with such grim realities. From time to time invitations come to an elected representative for him or her alone. One such arrived for me as an MSP in September 2000. I was asked to open the British Fair at Montclair, New Jersey, in the US. At the same time Susie was bound for Saint Petersburg in Russia with the Patrons of the National Galleries of Scotland so I had no qualms about going.

At the Fair I was greeted by my friend Dr Eugene Pugatch and by Mayor Robert Russo. The range of Scottish-American goods on sale was astonishing and included every kind of tartan and kilt brooches and plaids. It brought home to me the sheer numbers of Americans who are of Scottish descent and the opening was a cheerful and colourful occasion.

Afterwards Gene Pugatch drove me up the Hudson River to Hyde Park, the home of one of America's greatest Presidents, Franklin Roosevelt. The moment we entered the house, which contained a museum, I felt we were surrounded by a very friendly welcoming atmosphere. On the President's desk were some fluffy toys which had been given to him, and by complete contrast, in one of the first rooms we saw photographs showing the expressions of despair on the faces of all who found it impossible to get jobs during the Great Depression of the 1930s. Through the New Deal programme President Roosevelt had given these people hope.

As we walked around I came across a framed letter hung on the wall dated 26 June 1940. It was from King George VI and it was asking for help. In fact it was a request to the President for naval destroyers. On reading it I felt that one sentence could only have been written by Winston Churchill or as a result of his influence. It ran as follows "The need is becoming greater every day if we are to carry on our solitary fight for freedom to a successful conclusion." Under the Lend Lease Agreement 50 destroyers were sent, although the US was still officially neutral.

Most important of all I saw also the letter sent to the President by Albert Einstein warning him that the Germans were duplicating American nuclear research to create an incredibly powerful bomb which if exploded could destroy a whole port and some of its adjacent areas. Einstein asked for the setting up of experimental work through Government initiative. The letter was dated 3 August 1939, but it was not sent until after the outbreak of war.

President Roosevelt acted on this letter by setting up the Manhattan Project, which led in turn to the construction of the atomic bomb. It struck me as ironic that at a time when Hitler was engaged in murdering those of Jewish origin in secret throughout German-occupied Europe, one of the most eminent scientists of all time, a German of Jewish origin, was providing the President of the US with the key to ending the Second World War.

Gene Pugatch and I had been joined by Matt Nimetz, another friend from Oxford University. Gene was the Head of the Medical Faculty at Montclair Hospital and Matt had been a special adviser at the White House under President Johnson and became honorary US ambassador to Macedonia. It occurred to me that what we shared in common was our belief in democracy, justice, fair play, and respect for human dignity, all convictions which helped sustain the special relationship between Britain and the United States. President Roosevelt had added to that list with his four famous freedoms, freedom of expression, freedom of worship, freedom from want and freedom from fear.

His close friend Sir Winston Churchill, who outlived FDR by many years, had this final guidance to give to his country in his last speech to the House of Commons on 1 March 1955. "We must also never allow, above all, I hold, the growing sense of unity and brotherhood between the United Kingdom and the United States, and throughout the English-speaking world, to be injured or retarded. Its maintenance, its stimulation and its fortifying is one of the first duties of every person who wishes to see peace in the world and wishes to see the survival of this country." As it turned out one day there would be an opportunity for me to repeat these splendid words in the Scottish Parliament.

CHAPTER 13

A new MSP and a new Parliament

It has been instructive and extremely interesting to have been a member of three different legislatures, each with a vital role to play in the governance of Great Britain. After leaving the House of Commons my first reaction on becoming a member of the House of Lords was to say, "My God, they are all so old!" In the Scottish Parliament the impression was entirely different and I found myself thinking, "My God, they are all so young!"

Although the Conservatives had campaigned against the creation of a devolved Parliament, as soon as 74 per cent of the Scottish Electorate voted in favour in the referendum in 1998, I accepted the result as the will of a very substantial majority of the people. It was my firm conviction that since the electorate had made a final decision, the Conservative Party should enter the democratic process with a view to making the new body work in the best interests of Scotland and the United Kingdom as a whole.

All three Parliamentary Chambers have their own individual characteristics. The House of Commons provides a unique forum for major political debates, crucial votes and the noisy exchanges of Prime Minister's Questions. The House of Lords can exercise influence through the delay of contentious legislation for a limited period of time and many of the compelling arguments put forward there are included in the advice offered by civil servants to their Ministers. It offers a splendid ornate setting for high quality and often less partisan debate despite the frequently quoted jibe that its existence is "proof of life after death". The new Scottish Parliament in contrast is in many ways a young person's Parliament, full of earnest endeavour and the will to produce results quickly.

The major differences in structure between the fledgling body in Edinburgh and the House of Commons were obvious immediately. Most importantly the Regional List system, using a form of proportional representation, meant that no one party would ever be likely to have an overall majority, thereby making the prospect of a coalition government or a minority administration in Edinburgh inevitable. This meant that the largest party to be elected had to have regard to the views not just of any potential partner in the coalition but also of other parties. Initially Labour formed a coalition with the Liberal Democrats and more recently the SNP, as a minority administration, has had to win support for its policies from other groups.

The speed of delivery is very much quicker in the Scottish Parliament. Six votes in the House of Commons can take 90 minutes to record, while in the Scottish Parliament they are over within seconds with electronic voting. When I was an MSP, failing to press the correct button when required was regarded as one of the deadly sins. In addition members' speeches were time limited and a considerable amount of legislation was likely to reach the Statute Book.

Committees in the Scottish Parliament were designed to be a great deal more powerful than those in the House of Commons, since they contained the powers of both the Westminster Select Committees to take evidence and of the Standing Committees to scrutinise and pass legislation. This was important as there was no second chamber.

Early on at Holyrood, Maureen Macmillan the Labour MSP had a debate on a subject which had been swept under the carpet for years, namely a matrimonial partner exercising violence within the family home. She proposed that the aggrieved partner, often an assaulted wife, should have the right to apply for an interdict to prevent the violent partner entering the family home. Two-thirds of the MSPs listened to her speech and subsequently a Committee adopted her proposals as a Committee Bill which passed successfully through the Parliament. This is a procedure which is not available to Committees in the House of Commons.

I discovered during the selection process that the competition to get into the Scottish Parliament was even more intense than that for the House of Commons. Many people clearly saw the Parliament as a coming institution which would grow in power. I later learnt that the jobs associated with the Parliament, as in the case of the Parliamentary Ombudsman or the Children's Commissioner, were very much prized.

However it always surprised me that when groups of voters were dissatisfied with the policies of ministers, the Parliament itself would get the blame. This was because in the early years not everyone distinguished between the Parliament and the Executive. However when the Tories and the SNP unexpectedly defeated the Labour/Liberal Democrat coalition on the issue of fishing compensation, electors realised that the Parliament was where the Executive could be held to account. One or two Labour members had slipped away to their party conference and as Tory Chief Whip I had persuaded every single Conservative member to vote!

Finally the Scottish media show a great interest in the minutiae of what goes on in the Parliament and MSPs receive much more publicity than Scottish MPs in the House of Commons, often to the considerable irritation of the latter.

At the beginning I was involved in the controversy over whether the Parliament should begin each day's business with Prayers as in the House of Commons and the House of Lords. I prepared a Motion supporting such an arrangement and approached Alex Fergusson, the Tory MSP, whom I knew to be a son of the Manse and suggested that he might propose it, which he did.

Donald Dewar surprisingly spoke in opposition. Apparently he wanted people who wished to do so, to have periods of contemplation elsewhere without taking up the time of the Parliament. Alex Fergusson spoke well causing some laughter when he said he feared his father on earth rather than his father in Heaven. I intervened to say that this was not a party political issue but free vote territory and that I hoped Alex Fergusson would have the courage of his convictions and press the matter to a vote, which he did. The case for Prayers won decisively and after taking the views of the Scottish Interfaith Consultative Group the idea of having a Thought for the Day, lasting up to five minutes before Parliamentary proceedings, was agreed. These short addresses have proved to be thought-provoking and often very moving and the speakers have included the Dalai Lama and the late Reverend Dr David Steel, father of the first Presiding Officer.

Donald Dewar was not pleased that Alex Fergusson's Motion was passed and remarked to me sharply that it was the worst worded Motion he had ever seen. Since I had helped to draft it, I decided not to respond.

This episode did not detract from my great regard for Donald Dewar's abilities. As a young man he had been one of the finest debaters of his generation, as was John Smith and they were politicians in much the same mould. John Smith as Leader made the Labour party much more electable and Donald Dewar will always have his niche in Scotland's history for helping to deliver a Scottish Parliament. In some ways his erudite style of speaking was better suited to the House of Commons. The time limit on speeches in the Scottish Parliament sometimes gave the impression that he was ill-at-ease with the creature he had created. Perhaps this was because the momentum in the Scottish Parliament was far faster than in the House of Commons, with subjects coming up for immediate response. At First Minister's Question Time he did not always look comfortable when being cross-examined by Alex Salmond who one day would succeed him as First Minister.

Both Donald Dewar and John Smith were ardent supporters and close associates of the late Hugh Gaitskell, a former and, in my view, courageous Leader of the Labour party. While I was a student I had once met him in the somewhat unlikely venue of a petrol station in Oxford which gave me the opportunity to tell him I had enjoyed a recent speech he had made at the university.

Sadly, all three of them died before their time but their work and influence played a key role in modernising the Labour party, and, in the case of Donald Dewar and John Smith, leading to a landslide election victory in 1997.

I had practised law with John Smith and had taken part as junior counsel in many of the same murder cases. I had got to know Donald Dewar well at the junior Konigswinter Conference of students in Berlin. When former friends are elected to different political parties friendship does not normally extend to sharing confidences but expresses itself in a different way.

I once had a conversation with Donald Dewar telling him I had written a short book on my father's first flight over Mount Everest and that there was a photograph of him with a Prime Minister. Donald Dewar who had a wide knowledge of nineteenth and early twentieth-century history replied at once saying correctly that it must have been Ramsay Macdonald. I gave him a copy of the book which he kept and which after his death went with his collection to the Scottish Parliament.

He must have associated me a little with the Himalayas since he asked me when I was an MSP to host a lunch for Nepalese Parliamentarians in Edinburgh Castle. Arriving half an hour early I was dismayed to learn that the caterers had not arrived. I greeted the MPs from Nepal and I insisted, in order to gain valuable time, that their visit to Scotland would be incomplete without seeing the Crown Jewels. Historic Scotland had done a wonderful job in presenting their story, including the 150 years when they were hidden, before being rediscovered by the author Sir Walter Scott behind a partition. Fortunately the visiting delegation much enjoyed seeing the display of the oldest crown jewels in Britain and much to my relief by the time that came to an end the caterers had arrived.

During the first session of the new parliament one highly controversial matter in which I became involved was the discrimination enshrined within the Act of Settlement of 1700 against all Roman Catholics. This had suddenly resurfaced as a public issue. Although brought up in the Church of Scotland, I took up this issue with the Prime Minister, Tony Blair, because I did not like to see the State discriminating against a group of people because of their religious beliefs.

In a reply dated 23 October 1999 he told me:

"As you know, the Act of Settlement excludes from the Throne a person who is, or who marries, a Roman Catholic. The Act is a significant element in a political and constitutional settlement with complex historical roots which continues, 300 years later, to have wide-ranging constitutional implications for the United Kingdom, and indeed for the Commonwealth as a whole. The central point of the Act of Settlement is that the Established Church in England is the Church of England, of which the Sovereign is Supreme Governor. Therefore the Act does not prevent members of the Royal Family from becoming or marrying Roman Catholics but does remove them from the line of succession.

"The Government is conscious that this is a subject on which both Catholics and non-Catholics have deeply held views which need to be treated with respect.

"The Government has, however, no plans to repeal the Act; and any attempt to amend the Act of Settlement would in any case be complex in the extreme, as at least eight other pieces of legislation, some prior to the Acts of Union with Scotland and with Ireland, would also have to be amended or repealed. Moreover, in order to avoid any disputes over the Succession, identical legislation would need to be passed by at least fifteen other independent monarchies within the Commonwealth."

It seemed very clear from his letter that the Prime Minister had no intention of grasping this particular nettle. However as the matter was due for debate in the Scottish Parliament, I decided to press ahead and conduct a consultation with the faith communities in Scotland. Making use of Mr Blair's letter, I asked if it was the prevailing view in their churches to support an amendment to the Act of Settlement to remove the discrimination against Catholics and offered to place the responses in the Library of the Scottish Parliament.

Quite a number of replies had come in before the debate on 16 December on a Motion from Mike Russell, the Business Manager of the SNP, who spoke with his usual zeal. I followed him suggesting that this subject had come on to the Agenda "as a result of wholesale constitutional reform and the approaching millennium". I went on to say that "The important issue is whether there should be legislation that blatantly discriminates against a Christian religion. The subject is particularly relevant as we live in a multi-faith community. In the context of the millennium, it is intended to recognise and appreciate the contribution of all faiths and communities in our country. The heir to the throne can accede if he marries a Muslim, a Buddhist, a scientologist, a Moonie, an atheist or a sun-worshipper, but not if he marries a Roman Catholic. Leaving such a stigma in place when no other religion or faith is singled out is grossly unfair."

I made reference to the fact that when Mike Russell lodged his motion I had written to the Prime Minister who had replied that he had "no plans" to remedy the position and had claimed that it would be complex to reform the law. I said "That is absolutely right. Similarly, it was complex to reform the House of Lords, but that did not prove an insurmountable problem." I mentioned that, out of the nine responses to the consultation I had carried out, eight had been opposed to such discrimination. I quoted from

Cardinal Thomas Winning who said "Royal Commissions are normally established to tackle some thorny issue on which there is no wide consensus. The campaign to amend the Act of Settlement commands broad public and political support. Indeed, I can think of no major public figure prepared to defend the language of intolerance contained in the offensive clauses. What is now needed is a clear signal that this issue will be tackled, and tackled soon."

I also mentioned the position of the Church of Scotland, which had stated "It is the view of the Legal Questions Committee that the discriminatory provisions of the Act of Settlement have no place in our contemporary society. The Act was a product of its times and those are not our times. Thankfully, we live in a climate of ecumenical friendship and cooperation unknown at the beginning of the eighteenth century."

I again referred to Cardinal Winning who had summed up his views in a message to the Scottish Parliament saying "I wish all of you success in rooting out an offensive, embarrassing and anachronistic blot on our escutcheon." In addition a letter from the Hindu Mandir stated that "Hindus did not discriminate against anyone." Councillor Bashir Mann of the Muslim community confirmed "The Muslim Religion is against all kinds of discrimination on account of race, colour or creed. We would therefore support an amendment to the Act that would remove this flagrant statutory discrimination against the Roman Catholic faith."

Then I sought to come to the crux of the matter by placing the issue in its historical context. I said:

"This debate is a continuation of the debate in 1829 on the subject of Roman Catholic emancipation – enabling Roman

Catholics to become members of Parliament. The Prime Minister at the time was the Duke of Wellington, who had defeated Napoleon at Waterloo and who was on the side of emancipation. Lord Winchilsea attacked Wellington in language that was so offensive that it would not be tolerated today and he even went so far as to imply that the Duke was being disloyal to his country. The Prime Minister immediately challenged Winchilsea to a duel and on 21 March 1829, not long after first light, they met on Battersea fields with their seconds. When the moment to shoot arrived, the Prime Minister took careful aim and fired wide. Winchilsea, not wishing to kill his Prime Minister, fired in the air. He then wrote a grovelling letter of apology.

"A few days later, on 2 April, Wellington – in the face of the stiffest opposition in the House of Lords – spoke for Roman Catholic emancipation and made the best speech of his life. He said: 'I am one of those who have probably passed a longer period of my life engaged in war than most men, and principally in civil war; and I must say this, that if I could avoid by any sacrifice whatever even one month of civil war in the country to which I was attached, I would sacrifice my life in order to do it.'

"When the vote came, he obtained a majority of 105 – almost two thirds in favour.

"I hope that today our majority will be even more convincing. I hope that it will persuade the Prime Minister to put reform of the Act of Settlement firmly on the agenda. If the Duke of Wellington – who was, if I may say, even more right-wing than Mr Tony Blair, which is saying quite a lot – was prepared to take a stand on principle and bring in progressive reform, surely it is not too much to hope that our Prime Minister can show the same kind of moral courage."

Sadly, it was too much to hope, although I did not know it then. I finished by saying:

"The Act of Settlement... is neither in keeping with the spirit of the times nor consistent with the social inclusion that we wish to celebrate in the year of the millennium.

"Our vote today should serve as a signal that blatant and hurtful legislation discriminating against a religion is not acceptable, just as discrimination against a race or ethnic community is not acceptable. Today we have the opportunity to give an example to Britain, by recommending that such discrimination is an offensive anachronism that should be swept away. I commend the motion to the Parliament."

The motion was accepted unanimously and I followed this up with a further letter to the Prime Minister requesting that a team of experts be appointed to review the terms of the Act and to recommend a constructive way forward. The Prime Minister's reply came on 28 March 2000.

"As you know, the Government has always stood firmly against discrimination in all its forms, and will continue to do so.

"However, we have a heavy legislative programme aimed at delivering key manifesto commitments. There are therefore no present plans to review the Act of Settlement, as you have suggested. However, I am keen to monitor the ongoing debate about this issue and was interested to see the information which you have provided".

So his position was that while he was opposed to discrimination by the State against a major Christian religion, he was not prepared to do anything about it. He might have the power to start wars but the removal of a last obstacle to complete Roman Catholic emancipation was apparently beyond him.

It should be noted that throughout the debate I expressed no view as to how the Church of England should organise its affairs. It seemed to me that whatever the circumstances 300 years ago when Britain was under threat of invasion from Roman Catholic countries there had been no persuasive up to date case made for the State to discriminate against Catholics.

Interestingly enough I learned that resentment against the Act of Settlement had been smouldering away under the surface for many years and on a European holiday I discovered evidence of an unexpected supporter of change. Setting out on the track of Sherlock Holmes and the fictional great detective's struggle against the forces of evil led by Professor Moriarty, Susie and I visited the Reichenbach Falls at Meiringen in Switzerland. It was there that Holmes and Moriarty had their last desperate and fatal struggle, before falling into the foaming torrent at the foot of the Falls.

However, the outcry and disappointment from the readers of Sir Arthur Conan Doyle's works on Sherlock Holmes was so great that Holmes had to be brought back to life. He had not really died. By a miracle in his titanic struggle with Moriarty he had clutched on to the mountainside at the moment that Moriarty fell.

While at Meiringen we went into the Sherlock Holmes Museum, and there we saw a letter by Conan Doyle expressing his desire that the Act of Settlement be amended. So all I had been doing had been following a well-worn path, something which Prime Minister Tony Blair was not prepared to do.

The Act of Settlement debate was a one-off but it had made an impression. When the *Scotsman* newspaper awarded the prize for the best first speech in the first year of the Scottish Parliament, I received the rose-tinted glass trophy from the Labour Foreign Secretary, Robin Cook. Apart from winning a boxing trophy for defeating Cambridge in the boxing ring and a literary award from the *Yorkshire Post* for the best book by a new author in 1971, this was the first time I had won such a prize.

I had been friendly with Robin Cook at Edinburgh University, and had also been his local MP in Edinburgh West. When I had been a Minister he had shared car journeys with me and had come to see me on behalf of his constituents. On one occasion we walked together in a demonstration for more defence contracts for the employees of Ferranti of Edinburgh.

He had spoken extremely well as a relatively new MP seconding the Queen's Speech in 1974 and many years later he made a most memorable resignation speech at the time of the invasion of Iraq. This will be remembered as a case study in moral courage where an MP was true to his principles and convictions at the expense of his career. I regarded him as an extremely good debater and a great Parliamentarian, so it was a pleasant surprise to receive this award from him.

In the meantime the realities of hard work as an MSP took up much of my time. There were countless representations from constituents, all of which called for careful consideration and action.

Early in the Parliament news came through that the Intercontinental Tyre Company was to close its plant at Newbridge with many hundreds of jobs lost. MSPs who were interested or whose constituents were involved had a meeting. There Tommy Sheridan, the leader of the Scottish Socialist Party suggested that I put down a motion calling for a bigger redundancy package, which I did. The motion went through unanimously, and on the next day when the Vice Chairman of the Intercontinental Tyre Company visited Scotland he announced that the package to be made available to those made redundant would be increased by more than £1 million. I hope the motion made it more likely that this would happen and I was very pleased to receive a grateful letter from the Trade Union Shop Steward at the factory.

Halfway through the first Parliament another campaign caught the popular imagination. I had been given the role as lead spokesman on Justice issues, and it was noted that one Richard Crawford who had allegedly raped and murdered an elderly lady, had appealed against his conviction and had been released on bail. My point was that the presumption of innocence drops off after conviction and in any case the Prosecutor had not been given the opportunity to put forward the case for protecting the public. The decision had been made by a Judge in Chambers without any reference whatsoever to the Advocate Depute who had prosecuted. The public interest had not been represented.

Nobody paid any attention to my press release expressing grave concern, but shortly afterwards there was a great deal of attention. Crawford failed to turn up for his appeal, having jumped bail, and had disappeared, believed to be somewhere in the recesses of southern England. The police held a press conference warning the public that he was a dangerous man who should not be approached.

All of a sudden I was in demand from at least three radio programmes and three television companies. I appeared on the national news and argued that it was appalling that people convicted of serious crimes such as rape and murder should be granted bail so lightly. The public quite rightly expected the State to protect them from potentially dangerous criminals, and the law needed to be changed so that the rights of the public were put before the rights of rapists and murderers.

Crawford's mugshot was issued on nationwide television and luckily, just as I was finishing all the interviews, he appeared in a police station and gave himself up.

Not long afterwards the law was changed in Scotland and prosecutors were given the right to put the case to protect the public before bail could be considered. It had been an issue which for so long had been unnoticed and which came up to the boil prompting an immediate change of policy.

I shared the services of a Special Advisor called Ben Pinnington with the leader of the Conservative Group in the Parliament, David McLetchie. Much of his work was for the Leader, but every now and then we would discuss which public issues should be pursued. One day Ben asked whether it would be appropriate to start a campaign for a memorial to Princess Diana in Scotland. I told him that it was an extremely good idea but it had already been followed up in a number of ways.

However, I did feel that there was a strong case for a Memorial to the Queen Mother. Not only had she been a patriotic Scot brought up in Scotland, but she had given great encouragement to many charities including those involved with the protection of the environment, improvements to health care and with the advancement of education. She had been a tremendous support to King George VI and during the worst of the Blitz in London in 1940 had helped to raise the morale of the British people by visiting the victims of the bombing and their shattered streets. It has been claimed that Hitler was so infuriated by the positive impact which she had on the British will to fight that he referred to her as "the most dangerous woman in Europe".

I decided to float the idea of a Memorial to start the ball rolling and wrote to the First Minister, Jack McConnell, and to the Lord Provost of Edinburgh, Eric Milligan, to suggest that West Princes Street Gardens be renamed in memory of the Queen Mother or that some other memorial should be considered. The concept received considerable support from the local paper but was strongly attacked by the SSP leader Tommy Sheridan, well known for his republicanism.

Following his outburst, the First Minister, Jack McConnell, suddenly decided it was a cause worth supporting. I found myself acting as a Trustee under the experienced chairmanship of David Bowes-Lyon and meeting in Jack McConnell's office, which incidentally had been my office while Minister of Health in the Scottish Office. Evidently he liked it more than the Secretary of State's traditional domain. Some time later a national memorial garden was completed in the Royal Botanic Gardens, and memorial gates were constructed at Glamis Castle which had been the Queen Mother's family home.

Not all campaigns were resolved so easily. A proposal had come from the Home Office in Whitehall that a Reception Centre for asylum seekers should be installed in the former Royal Air Force quarters at Edinburgh Airport. The members of Edinburgh City Council were indignant that they had not been consulted about this, and when I discussed the issue with West Edinburgh constituents living nearby it was clear that there was intense opposition to the plan.

I had suggested that my old birthplace, Dungavel, might be suitable for such accommodation, and it eventually became a Reception Centre. I was unhappy about the proposal to site the centre at the airport because I believed it had a great deal of potential for expansion, bringing in its wake increases in tourism, trade, jobs and prosperity for the area. The site in question was also under consideration as a possible future Cargo Centre.

A debate was held in the Parliament and there was all-party support for the development of Edinburgh Airport on the site proposed for the reception centre. In any case Scots Ministers would decide on proposed compulsory purchase orders which would have had to be enforced for the Government to use this site. The Home Office in Whitehall realised that it had bitten off more than it could chew and withdrew its proposals.

The biggest campaign of all came up very suddenly and not long before the elections. The selection of candidates for the Regional List had been changed to a one person one vote system for members and I was chosen first on the Lothians List after David McLetchie so my prospects of being re-elected were reasonable.

Shortly before the election I learned that the great supersonic trans-Atlantic aircraft Concorde was to be withdrawn from service and that all of the world's most significant museums would be seeking to obtain one of the aircraft. Now, I was aware that not only had Scotland, with just 10 per cent of Britain's population, produced nearly a quarter of all Britain's greatest inventions, but that the wings of Concorde had been designed by Sir James Arnot Hamilton of Penicuik. Also Concorde had a special relationship with the Scottish Parliament as it had conducted a fly-past with the legendary Red Arrows on the day of its opening.

Concorde seemed to me to be a symbol of progress. While it could flash across the sky at incredible speed it was also worth remembering that at one time it had been no more than an idea in a man's mind. If a Concorde could be obtained by the National Museums of Scotland for its Museum of Flight, it would surely encourage education, employment and tourism in the East of Scotland and would be an opportunity to stress that Scots had always been in the forefront of driving forward the frontiers of technology and science.

I had a personal interest since the Museum of Flight was housed at the aerodrome at East Fortune in East Lothian. In the Second World War my father had been Station Commander at RAF Turnhouse and knowing that the RAF required a further aerodrome for spitfires he had chosen East Fortune. It's connection with flying dated back even before the Second World War when airships had taken off from there to cross the Atlantic. The site also possessed a hangar which would be ideal for housing Concorde.

If the National Museums were minded to put a persuasive case and the Parliament and the First Minister could be persuaded to give support, then just possibly we might succeed. I telephoned the National Museums. They were interested so I wrote to the First Minister in the midst of the election to the Scottish Parliament. At first there was no reply, and then shortly before election day, his junior Minister, Elaine Murray, confirmed on his behalf that he would give support.

The night of the election was the usual long drawn out and tense affair and the counting of the List votes went on until about six in the morning. However it was well worth the wait and I was pleased to be re-elected, once again, the third last MSP to be announced in the grand total of members. But I knew exactly which issue would be the first priority for me in the new Parliament.

CHAPTER 14

Concorde and Parliament at work

The newly elected Parliament in 2003 was still based on the Mound in Edinburgh, waiting for the time when its new home down the Royal Mile at Holyrood would be completed – at costs more than 10 times in excess of the original estimate! This gave rise to a prolonged political row over allegations of profligacy and poor judgement.

Jack McConnell, by now the First Minister, ordered an inquiry into the project to be chaired by the Conservative peer Lord Fraser of Carmyllie. His report was critical of the actions of certain civil servants but did not pin responsibility onto Ministers who in fact may have had more to do with the decision-making process than they were anxious to admit. However by the end of the Parliamentary session in 2007 this dispute had become yesterday's issue.

The Scottish Parliament had to be made to work in the best interests of those whom it sought to serve and cost overruns in this connection were sadly a familiar problem with some major capital projects.

After the election my first venture, as I had promised myself, was to organise the framing of a Motion to support one of the Concorde aircraft, which were soon to be withdrawn from service, coming to Scotland and suggesting it be put on display at the Museum of Flight at East Fortune. I told John Home-Robertson, the local Labour MSP, of the plan to raise the matter.

The idea appealed to him and he wanted the Motion to go down in his name as he was the member representing the Museum of Flight and before long approaching half of the 129 MSPs had signed. The lengthy Motion had been drafted in such a way as to present the entire case for obtaining a Concorde and referred to its special associations with Scotland, including the test flights carried out at Prestwick in the early 1970s.

On 18 June the subject was debated in the Parliament and won all-party support. John Home-Robertson put the case for the Museum of Flight and the benefits which would accrue to his constituents from having the aircraft in their midst.

When my turn came I stressed that the National Museums had backing from the Scottish Executive, Scottish tourist interests, East Lothian Council and a very large number of MSPs. I went on to argue that if Concorde did come it would help provide many jobs in East Lothian, would give a boost to tourism and encourage visitors from all over the world, as well as school parties from all over Scotland.

I kept the campaign going with an article in the *Edinburgh Evening News* and eventually the announcement we had hoped for was made. In spite of immense competition from all over the world, the National Museums had prevailed and British Airways had decided to donate a Concorde to them.

Here it must be said that the First Minister of Scotland had played a critical role. I had been the first to raise the subject publicly because I had foreseen that it was vital for the National Museums to get in their bid quickly with the support of Scottish ministers. But it was Jack McConnell who helped to clinch the matter. Apparently when asked how they would finance the presentation of Concorde the English museums had replied that they would rely on funding from the Lotteries. However in Scotland the First Minister had provided an extra £2million for this purpose.

What followed was a remarkable story in itself. Because the runway at East Fortune was not suitable for Concorde to land on, the wings had to be taken off the aircraft and the fuselage was placed on a barge on the River Thames. This extraordinary sight was photographed sailing past the House of Commons on its last journey out of London.

When the aeroplane reached Scotland it was taken by road with help from public spirited contractors, making the final part of the journey on a steel road laid down by the expertise of the British Army. This was all the more impressive considering that the aircraft even without its wings weighed over 50 tons.

Concorde was then put into a magnificent hangar, had its wings "sewn back" on again and has become, like the Royal Yacht Britannia moored in Leith, a symbol of national significance to Scots. As anticipated, the visitor figures to the Museum of Flight soared and the addition of further famous aircraft to the collection, including a Tornado Fighter Bomber and an RAF Jaguar, has enhanced that process. The arrival of Concorde gave me the opportunity to say that this development was confirmation that the Museum was "not just a centre of educational excellence, but one of the foremost aviation museums in Europe".

Back in the Parliament, education was one of the key subjects which would come up every week, and as Conservative spokesman I had my share of work. One of the issues which hit the headlines was the incidence of violence in Scottish schools, and the inability of a headteacher to exclude permanently the very small number of children causing persistent disruption.

The Labour/Liberal Democrat administration chose to leave responsibility for this issue with local authority officials and actually had a target for reducing the number of pupils being excluded from schools. The figures were shocking, as attacks on members of school staff were taking place frequently.

The figures for assaults had been steadily rising when the Executive chose not to reveal them annually. There the matter might have rested had it not been for the Freedom of Information Act. Under its provisions I asked each council for the up to date figures which showed an increase in violence towards members of staff. This underlined the fact that there was a growing problem which needed to be fully addressed. I called for headteachers to be given greater powers to remove unruly pupils from the classroom – if necessary permanently.

The Executive and in particular the Education Minister, Peter Peacock, appeared to have a hang-up about following initiatives taken south of the border. I had suggested a pilot scheme along the same lines as a new project in London to send the most able graduate teachers into struggling inner-city schools. My proposal was promptly condemned by the Minister, whereupon it was revealed that the English plan had in fact been endorsed by none other than Prime Minister Tony Blair. This gave rise to some wry comments about left hands not knowing what other left hands were doing!

Perhaps the most important theme for those of us on the Education Committee was how best to increase protection for children. In the wake of the Soham tragedy where two school girls were murdered in Cambridgeshire, there had been the Bichard

Report which recommended tightening up on vetting procedures for those working with children and young people. The committee spent many hours taking evidence and deliberating on this whole issue.

When the Children (Scotland) Bill had been debated in the House of Commons I had stressed the importance of the principle that the interests of the child must be paramount. In the Scottish Parliament a few years later the same principle was ardently supported.

Children's issues were uppermost in my mind at this time and not just because of prospective legislation. Gail, Lady Jopling had recruited me as a supporter for the new charity "Hope and Homes for Children," whose founders were the charismatic Colonel Mark Cook and his wife Caroline. At my invitation they came to the Scottish Parliament to talk about their cause and aspirations.

The charity had been brought into existence to benefit children whose parents had been killed in conflict or whose next of kin had lost their lives through illness, drought or famine. As I write, more than 10,000 children in Eastern Europe and Africa have been assisted through a most difficult and traumatic time in their lives.

At one of the first meetings in Edinburgh it was pointed out that the new support group based in the city would need somebody to take the chair. I looked around the table and saw that a dozen pairs of eyes had swivelled in my direction. Acting as chairman of the Edinburgh support group was a timely reminder that a small number of committed people can achieve a great deal, and they did with the very able help of the secretary, Mrs Anne Brotherston.

The support of national figures like the very popular Scottish comedian Ronnie Corbett and the journalist Kate Adie, well known for her TV reporting from the front line in war-torn situations, made a great difference.

"Hope and Homes" was not the only charity I supported while I was an MSP. As President of the International Rescue Corps I was able to arrange a reception in the Parliament, just after the terrible earthquake in Pakistan in 2006, for the volunteers who make up the Corps. The IRC, whose aim it is to save lives in emergency situations, always has a high-powered team of firefighters, paramedics and other specialists on standby. Time after time they have saved lives following earthquakes and floods and are particularly skilled at rescuing individuals buried under concrete.

In Pakistan, where there had been great devastation, acting with other charities, the IRC saved countless lives by establishing tented cities so that residents driven out of their homes would have access to food and water as well as clothes and warmth. They also saved lives in a few high profile cases where the local emergency workers had found the circumstances too difficult to deal with.

Charitable causes have an important role in the life of the Scottish Parliament and the support of so many MSPs for them seems to me to be an excellent example of participative democracy in action. Before devolution it was harder for such activities to take place on that scale as it was too expensive for many of the participants to reach the UK Parliament several hundred miles away.

One of the advantages enjoyed by MSPs is that they are able to speak on subjects even when they are constitutionally reserved to Westminster and one such deeply controversial issue was the future of famous Scottish regiments such as the Black Watch and the Argyll and Sutherland Highlanders. I had signed up to support the opposition to the Government's plan to amalgamate them all into one Royal Regiment as it seemed to me not so much a modernisation as a cost-cutting exercise.

On 1 December 2005 I asked the First Minister, Jack McConnell, in Parliament whether he would take up the matter of the retention of the distinctive regimental hackles, which are inserted into a soldier's Tam O'Shanter. He told me that the Executive had already made a number of representations before final decisions were announced. He went on to say that he had noticed I was planning to retire from the Parliament in 2007. This was true as after 33 years of being an elected representative, two as a councillor, 23 as an MP and eight as an MSP I had decided to pass the torch at a time when my supporters still wanted me to stay on.

The First Minister said to my surprise "If you will allow me to do so, Presiding Officer, I wish to take this opportunity to say publicly that he has been an outstanding member of the Scottish Parliament. I am delighted that he chose to serve here and wish him all the best in serving in the House of Lords."

Now when a Minister pays a compliment to an opponent it usually means one of two things – that he is being very generous or alternatively that he is being asked a difficult question and a kindly comment can serve to distract attention away from a none too satisfactory answer. Being uncertain as to which applied in this case I pressed on and asked him to agree that "to wipe out some of the last vestiges of Scottish identity will damage local recruiting," and lead to "some severe murmurings" among people like myself who once had the honour of wearing the black hackle.

He acknowledged it was disappointing that the "Regiments' original identities would not be retained completely" but that he would ask publicly for support for the new Regiment of Scotland whatever members thought about the decision to create it.

In 2006 I signed the "Save our Scottish Regiments" petition at the Scottish Parliament, which was to be handed over in the Houses of Parliament at Westminster on St Andrews Day. That day I said "Everyone knows that the Scottish Regiments have always acted as a major part of the backbone of the British Army. It is right and proper that there should be appropriate recognition of their outstanding worth. The petition puts down a marker that, in a time of uncertainty and volatility in the world, infantry soldiers will be required in peace-keeping operations."

Sadly the Government would not listen over the Scottish regiments and went ahead with the reforms which involved reducing the size of the army. Since then the issue has been superseded by a long running debate of far greater overall importance, namely the thoroughly inadequate funding of the British Armed Services which has been exposed as a result of having to fight two actions simultaneously in Iraq and Afghanistan.

It was not long afterwards that the Tercentenary of the 1707 Act of Union approached, and I found myself suddenly being cross-examined by the media over the conduct of one of my most controversial ancestors. Usually it is older generations who are asked to account for the behaviour of their descendants but in this case it was the other way round.

James Douglas, the fourth Duke of Hamilton was apparently a charismatic character who was popular with the Edinburgh crowd and was expected to lead a spirited opposition to the union of the Parliaments. However on the day of the critical vote he was absent, allegedly on account of toothache, but many of his colleagues believed the Duke was dissembling.

It is quite clear to me what happened. Somewhere along the way he changed his mind, seeing the benefits of the Union in terms of employment and trade with England and the colonies in North America. After the failed Darien Scheme in which so many leading Scots lost their wealth, the opening up of huge, new, lucrative markets was important. Furthermore, with a unified foreign policy the threat of civil war might be less. The point I made in front of the television cameras was that the Duke had been "insufficiently frank" with his Parliamentary colleagues over his change of mind and this was why he had been severely criticised.

However, it has to be said in his favour that he was a physically courageous man. In 1714 just before he was due to take up Queen Anne's appointment as Ambassador to France he was challenged to a duel by Baron de Mohun, an extremely violent man who had already killed at least one opponent and was reputed to be the best duellist in Britain. Not being a man to shrink from a challenge, the Duke met de Mohun in Hyde Park in the early hours.

The Duke was in less than perfect physical condition and no longer in the first flush of youth, but he still ran de Mohun through with his sword. His opponent, although fatally wounded, slashed at the Duke cutting an artery in his arm. It has also been claimed that General MacCartney, de Mohun's second, treacherously ran the Duke through from behind. There is some debate over which wound was the fatal one. What is beyond doubt is that by the time the sun came up de Mohun was no longer alive and a newspaper of the day subsequently reported: "Duke Hamilton is dead."

The news scandalised London society and Queen Anne was furious that her newly appointed Ambassador to France had met his end in such a way. A warrant was issued for the arrest of General MacCartney but he had fled to France.

My late uncle Geordie, the tenth Earl of Selkirk told me that the Duke was at fault and I later learnt why. The Duke had refused to pay £10,000 to his wife's mother, a payment which had been in the marriage contract. When his mother-in-law, Lady Gerard, died, de Mohun, a relative of hers, had taken up her claim and had thrown down the gauntlet to the Duke. I could not help reflecting that life should have meant more to each of the two men than the £10,000, even if it did represent a great deal of money in those days.

But the heroine of the story in the Hamilton family was the Duke's mother whose life has been written up admirably by Dr Rosalind Marshall in *Duchess Anne*. Her father the first Duke had been executed after the Battle of Preston and her uncle the second Duke had died of his wounds after the Battle of Worcester during the Civil War. She had married the Earl of Selkirk who was allowed to call himself Duke of Hamilton for life. He was an exemplary man, steady and safe as an MP in the Scots Parliament where he served as Speaker. Now that her volatile and erratic oldest son was dead she would bring up his oldest son, the fifth Duke who was just a small boy. For more than half a century she was the guiding light, holding the fortunes of the family together.

It had been a rather bizarre experience to be cross-examined in this way about my ancestor's behaviour, and I was amused when my old friend, now sadly the late Sir Neil MacCormick, Regius Professor of Law at Edinburgh University told me "You have made the inexplicable explicable and have refused to defend the indefensible."

On 22 March 2007 I prepared for my last speech in the Scottish Parliament on the subject of education, having already made it clear I would not be standing again in the forthcoming May election. As I walked through the garden lobby to the chamber, four MSPs spoke to me saying that they understood I was about to make a great speech.

Since I had made no such claim to anyone I suspected something was going on behind my back and I was right. My friend the Conservative Chief Whip and Business Manager Bill Aitken had e-mailed all 128 of the other MSPs saying that I was about to make a memorable last contribution.

During my speech I referred to the Children (Scotland) Act, which, along with the lead Minister in the Lords, Lord Fraser of Carmyllie, I had helped to pilot to the Statute Book in the House of Commons. The MSPs listened with some amusement when I told them that during the passage of the bill, I had been severely reprimanded by the Speaker Betty Boothroyd for putting forward too many amendments. These had in fact been responses to some sensible suggestions put forward by Labour MPs and in any case I was not repentant. What she said was "I know you meant well."

I urged them "Let us pledge ourselves to making sure Scotland will have an education system which looks up to our proud traditions. It must be a shining example to the world and second to none."

In the speeches which followed kind words were spoken about my parliamentary work and there were repeated mentions of my association with the Children (Scotland) Act which MSPs held in high esteem, from the Labour Minister of Education, Hugh Henry, Fiona Hyslop for the SNP and from Ian Smith of the Liberal Democrats.

Hugh Henry appreciated the fact that in the House of Commons I had been prepared to recognise the improvements contained in the Labour amendments, Fiona Hyslop mentioned my role in steering through this important legislation as it held "the interests of children as paramount in Scots law" and Ian Smith said that it remained "the definitive piece of children's legislation in Scotland".

Of course a House of Commons Minister is only one part of a large team, all of whom bear some responsibility, but if a piece of legislation catches people's imagination and is well drafted and stands the test of time it will be well remembered. The protection of children has always been at the top of my list of priorities.

I am reminded of the despatch of Sir Francis Drake to Sir Francis Walsingham "There must be a beginning of any great matter, but the continuing unto the end until it be thoroughly finished yields the true glory." Perhaps what we did in the House of Commons and later in the Scottish Parliament to further the interests of children represented the beginning and the continuation of that process, which others will take forward for as long as Parliamentarians remember that they are there to serve.

CHAPTER 15

Family connections – the Black Douglas, the Selkirk Settlers, and John Buchan's Canada

P ast family connections do not often impinge on the professional life of an MP or an MSP, but occasionally they can, and do, sometimes unexpectedly as in the case of the media's sudden interest in the rather erratic behaviour of the 4th Duke of Hamilton at the time of the Union of 1707.

The Black Douglas was another relative whose actions impinged on my life. Lying on his death bed at Cardross in 1329, King Robert the Bruce had asked his dear friend Lord James Douglas to carry out a last mission for him, as he knew of "no knight more valiant". He wished his embalmed heart to be carried to the Holy Land to do battle with the enemies of Christianity as a way of repenting his sins. Doubtless the king had in mind the occasion when he had killed his rival the Red Comyn in a church.

When Lord James arrived at Teba, north of the Rock of Gibraltar he was entertained by the King of Spain who on the next day engaged in battle with the Moors under the Castle of the Stars. There Lord James saw a Scottish knight, William Sinclair of

Roslin, surrounded by Moors and went to his aid. He was found dead surrounded by the bodies of his enemies but still in possession of King Robert's heart.

With the support of the Earl of Elgin and the Duke of Buccleuch and numerous members of his own family, my late uncle Geordie arrived in Teba, Spain, in 1989 to unveil a white granite memorial to Lord James Douglas donated by them from Scotland. The Mayor and citizens of Teba thought this might put their town on the tourist map of Europe and several thousand of them turned out to celebrate. At that time Susie and I were in the United States at the invitation of a family friend but our thoughts were also in Teba with Geordie and the Black Douglas.

Years later, in 2007, the Mayor and seventy residents of Teba came to the Scottish Parliament where I welcomed them in a large committee room. Because of the town's connections with King Robert the Bruce and Lord James Douglas they had wanted to see the new parliament and presented me with a photograph of the Castle of the Stars, which they told me is still in perfect condition after 700 years. The town regularly celebrates its ancient connection with the Black Douglas and they asked me if I knew what the great warrior had looked like. I realised I did not have an answer for them, but promised I would check and try to discover if there were any contemporary portraits.

I made enquiries and it emerged that there were no known paintings of Lord James completed in his lifetime, although in the church of St Bride in Douglas there is a chipped marble effigy above his last resting place. Even in its damaged state it shows a man in chain mail whose grim face suggests great strength and determination as though the last thought in his mind was whether he would be able to fulfil the wish of his great king and close friend.

Although there was no contemporary portrait, I was able to find out from various historical sources that the Black Douglas was dark with, apparently, a sallow complexion which was unblemished by scars or disease even at the end of his life.

The more I thought about it the more I liked the idea of retelling the Black Douglas's story through a commemorative painting of him which could be shown to the public. But who could take on such a task? I knew that Ronnie Browne of the famous Corries folk group had also trained as a painter and had taught art in schools. On behalf of the Directors of Lennoxlove House Limited, I approached him and he agreed to take on the commission.

The idea emerged to tell the story of the Black Douglas in a number of tableaux behind and around the central figure of the medieval knight clad in his chain mail with the casket containing Bruce's heart hanging round his neck. The background pictures show his own castle, which had been occupied by an English garrison, in flames after one of his assaults on it. Eventually he managed to destroy it completely as an English base.

There is a moon at the top of the picture which represents the Black Douglas' role as a feared specialist in night fighting. He was something of a medieval commando leader and is reputed to have clothed himself and his men in black over their armour to help conceal them during night raids. The Castle of the Stars also features in the picture with the Moors armed with their lances waiting to bring down the Black Douglas, something which the English could never do.

The picture was unveiled at Lennoxlove on 22 October 2007 by my mother. Since she was a Percy from Northumberland and considering the Douglases and the Percys had fought each other for centuries, I asked if she had any qualms about performing the task. She did not and agreed it was part of Scotland's story.

Another family connection which has involved me in present day events related to Canada and the people known as "the Selkirk Settlers". I first became aware of this piece of history as a student at Pau University where I was learning French. Completely by accident, near Pau Castle, I came across the grave of Thomas, the fifth Earl of Selkirk, which told me he had died in 1820 at the age of just 48. I was intrigued by the fact that his last resting place was so far from his home in St Mary's Isle, in Kirkcudbrightshire, and resolved to find out why.

I turned to my uncle Geordie who told me that Thomas' claim to fame was that he had chartered ships giving many hundreds of disadvantaged Highlanders the opportunity to buy large tracts of land he had purchased in Canada, thereby offering them the prospect of a better life in the New World. A seventh son who had unexpectedly inherited a vast fortune, he was much influenced by the progressive ideas of the Scottish Enlightenment. Seeking to put his ideas into practice, he encouraged the settlers to buy their homesteads at very favourable prices and allowed them generous credit terms. According to Geordie the founding of the famous Red River Settlement in the Midwest of Canada was the origin of the city of Winnipeg.

While I was a student at Edinburgh University I was sponsored by the British Information Services to take part in a debating tour of 29 Canadian Universities. While there I learnt that the descendants of the courageous "Selkirk Settlers" had succeeded beyond the wildest dreams of the first pioneers and that they continued to be very proud of their Scottish heritage.

Many years later, in 2003, this family connection cropped up again when I was invited to lead a Commonwealth Parliamentary Association delegation from the Scottish Parliament to Prince Edward Island and New Brunswick. By an astonishing coincidence this visit came at the same time as the bi-centenary of the "Selkirk Settlers" who had arrived on PEI with Thomas Selkirk on 9 August 1803 and made it their home. I was able to take part in the celebrations, where I paid tribute to the men and women who took their fate in their hands and made their way from Scotland to Canada, remembering them with "warmth, affection and pride".

More visits to Canada followed, although this time it was in connection with one of Susie's ancestors, namely her grandfather John Buchan, forever remembered as the author of that much filmed adventure story *The Thirty-Nine Steps*. In 2004 we received an invitation to go with the John Buchan Society, an association formed by ardent fans of his books, to visit Montreal, Quebec, Ottawa and Kingston on Lake Ontario.

John Buchan was created Lord Tweedsmuir when he was appointed Governor General of Canada in 1935. Aware that no American President had officially visited Canada, he invited President Franklin Delano Roosevelt to be the first. The timing of this trip was significant since conflict in Europe was becoming more likely with the rise of the European dictators.

In 1936, as already mentioned, President Roosevelt came to the Governor General's residence in the citadel of Quebec. Their lengthy talks were so successful that eventually FDR went outside to his official car, took the large Presidential flag, with its American eagle, off the front and presented it to John Buchan. From all that we were told, the talks played an important part in bringing Canada and the US closer together at a time when world war was only three years away. As for the flag it was given to Susie who passed it on to our son Charles to celebrate his second university degree in North America, at Colorado School of Mines.

On reaching Ottawa we were amused to hear that while attending St Andrew's Presbyterian Church, John Buchan learned that a member of the congregation was feeling the cold. He responded swiftly by sending the man several pairs of the Governor General's underclothes. We heard that they had protected three generations of Canadians from inclement weather!

John Buchan was not in the best of health when he wrote his last book *Sick Heart River*, in which the hero Edward Leithen accomplishes his last humanitarian mission and perishes in the snows of northern Canada. Only a few hours after completing the book, the author slipped in his bath, banged his head and died shortly afterwards. The Canadian Prime Minister, Mackenzie King, insisted he be given a state funeral in Ottawa and fourteen thousand people came to pay their respects at his lying-in-state.

We returned to Canada and the trail of John Buchan in the summer of 2007 visiting what was described to us by one environmentalist as one of the country's "best kept secrets". Tweedsmuir Provincial Park in British Columbia covers an astonishing 2.2 million acres. It was named after John Buchan as was the Tweedsmuir Glacier in the Yukon.

The nearby port of Bella Coola is known as the Grizzly Bear Capital of the World and my first encounter with one in the wild came when I was in a boat with Susie drifting down the River Atnarko. Suddenly we saw this mighty, muscular creature making its way up river on the bank. The grizzly paid no attention to us but we were left in no doubt that he was King of the Valley.

On our way home we went to Tofino on Vancouver Island. The whole of Canada is extremely beautiful but this coastal gem must number as one of the most exquisite places in the world with its spectacular views of tree covered mountains and gleaming beaches running into the Pacific Ocean. While we were there I visited a memorial to the Canadian servicemen and women who had made the ultimate sacrifice so that their fellow citizens would be able to continue to appreciate such beauty in the future. It made me think of the "Selkirk Settlers" who had also risked everything to create a better life for their children and their descendants. That too had involved hardship, fortitude and sacrifice and I was determined, if the chance ever came, to follow in their footsteps and go to the city of Winnipeg in whose early history they had played such an important part.

The opportunity arose in 2008 when I was asked to speak at the dedication of the Settlers Monument beside the historic Red River running through Winnipeg. Sculpted in bronze by Gerald Laing in the Black Isle in Scotland, this magnificent monument consists of a family group of father, mother and son depicted at the poignant moment of their departure from Scotland.

Thomas Selkirk had been much moved by the appalling distress caused by the Highland Clearances and he thought emigration to Canada could provide better opportunities for those who were struggling to survive. But a clash of cultures developed between the Settlers and the fur traders and adventurers, already operating in the surrounding area, which culminated in a fateful and bloody encounter in 1816 at the Massacre or Battle of Seven Oaks. Governor Semple of the Red River Settlement was killed with at least 20 of the Settlers.

The cold-hearted indifference of the landowners who engaged in the Clearances and the hot tempered aggression of the fur traders who killed the Settlers represented, I believe, aspects of the unacceptable face of capitalism. In contrast it was greatly to the credit of both the Settlers and of the Peguis First Nation, led by Chief Peguis, that they formed an extremely good and close working relationship which helped the new arrivals to survive.

Thomas Selkirk arrived accompanied by Swiss soldiers in the uniform of De Meuron's Regiment to protect the Settlers, reached an agreement with Chief Peguis and proceeded to arrest the murderers. The North West Company who employed them, reacted with fury and in the legal actions which followed in Montreal, Lord Selkirk was fined and had to pay ruinous expenses as the price for acting as the Settlers champion.

He returned to Britain and consulted his great friend William Wilberforce, the anti-slave trade campaigner. Thomas was by this time severely ill with tuberculosis and Wilberforce's comment was both poignant and timely – "the sword can outwear the scabbard" he warned.

The Earl, dying and heavily in debt, in a desperate attempt to recover his health, travelled to the fresh air of Pau, north of the Pyrenees. There his story came to a tragic end, as the grave stone I found all those years ago testified. Looking back he was, in that now unfashionable term, a coloniser on a massive scale but crucially he was also a philanthropist and an idealist who acted on his principles.

Back in Canada however the Settlers cause prevailed and their children and grandchildren succeeded beyond their wildest dreams. The settlements of farmers at Red River set an example and helped to open up the rest of Canada to new waves of immigration. My uncle, who took part in celebrations commemorating the Settlers in 1963, summed it up like this: "But in the end the Settlers won and the significance of their victory lies in the unity of Canada today."

When I spoke at the 2008 celebrations I described the story of Thomas and the Selkirk Settlers as one of both tragedy and triumph. He died prematurely in his 49th year but the legacy he helped create is tangible and lasting. I remember saying "Here in Canada, as you fly across Manitoba in the evening, you can see the twinkling lights of the great skyscrapers of Winnipeg founded on the blood, sweat, toil and tears of the Highland Settlers."

John Buchan made some observations which could apply not just to the Selkirk Settlers but to all those other Scots who left their native shores and spread their influence throughout the world. He wrote "The Scots are perhaps the most famous small nation since the Ancient Greeks because they have not all stayed at home. We have two natural gifts when it comes to seeking our fortunes, which sell high in the right market. One is the ability to live anywhere in the world and far more happily than anyone else in real isolation. And we have a genius for survival. Survival is not an art, still less is it a science and least of all is it an accident." I feel these words might have been written with Canada's Selkirk Settlers in mind.

These were not the only family connections which exerted an influence on my life. Much nearer to home there was the case of my own father who was a pioneering aviator of some renown. His most famous exploit was in 1933, when along with his friend David McIntyre he made the first flight over Mount Everest. Later they went on to establish Prestwick Airport and to found a factory for constructing aircraft – an industry called Scottish Aviation.

Nearly eighty years ago it was just technically possible to attempt such an aerial exploit and they flew towards the mountain in open cockpits using heated oxygen tubes to allow them to breathe and wearing specially heated clothing. My father later recounted the dangers they faced, speaking of being "caught in a tremendous down rush of air" which caused their experimental Westland aircraft to fall several thousand feet. However, they managed to scrape over the north-east ridge of Everest and circled round until they were high enough to soar over the summit itself. I remember when my mother saw the film of the flight taken from David McIntyre's aircraft, and all the risks involved, she said she was very glad she had not been married to my father at the time.

All this excitement had taken place almost a decade before I entered the world but it was a tale which I grew up with, being well aware that if anything had gone wrong at 31,000 feet I would never have been born! But I was, and some 40 years later when I was an MP I wrote the story of the flight in a book entitled *The Roof of the World* in which I tried to capture the spirit of adventure and the sheer exhilaration of the men who were the first to see Mount Everest from the sky.

Down in Yeovil the Westland aircraft makers had not forgotten the flight either or the part their aircraft had played in it and on the 75th Anniversary I was asked to give a lecture at Aerosystems International. It was a talk which I had delivered on many previous occasions and in which I portrayed the flight as an example of humankind constantly striving to drive back the frontiers of the unknown.

I like to end by quoting the words in *The Pilot's Book of Everest* written by my father and David McIntyre, which shows how moved these two pilots were by the grandeur of the landscape they had witnessed from their cockpits. They wrote:

"No man can come close to the great peaks without acknowledging a sense of awe and understanding something of the fascination they hold. We saw the mountain on both occasions in high sunshine when there were few shadows to shroud her mystery.

In softer lights one might expect to feel something of the romance of these enormous masses of rocks and ice. Something of the mystery has been overcome and something of the unknown has been revealed; yet the Mistress of the World remains remote, immense and magnificent. The best that we could bring back was but a faint impression of her dignity and beauty."

On the subject of family connections the political philosopher Edmund Burke had this to say:

"People will not look forward to posterity, who never look backwards to their ancestors."

I cannot pretend that the loss of my uncle George, Duke of Northumberland, fighting with the Grenadier Guards near Dunkirk in 1940 or the loss of my uncle David, bringing back important photographs before the American invasion of Southern France in 1944, have not influenced me. I am also proud of the actions of Colonel Lord Henry Percy who won the Victoria Cross during the Crimean War at the Battle of Inkerman or Acting Colonel Angus Douglas-Hamilton, a first cousin of my grandfather, who won a VC posthumously at the Battle of Loos in 1915. After all, these were examples of men performing courageously above and beyond the call of duty.

Examples are not restricted to those who exhibited physical courage – a great uncle on my mother's side, five generations back, left his entire fortune to the United States of America, a somewhat unusual thing to do in 1829. The details of the will were hurried down the Corridors of Power in Washington, and were placed on the desk of President Andrew Jackson. The bequest was for the creation of an establishment for the increase and diffusion of knowledge. President Jackson informed Congress and the gift was accepted in 1836. Its value exceeded 100,000 gold sovereigns and on being re-coined it was in excess of half a million dollars. My relative, of whom I am very proud, was called James Smithson and his action sparked off the process which led to the creation of the Smithsonian National Museums in Washington.

Some of the colourful characters who have enlivened my family's history have indeed been an inspiration to me but when the chips are down, in the rough and tumble of political life, ultimately it has been my experience that every aspirant for elected office has to make their own way entirely on their own merits. When asked whether family background was a plus or a minus, I have always given the same answer. All that matters is if you can deliver the goods.

Afghanistan and the future of devolution

My return to the House of Lords after leaving Holyrood in March 2007 has brought with it fresh opportunities including the chance to contribute to debates on defence issues, on which I have some personal knowledge. I had joined the 6th/7th Battalion Cameronians (Scottish Rifles) at the age of 19 as a Territorial Army soldier and was commissioned shortly afterwards. However, within six years the Labour Government decided to axe three quarters of the Territorial Army and, during my degree exams at Edinburgh University, I was one of those made redundant. Four years later, however, the TA's fortunes changed as the Conservative Government decided to expand their numbers and I found myself a soldier again.

All my personal reports said much the same thing. I was considered to be a good officer but needed to put in more training. I went on the Lieutenant Captain's course at Warminster where I was most impressed by the quality of the members of the Parachute Regiment, the Royal Marine Commandos and the Scottish officers. One morning while attending our course, the news broke of the shootings in Londonderry which became known as "Bloody

Sunday". As well as being shocked at the number of deaths, I remember thinking what would matter was who had fired the first shot, a controversy which has continued to this day.

By the time I became an MP I was a Captain with just on ten years service. In those days Territorial soldiers were not used as front-line troops. All that has now changed and they are now treated almost as part-time regulars. The Armed Services have shrunk enormously and it seems clear to me that they are being asked to do more and more with limited resources.

In the House of Lords, in the Spring of 2008, Baroness Park put forward a motion for debate about resources for the Armed Services and the former Chiefs of Staff seized upon it as an occasion to criticise the Government and argue strongly for more funding. I took part in the debate stressing that ministers had an "inescapable duty" to uphold the Military Covenant – the agreement whereby members of the armed forces put their lives on the line on behalf of their country and the Government gives full support to them and their families in return.

By this time I was an honorary Air Commodore to 603 (City of Edinburgh) Squadron and had become President of the Scottish Veterans' Garden City Association, the largest British charity for providing housing to servicemen and women who have an element of disability.

If I was going to continue to talk about military matters I felt it was important to get at least some idea of what life in a current war zone was like, so in the summer of 2008 I took the opportunity to join a delegation travelling to Helmand Province in Afghanistan to visit the troops. That was how I found myself coming in to land in a military aircraft under cover of darkness at Kandahar Airport. We were told we would be landing in ten minutes but nearly 50 minutes later we were still in the air. After we came down we learned that beforehand rockets had been fired at the aerodrome by the Taliban. Once you are on the ground it is quickly brought home to you that the fighting is for real when you see young servicemen and women with their weapons slung over their shoulders or with automatics strapped to their waists. When I had been a volunteer soldier after an exercise we had been used to returning all weapons and ammunition to the Armoury

Next day we were taken to Lashkar Gah, where we were given excellent briefings about the current situation. Getting there was a memorable experience, flying very fast in a helicopter just above tree level. If anyone had been minded to take a pot-shot at us we would have been moving far too swiftly for them to succeed. When we came in to land I noticed that a serviceman had taken up position behind the heavy machine-gun at the rear of the helicopter.

The day before Governor Mangal of Helmand Province had a close shave when his helicopter was hit by a rocket-propelled grenade which went through one of the blades. Miraculously the helicopter stayed in the air. We realised that the spare blade we were carrying in our helicopter was to make the machine which carried the Governor airworthy again.

Before leaving Lashkar Gah, I asked a Lieutenant Colonel what would happen if one of us tried to go shopping in the town. I was told that on a first occasion you might get away with it but if you tried it again you would be shot dead. I was sad to learn a few days later that a journalist had in fact been killed there just before we arrived. It is as important for members of the media to be as carefully warned about the risks as those serving with the military.

A visit to Camp Bastion, the British forces base, filled me with admiration for the professionalism of all branches of the armed services. The medical facilities were particularly impressive as was the expertise of the medical staff, who had saved many lives there. I will always remember seeing a nine year old Afghan girl who had lost the lower part of her left arm as the result of a suicide bombing attack on civilians, who was in the hospital with her father. The helicopter rescuing her had been fired on by the Taleban. This episode seemed to me to symbolise the difference between the two sides, the mindless violence against civilians on one hand contrasting with the desire to establish the rule of law and effect reconstruction on the other.

I asked the Afghan general whom we met how long he wanted the British forces to stay and he replied, slightly to my surprise, "Sixty years." Whether Britain remains there for a long time or not will of course depend on what level of resources successive governments are prepared to commit to finish the job. I arrived back in London just too late to participate in the debate in the Lords on the centenary year of the Territorial Army Reserve.

Just as challenging as this visit, but in a different way of course, has been the opportunity to serve on the Commission on the future of Scottish devolution, chaired by Sir Kenneth Calman, which was set up in 2008. The Commission has included representatives of the academic world, trade unions, industry and commerce and members of the political parties which support the Union.

We were asked "To review the provisions of the Scotland Act 1998 in light of experience and to recommend any changes to the present constitutional arrangements that would enable the Scottish Parliament to better serve the people of Scotland, that would improve the financial accountability of the Scottish Parliament and that would continue to secure the position of Scotland within the United Kingdom."

The Calman Report's recommendations were unanimous and were published on 15 June 2009. Among the most important of its proposals were increased tax raising powers for the Scottish Parliament. In my view the editorial in *The Times* summed up much of the immediate reaction by saying "This report opens a serious debate on the nature of devolved power...it goes a long way towards correcting the flaws of devolution. It deserves support from both sides of the border."

My views on the value of the Union were published in *The Holyrood Magazine*'s special publication "Scottishness: Reflections on Identity," and I noted then that I had both Scottish and English ancestors – the Douglases and the Percys – who over the years had killed each other in very considerable numbers. Since my father was a Douglas and my mother a Percy it seemed to me that there was a great deal to be said for both families. In my humble opinion the Douglases were better fighters but the Percys were more numerous!

What seems important to me is that the Union of the parliaments replaced centuries of cross-border warfare with a much more modern and productive partnership. I personally am proud to be both Scottish and British and do not wish to have to choose between the two.

The Scots have always had the ability to look beyond their own shores and boundaries and nowhere is this more evident than in the remarkable list of scientific breakthroughs, whether we are considering James Watt and the steam engine, Alexander Graham Bell's creation of the telephone or John Logie Baird's invention of television. These were all revolutionary advances which benefited the citizens of the world, not just those living in Scotland. Similarly Joseph Lister's discovery of antiseptic, Sir Alexander Fleming's pioneering research into penicillin and the breakthrough made by Sir James Young Simpson with the use of anaesthetic, all helped to save countless lives around the world. Scottish credentials for transforming life in the Third World are beyond doubt through medicine, teaching, engineering and administration.

For the Scots who have remained in Scotland, and those who have become Scots by virtue of settling in the country, the debate as to which areas of policy should be dealt with locally, nationally or at United Kingdom level has been on-going for decades. The all-Scotland Referendum in 1998 resulted in an overwhelming majority in favour of the creation of a devolved Scottish Parliament. This outcome caused the Conservative Party, which had campaigned for a "no" vote, to decide, despite some few voices of dissent, to take part fully in the new politics.

During my eight years as an MSP the members of the Conservative Group performed strongly at Holyrood, punching above their weight and latterly, under the redoubtable leadership of Annabel Goldie, their influence has grown steadily. I firmly believe Scottish Conservatives must never withdraw to the political sidelines and must be prepared always to examine fresh ideas on their merits. As the oldest and most resilient party in Britain they must continue to fight for the best interests of their constituents within the United Kingdom.

As I write there is a good deal of cynicism voiced about politicians and their activities. Against the background of recession there has been a huge adverse reaction from the electorate to the publication of details about the way in which the allowances system was operating in the United Kingdom Parliament. As it happened I was previously appointed to the panel which reviewed the allowances available in the Scottish Parliament, which reported in 2008 and tightened up the system in various respects. New arrangements are now being put in place for MPs which are intended to restore trust and confidence.

Yet I believe that in spite of these events there is still a lot to be said for the view of the Scottish historian F.S. Oliver who believed that: "With all the temptations, dangers and degradations that beset it, politics is still I think, the noblest career that any man can choose." We must add of course nowadays the words "any woman". Looking back over 33 years as an elected politician who has served in three parliamentary chambers, I do not agree with the view attributed to Enoch Powell that all political careers end in failure. How high a politician can climb up "the greasy pole" is not what matters most. What really counts is whether an elected representative has managed to be of service to others, and has stood up in a principled manner for the best interests not only of the party, but of parliament and, above all, the people. As Sir Winston Churchill wrote in his book *My Early Life*, the world "was made to be wooed and won by youth". So I would urge young people in particular to get involved in political activity and public service because there will always be much urgent, worthwhile and fulfilling work to be done.

Index

Abrahams, Eric 35, 38
Act of Settlement 238-44
Afghanistan 275-8
Aitken, Jonathan 24, 29
Ali, Tariq 34-6, 38
Alnwick Castle 4
Ashdown, Paddy 179-80

BBC 48-9, 51-3
Benn, Tony 187, 189-90
Berlin Wall 25-6
Berlin Wall Museum 76
Black Wednesday 196, 211
Blackford, Group Captain DL 66, 68-9
Blair, Tony 206, 238-45
Boren, David 31-2
Bowes-Lyon, Elizabeth (The Queen Mother) 1, 201, 247-8
Buchan, John 13, 96, 194, 226, 267-8, 270
Buganda 45-6
Bullock, Sir Allen 56

Callaghan, Jim 101, 108, 110, 112
Calman Report, the 278-9
Cameronians (Scottish Rifles) 23, 48, 88, 92, 160, 184, 213, 275
Campbell, Menzies 84, 91, 174
Chamberlain, Neville 62
Channon, Paul 165
Charles, Prime Minister Miss Eugenia 116-9
Children (Scotland) Bill 254-5, 261
Churchill, Randolph 32
Churchill, Sir Winston 2-3, 46, 62-3, 66, 72-3, 90, 112, 204-5, 210, 231-2, 281
Clydesdale, Angus, Marquis of Douglas and Clydesdale, and the 15th Duke of Hamilton 4, 8, 21, 92, 94, 186, 190, 213

Community Charge 141-7, 163, 175-8
Concorde 215, 249-53
Cook, Robin 87, 137, 201, 245
Crathorne, Lord 207-8
Creagh, Rosemary 134

De Wet, Carel 34
Devolution 105-6, 109, 208-9
Dewar, Donald 25-6, 37, 53, 96, 107, 154, 165-8, 174, 198, 215, 236-8
Disclaimer of the Earldom of Selkirk 182, 185-190
Douglas, James: the fourth Duke of Hamilton 258-60
Douglas, Lord James (The Black Douglas) 263-6
Douglas-Hamilton, Alasdair 185, 190
Douglas-Hamilton, Douglas, 14th Duke of Hamilton (father) 2-10, 19-21, 28-9, 38, 45, 87, 90-2, 100, 250
boxing 4, 10, 20, 90
First flight over Mount Everest 58-60, 91-2, 128, 180, 238, 271-2
Hess 55-74
Douglas-Hamilton, Susan 2, 96-9, 121, 151, 194, 214, 216-7, 220, 228, 230, 244, 264, 267-8
Douglas-Home, Sir Alec 37, 52-3, 62, 105
Douglas-Home, William 37
Driver, Jonty 42-3
Dunblane shootings 200
Dungavel 4, 6, 249

Edinburgh University 40, 44, 47, 50, 53, 137, 266, 275
Elizabeth II, Queen 1-4, 213-5
Eton 10-18 passim, 23
Ewing, Margaret 214
Ewing, Winnie 79, 91-3

Fairbairn, Sir Nicholas 84, 96, 110, 172-4
Falkland Islands 123-7, 138, 167
Fergusson, Alex 236
Firearms amnesty 159, 161
Fonda, Peter 217
Foot, Paul 29, 31
Forrester, Ian 97
Forsyth, Michael 155, 163, 172, 180, 191, 194-5, 199, 209
Foulkes, George 87-8, 137
Freeman, Lee 217

Gabcik, Josef 221-5
Gandhi, Indira 129, 131
Gibraltar 139
Gladstone, Willie 13, 23
Gloyer, Bob 79-80
Goebbels, Josef 74-5

Hague, William 173, 206-7
Hailsham, Lord 115, 141, 187
Hamilton, Duke of (See Douglas-Hamilton, Douglas)
Hardie, Andrew 214
Harper, Robin 212
Haushofer, Albrecht 55-76
    letter to the Duke of Hamilton 63-4
    Moabit Prison 73-5
    peace plans for German Resistance to Hitler 72
Haushofer, Heinz 58-9, 75-6
Haushofer, Karl 56, 58, 62-3
Haushofer, Martin 73-4
Heath, Edward 92, 95, 105-6, 112, 155, 207
Henry, Hugh 261
Heseltine, Michael 177-8, 196
Hess, Rudolf 55-76
    Flight to Scotland 69-72
    Spandau Prison 58, 72
Hess, Wolf Rudiger 57-8
Heydrich, Reinhard 220-5
Hitler, Adolf 55-78 pasim
    German Resistance to Hitler 62, 68,

72-4, 76-8
Home-Robertson, John 252
Houghton, Roger, Vice Captain of the Cambridge University Boxing Team 20-1
Howard, Michael 25
Howe, Sir Geoffrey 136, 176-7

Jopling, Michael 113-4
Jowell, Jeffrey 24, 36, 41

Karnad, Girish 130-1
Kennedy, John F. 26-8
Kenyatta, Jomo 45
Khrushchev, Nikita 28-9, 90
King Jr, Dr Martin Luther 39, 49
Kinnock, Neil 180
Kirkwood, Richard 29-30
Kubis, Jan 221-5

Lang, Ian 170, 179, 188, 193-4, 208
Lee Kuan Yew 182-3
Lenthall, William 214
Lind, Harold 24, 26, 36
Lockerbie 165-171
    release of Al Megrahi 171

Maclean, Sir Murdo 114-5
Macleod, Iain 33
Macmillan, Alexander 89
Macmillan, Harold 25, 89-91, 95-6, 183
Macmillan, Maureen 235
Mandela, Nelson 41-2
Maxton, John 150-1, 158, 178
McConnell, Jack 248, 251, 253, 257
McDonnell, John 35-6
McIntyre, David 91, 271-2
McLetchie, David 210, 247, 249
MI5 57, 60-1, 63-9
MI6 134
Mussert, Anton 228-9

Nimetz, Matthew 231
Nuremberg War Trials 72

Olympic Games, Berlin 1936 55, 60, 66, 71, 74
Oppenheimer, Harry 40-1
Osler, Maeder 42-3
Oxford Union 23-39 *passim*

Peacock, Peter 254
Percy, Elizabeth (mother) 4-6, 9-10, 29, 38, 95, 192
Poll tax (*See* Community Charge)
Pratt, Garth 29, 34-5, 38
Pugatch, Dr Eugene 230-1

Reith, Lord 48-9
Renton, Lord David 192, 207-8
Revaluation (*See* Community Charge)
Ridsdale, Sir Julian 121, 123
Rifkind, Sir Malcolm 47, 51, 84, 86, 96, 106, 127-8, 135-7, 151-2, 165-6, 168, 172-3, 193
Rizvi, Mo 132
Roberts, Violet 63-5
Robertson, George 200-1
Robertson, Major "Tar" 66-9
Robertson, Raymond 210
Rockefeller, David 216
Rodger, Alan 189
Roosevelt, Franklin Delano 194, 230-1, 267
Ross, Willie 104, 106
RTM (rent-to-mortgage) 163-4
Russo, Robert 230

Salmond, Alex 33, 237
Schlabrendorff, Fabian von 57
Schuschnigg, Dr Kurt von 57
Scottish Office 153-81 *passim*, 192-3, 199, 201-2
Scottish Parliament 233-262 *passim*
Selkirk, Geordie 124, 149, 182-6, 188-9, 260, 264, 266
Selkirk, the Earldom (*See* Disclaimer of the Earldom of Selkirk)
Selkirk, Thomas, the fifth Earl
  Selkirk Settlers, the 266-7, 269-71

Sheridan, Tommy 246, 248
Smith, Ian (Prime Minister of Rhodesia) 43, 50, 52-3
Smith, Ian (Scottish Liberal Democrat) 261-2
Smith, John 84, 128, 130-1, 196, 198, 237
Stauffenberg, Colonel Claus Schenk von 57, 72, 76-6
Steel, David 52, 212, 214
Stewart, Allan 172, 188
Stewart, Frances 8
Suzman, Helen 41-2

Territorial Army (*See* Cameronians)
Thatcher, Denis 150
Thatcher, Margaret 99, 105-6, 111-2, 118-9, 140-1, 148, 151, 154, 158, 164-5, 169, 174, 180
  Falklands 127
  leadership election 177-9
  RTM (Rent to Mortgage) 162-4
  Community Charge 141-7
Thomas, George 99, 103
Thompson, Alan 50-1
Thompson, Scott 43, 4
Todd, Garfield 33, 43, 52-3
Todd, Judith 52-3
Tweedsmuir, John 226-9

United Nations 89-90, 137-9

Verey, Charles 15, 16

Walker, Bill 172, 195
Walker, Harold 123
Whitehead, Philip 33, 51-2
Whitelaw, William 125
Wilson, Brian 174
Wilson, Harold 52, 95, 101, 104
Wisdom, Judge Norman Minor 50
Wright, Reverend Dr Ronald Selby 97

Younger, George 120
  Community Charge 142-3, 147